Entertaining the Tommies

Entertaining the Tommies

Two Accounts of British Concert Parties
'Over There' During the First World War

Modern Troubadours

Lena Ashwell

My Greatest Adventure

Ada L. Ward

LEONAUR

Entertaining the Tommies
Two Accounts of British Concert Parties
'Over There' During the First World War
Modern Troubadours
by Lena Ashwell
My Greatest Adventure
by Ada L. Ward

FIRST EDITION

First published under the titles
Modern Troubadours
and
My Greatest Adventure

Leonaur is an imprint of Oakpast Ltd
Copyright in this form © 2018 Oakpast Ltd

ISBN: 978-1-78282-754-2 (hardcover)
ISBN: 978-1-78282-755-9 (softcover)

http://www.leonaur.com

Publisher's Notes

The views expressed in this book are not necessarily
those of the publisher.

Contents

Modern Troubadours   7

My Greatest Adventure   199

Modern Troubadours

Contents

Foreword	11
Beginnings	13
In France	38
Malta, Egypt, and Palestine	67
Raising the Money	95
Back in France	108
The Firing Line	126
Repertory Companies	145
The Devastated Areas	162
Work at Home and Demobilisation	172
Recreation and the National Life	179
List of Artists	193

Foreword

This account of the work of the singers, musicians, and actors who undertook their not altogether unimportant work in the Great War, under the title of *Concerts at the Front*, cannot be in any way considered as a complete record. The experiences of over six hundred people whose impressions were chaotic no one person could write down, but such as this record is, it could not have been written without the letters and diaries of—

Esmé Church
Kate Coates
Cicely Hamilton
Olga Hartley
Gertrude Jennings
Yvette Pienne
Paget Bowman
Tom Burrows
Theodore Flint
Gale Gardner
Frank Macey
R. MacLennan
and Stanley Worrall.

Invest me in my motley, give me leave
To speak my mind, and I will through and through
Cleanse the foul body of the infected world
If they will patiently receive my medicine.
                                    As You Like It.

Orpheus with his lute made trees,
And the mountain tops, that freeze,
Bow themselves when he did sing:
To his music plants and flowers
Ever sprung; as sun and showers
There had made a lasting spring.

Everything that heard him play,
Even the billows of the sea
Hung their heads and then lay by.
In sweet music is such art,
Killing care and grief of heart,
Fall asleep, or, hearing, die.
                                    Henry VIII.

CHAPTER 1

Beginnings

Orpheus with his lute was also a Fisher. Does not the playing of music incite men to lay aside their cares and the turmoil of the daily struggle; to let something beautiful, invisible, and healing cleanse and beautify their souls? Is there not something in the idea of Blake, Shakespeare, and many other writers that in sweet music, the music of the lute, the music of the spoken word, the music that stirs and quickens the soul, there is a power which is preparing the souls of men for something greater? Killing care and grief of heart, the troubled personality falls asleep, and hearing, dies; because the Fisher with his magic sound prepares for the new kind of life, the life of courage and self-denial, the life which some day will enable the human being to overcome evil with good.

When sending over a new concert party to France, I implored the artists to remember and to note things of interest, and to write me descriptions of what was happening to them; and almost every time I was disappointed, because when they wrote or spoke they could only mention meals and journeys, what they had had to eat, and the number of concerts they had been able to give. The reason was not dullness of soul or greediness of body, but that the whole experience was so overwhelming, so moving, so terrible that one's littleness was stunned and could not find expression. It is easier to describe a little tennis-party at a country vicarage than seeing a world in arms—suffering, wounded, muddy, weary, smiling, and tortured; try to express, try to give even a small impression—that is beyond description.

To stand, as we did so often, on some piece of rising ground to watch regiment after regiment going down from camp to entrain for the line, to watch those thousands going forward with a smile to death, sacrificing self for an ideal, for freedom of small peoples, for an empire in danger of destruction, for Country, for Home, for wife and child, that women might not be ashamed of them, that God might know that they could play the game, who can describe this?

The young lieutenants marching just a little in front of their men, the "Captains Courageous," the youth, the beauty of manhood when stirred to nobleness, the wonder of courage and gladness in the fight, might well be impossible to speak of or write about. The tears might blind one's eyes and mark one's face, but these signs of sorrow must not be seen, for we were there to help.

In a crowded hut or tent filled with smoke and packed to suffocation, one felt the hunger of the souls of men, the aching, wondering query in their hearts. Many have found some answer now, and "when the barrage lifts," perhaps we too shall see, "no longer blinded by our eyes."

But we could find no words or tongue to express the suffering of our hearts, the aching sympathy, to see great battalions moving up to the line, and welcome a few men back, to have a concert interrupted with the sudden roll-call of the men who were to join their regiments at once, to see the men respond to their names and go out and up the line, to hear a whole massed audience singing as their last experience before going up to the blood and horror, "Lead, kindly Light;" these are not experiences which can be described, they cut too deep into the soul. When in some chorus, "The long trail, the trail that leads to home," thousands of voices would give some expression to the deep sentiment of the British for "roses," for "flowers," for "Home," for "Flo," one's whole body shook and trembled in response, and one wondered if the music of the spheres, the great invisible choirs, were perhaps giving voice through these human hearts to the eternal desire for beauty and goodness.

So, when I am asked to write a little book, the experiences of six hundred artists, who many of them worked, with short intervals of rest at home, right through those four years, from 1915 to 1919, you can, I am sure, believe that no one realises more acutely than I do that the task is impossible. It cannot be done.

I pray the readers of this book to forgive my incapacity, and the artists to forgive me for not mentioning all their names when trying to narrate not only my experiences but theirs, and to believe that I am, in as faithful a way as possible, giving a tiny record of the great experiences which we, all six hundred of us, went through.

When, in the early morning, in February 1915, we were getting into the harbour at Havre, I rang for a cup of tea, and the stewardess in a chilly tone remarked, after a silent contemplation of my face, "If I were you, Miss, I should leave well alone," I lost courage, I betrayed my birthplace, the sea, and gave way to the subtle suggestion. Tiredness, I think, often makes people seasick, and it was not only the excitement of getting off at last, the weary waiting at night on the quay, the long standing in the queue before we filed in one by one for the examining of passports, and all the annoyance of perpetual delays.

The work of organising had been pretty considerable. War-work and "business as usual" was a quite impossible combination. One cannot serve two masters, though of course most of us did our best. I had undertaken to send concerts to the Front, which meant finding the artists and also the money to pay their expenses, but I had also to keep the Kingsway Theatre open, or pay the expenses of it when closed. I had just finished playing in the revival of *Fanny's First Play*. This, my first journey to France, had to be a short one, as I had to come back for rehearsals of a play to be produced at the Coliseum. The Kingsway was shut, but the rates and taxes had to be paid. I wonder how many people who were fortunate enough to have short leases, or who were able to break the lease in these first years of the war, and leave all the responsibility upon the wretched landlord, mention these moments of agony when complaining of the avaricious landlord who, afterwards, when there was a demand, tried partially to cover some of his losses? I, like many others, had a distressing struggle with property that no one wanted during the early days of the war.

Of course one's heart was in war-work, and "business as usual" made one groan in spirit, it seemed so absurd and selfish; and, besides, I had always longed that artists might have their proper recognition as a great arm of National Service. In our professional capacity we might be of as much use and as real a necessity as the Red Cross or St. John's Ambulance, for does not the soul of man need help as much as his body?

It is always to me curious, the suspicion of the English people with regard to the theatre, and that wicked creature, the actor. I used to be glad that my hair was white, and that I have achieved a certain measure of solidity of figure, because when arriving at a Y.M.C.A. meeting, I could feel the sigh of relief and security. Here was no "*Siren come to tempt St. Anthony*," but a Mrs. Grundy in whom they might perhaps place confidence.

On one occasion, after a heated appeal to the Council of that great organisation, a real old Puritan said "it was very strange that a woman who was obviously a good woman, such as Miss Lena-r-Ashwell, should hold such perverted views. It was well known that, on the deathbed, nothing was of any avail but Grace."

Of course, the why and wherefore of the national indifference to one of the greatest assets of national life is a long story, and this is not the place to tell it.

But in October 1914 I tried very hard to get the entertainment of troops put on national lines, and was interviewed several times on the scheme of "every camp its own theatre," and the organising of the work by professional actors, but there was little interest shown. This effort, meeting with no success, was followed by the formation of a Representative Committee—which I invited to organise an appeal to the War Office—a gathering together of noted musicians and actors, with representative generals and bishops of the Church as a guarantee of our respectability and good faith. An appeal was formulated and sent to the War Office that recreation should be organised, that the movement should be national, as national as the Red Cross, but our offer was refused.

We were still considered "as useless as an actor, a billiard-marker, or a golf professional." I do not know how the golf professional or the billiard-marker felt when they read this sentence in the *Ordeal by Battle*. I expect they were in the army, but I felt very sad and disheartened, and threw more energy than ever into the work of the Women's Emergency Corps.

When I read the first six months' Report of this organisation, it takes my breath away; the tremendous amount of work that was done, and the way that it gave birth to many greater efforts—the National Food Fund, the Women's Legion, the Women's Volunteer Reserve, amongst many others. It was carried on even when its vigorous children left it, but its first six months were surely very valuable. The first suggestion of this organisation was due to Miss Decima Moore: she and Miss Eva Moore, the Hon. Mrs. Haverfield, and myself were the original workers—all but one actors—and Miss Gertrude Kingston lent the Little Theatre.

One never-to-be-forgotten day, when I had quite lost hope of the drama and music of the country being regarded as anything but useless, Lady Rodney called on behalf of the Women's Auxiliary Committee of the Y.M.C.A. She had just returned from France, and came from Her Highness Princess Helena Victoria, Chairman of the Committee, to ask if it was possible for a concert party to go to Havre. Of course I accepted with enthusiasm, hurried to a friend of mine whose name I should love to mention but dare not, who gave me the first cheque to pay the expenses of the first concert party. Mr. Theodore Flint, who went ahead to make the arrangements in January 1915, was the first of our artists to land in France.

Every concert party that followed was made up on more or less the same plan: a *soprano*, *contralto*, instrumentalist, tenor, baritone or bass, entertainer, and accompanist.

H.H. Princess Helena Victoria and her committee had been able to make arrangements with the War Office that, owing to the very suffering state of the men at the base camps who had passed through a very difficult period of fighting, and were to be at the base for rest and further training, this experiment of sending recreation should be made.

The conditions were: no advertisement, no making use of the war to aggrandise one's professional popularity, that every artist should be personally known to me, and that I should be able to guarantee their suitability to Her Highness and the committee, and that every artist should become known to Her Highness, who became personally responsible for them and their conduct. They were to work with the Y.M.C.A., who would look after the billeting arrangements in France, and places, times, etc., for the concerts.

The experiment was tentative. There were grave doubts on the part of the Y.M.C.A. as to what unknown terrors they were letting loose upon themselves. Of course people are afraid of the unknown, and there is a great prejudice amongst a section of the nation against artists, especially actors. To them we are a class of terribly wicked people who drink champagne all day long, and lie on sofas, receiving bouquets from rows of admirers who patiently wait in queues to present these tokens of rather unsavoury regard. I think some expected us to land in France in tights, with peroxided hair, and altogether to be a difficult thing for a religious organisation to camouflage.

Some good things did come to us through the war, and one of them was the breaking down of barriers due to misunderstanding, and perhaps one of the biggest barriers has had large gaps made in it by the co-operation of the actors and musicians with the Y.M.C.A. So many of those working with the Y.M.C.A. who had never been to a play, and thought with the Puritans of old that all recreations were evil, and that the only safe interests in life were a sound banking account and a large meal, took to plays like ducks to water, and are now some of the most splendid workers in the demand for sound and wholesome recreation for the people.

For the laughter, the interest, and the music was more than mere "amusement" to those armies of men. One chaplain from the other side of the world came up after one of the performances and said, "I am a Puritan, with a Puritan's view of the theatre—and you know what a deep prejudice that is—but I cannot tell you how grateful I am that my boys should have this hour of happiness; you don't know what it means to us." And when he tried to tell me what it did mean there were tears in his eyes. A tremendous barrier had evidently gone down when he could speak from his heart in praise of drama and music.

At home, in peace-time, music is so often a mere accompaniment to something else in life—conversation or a meal. Drama is so generally overloaded with stage effects and pomp and circumstance that its primitive elements are extinguished. Artists are "unproductive workers," to use the language of bygone philosophers—those strange people who created a science of political economy divorced from ethics, demanded a religion devoid of mystery, and named the chaotically unreasonable result "Rationalism."

But out there—where life and death were stark realities, where life was swept bare of all artificialities and death was abroad, visible and undisguised—there, music, the straightest road to the unseen world of spiritual beauty, fulfilled more than its tangible function of cheering up the men, although that is "a work of great military value," to quote the words of a distinguished doctor after a concert in a rest camp; it was more than food for their spirits, hungry for loveliness after the abnormal hideous experience of weariness or pain and tension. Music ministers with magical results to minds distressed, destroying the seeds of despondent thoughts, the black moods that dullness, pain, or loneliness sow in the most gallant hearts, for "*where music is, there can no ill thing be.*"

I could not go with the first party that went for a fortnight on 15th February 1915, and gave thirty-nine concerts in fifteen days, but I got away in the middle of March after organising the first *matinée* at the Coliseum.

Memories of that time come flowing into one's mind, and it is difficult to pick out the most interesting. Some of the mornings were sunny and warm, and at Havre I used to lie in bed and watch troopship after troop-ship arrive in the harbour, quite undisturbed by the first submarine menace. All the men were singing as the ships came in. Those in the bow generally struggled with the "*Marseillaise*" out of politeness and goodwill, but those in the stern were determined to let the French hear "Tipperary." Everybody was in picnic mood, that first beginning of the landing of Kitchener's Army.

At the concerts I met many men of the "Contemptible Little Army." How like us to keep that as the name for the greatest "Little Army" that ever fought in the history of the world! Will not Mons, Maubeuge, and the Marne rank with Marathon? These men were quieter and graver than the New Army. They were still weary after that fortnight without sleep, fighting and retreating, fighting and retreating, the hardest kind of fight.

I have a lucky bean, presented to me by a sergeant who had been in the South African War, the Egyptian Campaign, and who gave me his little lucky bean as a souvenir of Mons, Maubeuge, the Aisne, and Ypres. I was very touched and flattered, but very loath to take it. One is always afraid that with the bean one may be taking the luck.

It is, perhaps, not generally known that both Havre and Rouen had at that time just been evacuated at very short notice, and the troops had even been on the boats, placed like very well-packed sardines, waiting to be taken farther south—the Germans were within five miles of Rouen. The French were on the point of making any terms which would save the beautiful Cathedral. The Uhlans were in the Pas de Calais, and in those early days one felt how very near the Germans were to taking the coast.

Kitchener's Army were sometimes embarrassing by their reckless disregard of regulations of giving away their badges. In those first concerts we were covered with badges of the different regiments.

The first concert was at No. 15 in the Harfleur Valley. The valley was a sea of mud, with tents and a few huts, and as a pathway through this sea of stickiness there were duckboards to walk on. If you fell over, you were done in, for the mud was ankle deep, and very often knee deep. We wore top-boots. The winter had been very cold and abnormally damp, and the cold and rain and mud without made a very great contrast to the fog of smoke and the heat within the huts and tents. There was a great concert in the new Cinema Hut, which we, the Concert Party, opened in great style. The base *commandant* and the officers of the base were all present. The wooden hut was packed to suffocation. No one would ever believe now that human beings could take up so little room. The men had been waiting for hours and smoking incessantly, and the fog of smoke and the heat within the hut was a tremendous contrast to the cold, rain, and mud without.

The acetylene lights were very new and very glaring, and quite suddenly they all went out. We were all sitting on the platform, as we always did, partly because there was nowhere else to go, and partly to save time. The concerts had to be fairly short—two hours at the most—and there was no time to spare for entrances and exits. When the lights went out there was a rush for candles, and a row of candles was lit in front of us and along the side of the hut. No one can imagine how hot rows of candles can be. The heat of the candles, the smoke, the enthusiasm, the terrific roar of response to our small efforts were quite incredible.

Ivor Novello, who was one of the party, had just written "Keep the Home Fires burning," and when he sang it, the men seemed to drink it in at once and instantly sang the chorus, and as we drove away at the end of the concert, in the dark and rain and mud, from all parts of the camp one could hear the refrain of the chorus.

The general drove me away from this concert, as it was more or less an official affair, and I felt like several queens—in fact, like the whole of the Royal Family rolled into one—for there was no longer any doubt for any one who was present that artists were of real use, real service to the nation, and powerful agents for happiness.

After the terrible Battle of St. Eloi, the little concert party was in Boulogne. There were not enough hospitals. Every ward was full, and there were wounded and dying in the streets. A nurse, writing from the hospital at Wimereux, said that:

"They came and gave a concert in the orderly room, as the men in hospital were too bad for us to have a concert in the hospital itself; but afterwards those kind people came into each ward and sang softly, without any accompaniment, to the men who were well enough to listen, and the little Canadian story-teller went round and told his stories to each man in turn as they were having their dressings done, the result being, that instead of a mass of suffering humanity having their wounds dressed, the men were happy through the time that is usually so awful. It really was too nice, and so kind of those concert people to do it, as it must have been a very trying job for them: the sights and smells are gruesome. Altogether it has been such a boon to have them about through this awful week, and they have worked so hard and so cheerily, and have done good to the whole place."

After the hospital concert, which was part of the day's work every day, the artists generally went through the hospitals and gave individual entertainment in the different wards. It was always very extraordinary, the way that music seemed to change the entire atmosphere. It was often very distressing, going into the ward, so black the suffering, so tense the atmosphere. It seemed impertinent to intrude, and yet the first strains of music seemed to break up the spell of pain. Men still in their blankets on stretchers just placed in the wards from the train which had come down the line, apparently indifferent to life, concentrated in suffering, would, after a time, become interested and forget, and join in the concert.

Such funny places were turned into hospitals. The railway station on the quay at Havre, the great big buffets still in the glass-roofed hall, the Casino, the racecourse at Havre—any place that was big enough became a huge hospital. In the Casino we at first used the steps in the big entrance-hall as a platform, the beds in rows below one and on the landing above. During the whole of the first concert they were unloading a convoy of wounded, and carrying them on stretchers through the audience past the performers, up the stairs. Nearly every one, however badly wounded, craned his neck to see and hear all he could. On the racecourse at Rouen our first concerts were given on the Grand Stand; a tarpaulin was stretched over the front to keep out some of the weather—it was bitterly cold. A huge coke brazier was put at one end of the stand, where the artists kept warming their fingers. The artists were cold enough, but what the audience felt like, one cannot guess. But not one of these boys in blue moved until the end.

The next concert the weather was warmer, and I can still see the crowded stand filled with boys in blue, the rows of beds with red blankets, the rows of tents with the flaps fastened back so that the men within could hear the concert, and the great distance of silent listeners by which one could realise how far the music and the voices travelled.

A few incidents stand out which the flood of after events can never wash away. I met with an incident, the pathos of which must fix itself in my mind as long as my mind and body keep company, and perhaps long after. Close to the tent where we were playing and well within reach of the shouts of laughter, lay a wounded German prisoner. The long tent where he was lying contained no bed but his, and on that bed, close to the open end of the tent, and in full view of all who came to look, he was propped up in a half-sitting position, waiting for the end. With shattered limbs, shot through both lungs, his face as white as the bandages that hid so large a part of it, he remained, a motionless

21

wreck of a man, never by any human possibility to move from that bed again. At either end of the tent sat a sentry with a loaded rifle.

At No. 7 Stationary Hospital in Havre we played on a veranda, the patients filling the enclosed courtyard. The windows overlooking it were filled, and the roof of the largest building made an excellent, though somewhat elevated, gallery. There were two barred windows on the right, one filled to suffocation with German prisoners, who obviously understood English, and laughed most heartily at the jokes in the plays. The contralto once hesitated, finding herself well in the middle of a verse about the *Kaiser*, but the bandaged *Fritzes* did not seem to mind a bit.

At the other barred window were two officers, the elder obviously a Saxon and the other equally obviously a Prussian. Very early in the programme the Prussian youth withdrew, noisily and contemptuously, and evidently sat alone with his thoughts, for the men from the crowded window gradually joined the Saxon officer, and both windows were filled. I suppose being young, and hearing the laughter and enjoyment, the young Prussian could not long enjoy his isolation, for he quite unexpectedly returned to the window, and when the men saw him they dropped from the window and shrank away like drugged flies. It was a complete revelation, quite hideous to see.

This, my first week in France, was the week before Easter, and Good Friday was, of course, a difficulty, as we could not give a concert; and so the party divided into two and sometimes three, the singers singing sacred songs in the different camps. One of the Y.M.C.A. directors invited me to recite something of a religious nature. I had, of course, no books with me, but after digging in my memory I was able to write out "*The Faithful Soul*," by Adelaide A. Procter; "*Abou Ben Adhem*," by Leigh Hunt; and others of the same calibre.

On being deposited at the hut, I was met by the Y.M.C.A. in charge, a very tousled fellow with longish curly hair standing well up from his forehead. He asked me what I was doing there in his camp on Good Friday. I said I had been asked to recite, and he told me that it was quite out of the question, and it was useless to press it as he never would permit such a thing. Seeing that there was some sort of service going on, I asked with much humility if I might be allowed a chair to sit at the edge of the congregation, as I realised that my position at that moment was distinctly that of an outcast. The car could not return for some time to pick me up, or I would have gone back to the hotel. I was grudgingly given a chair, but watched the men, however, and I could not help knowing that the beautiful poems would have made them happier than the somewhat dreary discourse, for there is great inspiration in noble verse.

The first public performance I remember was at the Folies Bergères in Rouen. Captain Braithwaite, Miss Lilian Braithwaite's brother, took the chair for that concert, and it was a very wonderful evening. It was then I ventured for the first time to recite a serious poem instead of the humorous ones to which I had hitherto confined myself. I was urged by Madeleine O'Connor, singer, lecturer, and journalist, who was living at the Base working for the Y.M.C.A., to do serious poems, and having learnt *Abou Ben Adhem*, and some Elizabethan love lyrics, I was ready, and was very much astonished at the deep interest and very real response the men made. She has sent me this from her diary, which gives a very vivid description of the occasion:

Went in early to Rouen and found Lena at her hotel, having a much-needed rest in bed. She is very nervous, as they are having a huge concert in the theatre tonight. She asked me to hear the poems she and F. have selected for her to recite. I was so disappointed at first, all rather light, quite charming, but not what is expected of her. I told her this, and she said the navvies at Havre loved the Elizabethan sonnets. I told her the men are so excited at the prospect of hearing her, and are always asking me, 'What is she going to recite?' They are hungering to hear her in something good. We all sing rot at first and end by finding they have better taste. She sat up in bed and let herself go in the sonnets and '*Abou Ben Adhem*,' and I knew it was the very thing, so I implored her to include them anyway. Left her, telling her not to see too many people and tire herself out; every one is wanting to see her.

Went to camp. . . . Got off early, and was given a lift in a lorry down to Rouen. Arrived at theatre. What a night!!! It's the first time they have given a show in the theatre, packed; all the 'Brass hats,' 'Blood oranges,' and the bright uniforms of the French officers made it look extremely gay, the men packed everywhere, sitting on each other's laps, a few young Christians. Although I see hundreds of men every night, it was an amazing sight to see this theatre packed with only men in khaki (one box with the English chaplain's wife, etc.), and the lights seemed so glaring, and the French advertisements on the safety-curtain amused the men, who tried to puzzle them out; they were half wild with delight, pretending they were in a theatre at home. Went round to the back, found the whole party very nervy; Lena, white, strained, intensely nervous, told me F. did not approve of her changing her pieces.

He was awfully ratty with me, asked me what business had I to upset her; but I know Lena and the men, and felt quite confident, told her she would get them; she nodded, very mute. Ran back to front of house, up went the curtain. Such cheers! Everyone had a wonderful reception as they came on. How splendid to hear a good violinist again! F. is an exquisite accompanist; what a moment in their lives! Then came Lena, looking rather pathetic, but very sweet; her dress is charming; it gave me a pang to see a pretty frock. The men went mad and cheered and roared their welcome. She meant so much to them and it was the first time they had seen her. She began with the sonnets. What a delight it was! You could have heard a pin drop, the whole atmosphere changed, the men around me leant forward, looking and listening; they let her go on from song to song, almost quietly, they were sucking it in.

She led them from the first moment. I was so nervous that my knees shook. Then when she had finished they tore the house down; she looked so happy. I was completely justified; but later, after many encores, when she gave them *Abou Ben Adhem*, it was indescribable. As usual when I am overwrought, I wept, and felt so proud; Lena at her greatest best had penetrated into all our hearts. As I came out that night one of our orderlies said to me chokily, 'It was all you said, Mrs. . . . Miss Ashwell gave us what we were longing for.' . . . Must write and tell H. J. After last night I am more convinced than ever the men are hungering for good stuff. It's an awful injustice to treat them to slop.

It was during this first visit to Rouen that I first made the acquaintance of a Y.M.C.A. driver, Mike, who was a constant joy to all of us. He was a very fine mechanic and a splendid driver, with an almost ungovernable temper. He was not quite conscious, I feel, of the full humour of the things he often said.

Once, when nearly running over some chickens on the road, and having just escaped taking the life of a dog, he was asked what animal he found most dangerous to a motor driver. He considered this for some time, and then said, "Well, on the 'ole, I thinks women."

One of the voluntary workers at the base was the Hon. Mr. ——, who was tremendously fervid in his anxiety about the souls of the people whom he met. He attacked Mike, who was anything but polite in return. When the Y.M.C.A. leader remonstrated with him, and told him that "he must remember that he was working for the Y.M.C.A., and therefore must give a civil reply, also that the Hon. Mr. —— was the son of the late Earl —— and brother of the present peer," Mike replied, "Oh, I thought there was something wrong with 'im. That's the worst of them there haristercrats. They either takes to drink or to religion; they don't know no middle course!"

His fury at the incompetence of some voluntary workers who were driving cars he sometimes found impossible to express. A noted writer on leaving the Base was being seen off by Mike, and she described to him with heartfelt admiration her appreciation of the marvellous work done by the voluntary workers, and especially picked out one of the voluntary drivers, a man who drove his car but left others to keep it clean and mend it. She said that this man had said how happy he was in his work, that he not only enjoyed driving the car, but that all the work he had to do filled him with the greatest happiness he had ever known in his life.

Mike controlled himself at that moment, but on returning to the headquarters repeated these expressions of admiration with rage and disgust, and ended up by saying, "Mr. —— drives his own car, does his own repairs, cleans his own car, says he has never been so 'appy in his life, well, wot does 'e come 'ere for? To be 'appy?" He was always a joy to us, and later on played in some of the plays.

I think it was on the Easter Monday that, after a concert on the Quai d'Escale, at Havre, we had the tremendous joy of giving a special concert on the Hospital Ship which was lying alongside the quay, gradually filling up with men going home to Blighty. It was all very strange and very wonderful. Bandaged men lay upon their beds around us. More bandaged men limped along, some of them leading comrades who will never see any more. It seemed little short of a miracle that they too could seemingly forget, and laugh and sing choruses with the others.

On the journey back I had my first experience of the conditions produced by a submarine. We crossed at night, and quite suddenly I was awakened by the peculiar motions of the ship. She seemed to be quivering like a startled animal, and evidently was taking the most zigzag of zigzag courses. Of course one knew at once what was the matter. I found myself solemnly putting on my hat, and then wondering why I was putting on my hat, and answering myself that it would help me when I was in the water, because it would prevent my hair getting in my eyes. I then of course realised that that was nonsense, and as I could not find any one moving when I opened my door, I retired again to bed. I do not think then, though one was nervous, one had realised at all what being torpedoed meant. That of course came later.

From then until I went back to France in June, I continued the effort of "business as usual," together with the finding of artists, arranging of parties, and raising of money.

The one thing that one was grateful for in the steady increase of the number of the parties asked for and sent was the firm belief of the committee that in the summer we might relax our efforts, as entertainments would obviously be wanted only out of doors. So when I started back in June, though funds were low I was not very much disturbed.

On this visit we made our first journey to Abancourt, which is about fifty miles from Rouen, on a railway siding. It is a high plateau where, at this period of the war, we had one of our big forage camps. I was told it was twenty miles from the French front line. The men were mostly wharfside navvies from the Thames and the Tyne; before Lord Derby's Dockers' Battalion was born or thought of these men were at work in France, unloading and reloading the thousand and one things from England which are so vitally necessary to the maintenance of an army abroad. This is work, to which they have been fitted by lifelong custom—hard work at all times, doubly hard in time of war. Few departments in the service are less remembered by the general public at home, and few deserve more. It is very difficult for people who have not had the experience to realise the monotony of life when life consists of hard work, rigid military discipline and nothing else, when one's world is suddenly a group of bare huts and a sea of mud.

These men had had nothing to break their monotony and were almost hysterical with joy when our little party of eight, very dusty and very weary after driving fifty miles—and incidentally giving another concert on the way—came into the camp.

The concert was in a tent. We had a quartet from the *Gondoliers*, and then "Van Tromp was an Admiral"—only this time, of course, he was Von Tirpitz. Sir John Jellicoe admirably filled the place of Admiral Blake, and the great North Sea was swept with thunderous applause.

Never surely did singers have a more gracious audience, moved at a touch to laughter, and spellbound by such music as Schubert's exquisite little "*Moment Musicale.*"

Of course we had at the end some chorus songs, and the little French officer in his light blue uniform, sitting with the other officers in the front row, seemed quite carried away by the then popular "Are we all here?" He shouted "Yes!" in all the wrong places, and added to the laughter and enjoyment of the song. Afterwards he told me it was the happiest evening he had spent since August 1914. "Are we all here? Yes," he said in a shaking voice, "and we stop here, yes, until we have won the war. Yes, yes, yes!" and his eyes filled with tears as he disappeared into the darkness. He was the son of the famous Captain Dreyfus.

The officers were very proud of a bath they had made, there being no water for miles round; a great hole had been dug in the ground, and lined with tarpaulin. Into this they had carried water and made themselves a swimming-bath. They called it "Tarpaulin Bath," and everyone seemed to regard it as a gorgeous recreation to be allowed to swim in it. About two strokes would take any one across the bath.

How nice the officers were to us! How glad to see us! And what wonderful thoughtfulness had gone to the preparation of our meal. Even tents with bare wooden tables and candles stuck in bottles with a few, a very few flowers, one felt had taken a good deal of thought to make the most of, for our entertainment.

For a long time I kept the funny little bouquet that the men presented that night. There were, apparently, no flowers on the plateau and yet they had contrived somehow or other to get quite a nice, tight little bunch with cut paper all round them, rather like a superior and more tightly packed sheriff's bouquet.

It had been arranged that Mike, who was the best driver at the base, should lead the way out of the camp, as he was the only person who knew the road; but our friend the voluntary driver had an independent spirit, and as we found some difficulty in starting, he whisked off in the moonlight the wrong way and disappeared. Mike groaned, and cursed him as he tried to make the engine start. The men were all of them grouped to give us a good send off, and, as the engine refused to start, they, I think, sang every song they had ever heard—"Auld Lang Syne" several times, all the bits of chorus songs they knew, and suddenly, to my intense surprise, they burst out with "Here we go gathering Nuts in May."

You can imagine our astonishment at hearing these grown men singing this nursery song in wartime. We listened more intently and found they had slightly changed the words, and were singing, "Here we go gathering oats and hay, oats and hay, all the day." We left the cheering, happy crowd singing away in the moonlight.

What a moonlight night it was! And they went over and over again the songs and stories they had heard, a happy memory in the monotonous dull work of "gathering oats and hay."

Of course we had to drive after the voluntary driver who had taken the wrong turning, and found ourselves "somewhere in France," in the middle of the night, quite unaware of our direction. The signposts in France are very hard to read, and we spent some considerable time in climbing up the signposts, lighting matches, and trying to find where we were. We took the wrong turning and found ourselves on the road to Paris, and wandered about most of the night, first in search of the wretched independent voluntary driver, and afterwards, having given up pursuing him, we found the right road, and though it was a lovely night, we were very thankful when, in the wee, small hours, we got back to the hotel in Rouen. The next day he expressed no repentance for leading us such a midnight dance.

There was a lovely story about Abancourt. When the first Y.M.C.A. tent was opened, someone had the bright idea of sending a man who had been a lecturer to speak to the men on Germany. He had been a student there, and so he told them at great length about the German customs, the German Christmas, and the German life. The following day the Censor, going through the letters, found reason to prevent the lecturer discoursing further on his German experiences. For one of the men solemnly wrote to his wife the whole story, as far as he could remember it—the story of the German Christmas, the German character, the German virtues —without any comment, but in a postscript said: "If all this is true, what I want to know is, what the bloody hell are we doing here?"

The first of the concerts we gave in the open was at Forges les Eaux, so called because of the iron spring that was discovered about 400 years ago. It has been a watering-place with a Casino and a Hôtel des Bains ever since. I believe that Edward VII. was often a visitor. The water is very palatable and distinctly tastes of iron. Forges les Eaux was the horses' hospital, a wonderful example of humane organisation. The horses had their operating theatre, sterilising apparatus, chloroform nosebags, surgical instruments and pills—a fearful sight those pills, rather like cartridges in size and colour—doses and tonics, just like their human brothers. The nurses were men who went round the wards changing the dressings and bathing and tending the wounds. Patience, gentleness, consideration—these, too, have their part in the great enterprise of war.

Though it was hot that June, the first thing that I noticed was the absence of flies. Generally flies and horses seem to go together, but in this hospital cremation was the word. Everything to be destroyed was burnt at once.

We opened a new tent on the racecourse, In a thunderstorm. The noise of the rain and of the hail on the roof must have deafened the audience as much as it disconcerted us.

The officers' mess at Bapaume was a fine *château* on a hill, with a wonderful view looking down from the hills on to the delightful little town. Rouen was always tremendously lighted, as though Zeppelins and aeroplanes were unknown. The garden was lighted with Chinese lanterns when we had supper under the trees.

We opened a new hut at Bapaume. It was a tremendously big one. Major Barnes was C.O. there, always a good friend to our work, throughout all the war. His camp was one of the great Motor Repair Depots in France and was, I think, the first for that work. In 1914, when the evacuation of Rouen took place, this depot had to be evacuated at a very few hours' notice, and it is something to be proud of that they had such a complete control of the work that not a bolt or screw was left. On the return of the army they restarted the work in the same spot, and at this time it was a vast camp where there were all the spare parts of all the cars used by the army. The damaged cars used to come down to this base to be refitted.

The organisation must have been tremendous. It was a very difficult camp to find one's way about in, and at the end of the concert Major Barnes used to ask the men to form a pathway to show us the way out. So we went out from the hut between two rows of men, all lighting matches to show us the cinder path. But who could look at the cinder path when all those faces were illuminated in the darkness as the matches were lit and held in front of them?

In Rouen, at the Bakeries, I saw how the army made its bread. The bakehouse was a huge field, with a sort of trench dug the whole length of it, forming a tunnel. The bakers simply packed the faggots into the tunnel, and when it was glowing with heat, put in the dough and left it there all night. It was bread in the morning. This method, I believe, originated in India.

Into the hospitals we went, of course, with our music, our little songs and poems, into the atmosphere impregnated with pain and the awful blackness of concentrated suffering; but there was always the same mysterious magnetism which changed the atmosphere and made way, at any rate, for a temporary happiness.

At one hospital there was a boy whose face was grey and tense with pain. His shoulder was in a surgical bath, with all his nerves exposed; the perspiration poured from his forehead. I went and sat beside him and put my hand on his head, and presently, as the strain relaxed, he began to cry. Why should not a man cry? The other men in the ward all turned away, hating to see his weakness, and I crept away while his sobs broke the silence of the ward. After the concert I went back to listen to the singers, who were going round visiting the cases too ill to be moved. The *soprano* was singing a chorus song to a violin accompaniment, and the boy was singing louder than any of the rest. At any rate for a little while the tension had gone and he was able to forget the pain.

The most terrible side of the war, and no words can paint the horror and unutterable cruelty of it, was the sight of scores of men gasping for their very life-breath, some of them blue in the face as in the agonies of drowning, those who had just been gassed.

While the story of Neuve Chapelle was still poignantly painful, I met an uproarious company of men in hospital blue, bandaged, shuffling, and limping, on the way from a hospital concert, and found it difficult to believe that they were truly fifty men from out of hell, mangled in that heroic charge.

The most pathetic sight almost is to see the patients who have been severely wounded by lyddite explosion; their poor faces, stripped of all the skin, are swathed in cotton-wool and bandages until their heads appear out of all proportion to their bodies. In the midst of the mass of bandages are cunningly arranged funnels which lead to the patient's eyes and enable him to have a somewhat constricted idea of what is passing in the outside world. His hands, too, may be swathed in bandages until they are larger than boxing gloves, but that does not prevent him from "showing his appreciation in the usual way." The pathetic way in which those two eerie funnels attempt to follow your every movement show that, despite the terrible handicap of smothering bandages, he is not missing anything he can help.

It is only natural that hospital patients should enjoy most what they can appreciate with the least effort, and it can be therefore readily understood that the ballad-singers, and above all the instrumentalists, should be most popular in the hospitals. The last movement of the Mendelssohn Concerto and the Intermezzo of the *Cavalleria Rusticana*, Handel's "Largo," were always much loved in hospital. When the nursing sister would have kept a Serious Cases Ward sacred and undisturbed, the men asked that some music might come in to them. Literally, music is what they crave for, even when they are dying.

On one occasion there was a man in very great pain; his tense face strained and infinitely weary, he was waiting for the music to start. When the violinist passed him he said, "Give us something nippy, Miss." She went up to the top of the room and played the gayest tune she knew, but when she looked for his face at the end of it, she saw that he had passed on to the Great Unknown while she was playing.

That music is the medicine of the mind was happily illustrated on many occasions. A soldier who had been badly wounded and had endured racking pain for many days fell into his first sleep listening to music. For seven hours he derived the benefit of *"sleep that knits up the ravelled sleeve of care,"* after he had been *"lulled with sounds of sweetest melody."*

We are beginning to learn many things about the power of suggestion, and a very good example, I think, we came across, with a man who had been given up as hopeless. When the entertainer was telling him some amusing stories, he asked if it was true that he was "for it." The entertainer assured him that he was not going to die, that there was no reason that he should imagine that he was so severely wounded, and, having cheered him, went away. There was lively disagreement between those who felt that the entertainer was quite wrong, when he knew that the man was dying, to persuade him to the contrary, and thus cut short his time of preparation for another world. The discussion was very heated, and some bitter things were said which made me remember the incident, and afterwards, on a subsequent visit, a nurse told me that the man had recovered—at any rate he had been sent home to England.

A very touching incident which happened was when Mr. Ernest Groome sang the old favourite "Mother Machree." Among the audience was a soldier who had been through severe fighting, and received such severe injuries that his mind was a complete blank. He had no memory of his past, and his words were a meaningless babble out of which the nurses could make nothing coherent. But by one of those sudden and curious mental effects which are sometimes produced upon the deranged mind, the man caught upon the word "Mother" in the song, and when the singer had finished, he still went on repeating the word "Mother" with a half-vacant mind, till its constant repetition seemed to give him the key to his memory, and unlock the recollection of his previous life. He has now recovered and is a perfectly normal and sane man. Many seemingly miraculous cures of deafness, dumbness, and blindness in soldiers have been effected by means of an accidental appeal to the emotions.

When Miss Carrie Tubb and Miss Phyllis Lett were in France in September 1916, with the Westminster Singers, they all agreed that the taste of the soldier audiences was extraordinarily good. They loved the old folk-songs. For instance, they never tired of "Annie Laurie," and they were very appreciative of the old English catches, "Would you know my Celia's Charms?" which is nearly two hundred years old, and they loved Sir Frederick Bridge's "The Goslings," but above all, "Drink to me only with thine Eyes" had immense popularity. They were very proud of a remark made by a soldier in finishing his speech. He said that the voices sounded like a lovely chord.

I believe there is something that connects rag-time with war, because, as Julius Harrison wrote in the *Musical Times*, "There is real genius in these despised tunes. Could you but hear these music-starved men shouting out these songs with full lung-power, you too would come to the conclusion that rag-time seems to quicken the pulse of the soldier in the most extraordinary way. They seem to be the external expression of his whole emotional being."

It is not only the suffering of war one is made to realise, but it is also the dullness, the monotony, the dreariness of the lives of thousands of men; and of all dreary spots, I do not suppose there is any drearier than Cinder City in the docks at Havre, a great mass of railway lines and huts on a piece of marsh land reclaimed from the sea and filled in with cinders. Here lived thousands of transport workers doing dockers' work between the quay and the railway. Many of these men had been in the trenches and had been invalided from the fighting line though they were not ill enough to come home.

It was amazing the way every Cinder City Tommy had made a garden. Who would have believed that flowers would grow in cinders? But they do, and where Tommy found that the hardiest flowers would not grow, he made wonderful patterns of coloured stones and grass—a pathetic witness to the human being's longing for beauty and colour.

The Convalescent Camp at Havre was, at the beginning, a very arid place where a great deal of refuse had been thrown. When I saw it in March it was very dreary. In June it was already a garden. Everywhere where the English stayed, even for a short time, Tommy made his garden. No wonder that sometimes the French were a little uneasy. I do not think any other nation would be impelled to plant flowers—vegetables, perhaps, but not flowers—the way the English did, and what with the Harfleur Valley filled with roses, and ramblers climbing over the new huts, and the immense erections for baths, no wonder that the Frenchman sometimes wondered if the British meant to remain for ever.

In Rouen we gave a special concert for the hard-worked surgeons and nurses. Most of them had been out there since August without rest or holiday.

The concert was given in a hut, No. 27, which was on the roadside, and during the concert one always prayed that there might not be too many motor-lorries passing. The motor horns do not always punctuate one's recitations in the right place. There were over six hundred nurses and R.A.M.C. doctors, Just a few from the many hospitals who could be spared for a few hours. The Y.M.C.A. collected them in motors and brought them out to the hut, and took them back again at the end of the concert.

Colonel Jopp took the chair that night, and made a most delightful speech, and, amongst much cheering, I was presented with an enormous bouquet. The concert being late, the supper that was given us afterwards was late, and we started back for Rouen after hours. It was quite dark when we started back, and just outside the town we found our way barred by a French sentry. We explained who we were to no purpose. The sentry merely said, "I have my orders. No one may pass." We had resigned ourselves to sleeping in the car, though a Ford meat-safe is not always the most comfortable place in which to spend a night; but one of the company finally prevailed upon the sentry to send for his superior officer, who came and gave the necessary instructions for us to pass through. I do not know who was the most relieved, we or the sentry.

On another occasion, returning from a concert in the dark, we lost our way and arrived at the station, but the level-crossing gates were locked. We knocked up the stationmaster, who was fast asleep, and who was naturally very irritable, and said that for no one would he unlock the gates, not even for General Joffre himself—a refusal which caused a very long detour, and we got home about 4 a.m.

No. 2 Territorial Base Depot had at that time the largest hut in the base, and it was one of the most delightful audiences that we met, and we all enjoyed our visit to the mess, where Colonel Crawley treated us with that delightful courtesy and consideration which seemed to belong to all the dugouts. One of the most embarrassing moments of my life was on an occasion later on in the war when I happened to be touring round on my own, taking a general supervising visit to sort out disagreements and adjust deficiencies, and have a peep at the different concert parties, both permanent and visiting. I wrote a little note to Colonel Crawley from the Y.M.C.A. hut, and said I was there and would love to pay my respects to him. He came out at once and asked me to come into the mess, and, without realising, I did so.

Apparently hundreds of men stood up and waited at attention whilst we went through the mess, and though actors are accustomed to receiving a good deal of attention when on the stage, I think they find it somewhat embarrassing when any notice is taken of them when off. But of course all the standing and the attention I received was not because I was an actor, but only because I was a woman. There is something in the old copy-book saying: "*Manners maketh man.*" He told an orderly to get me a table napkin. There was a great delay, and a second request for it. One at last was brought, which was evidently not quite fresh from the linen-cupboard, and when the colonel remonstrated, the wretched orderly said that there were no clean ones.

The colonel was rather unhappy because he said that I would remember his mess as deficient in table-linen; but though I remember the incident, of course, I remember much more vividly the delightfulness and kindliness shown to us. In his delightful letter you notice that he says that these glimpses of civilisation (namely, the concerts) have had an ennobling effect upon them, and seem to take them out of the drab surroundings there. There are drab surroundings and desperately grey lives even when there is no war. In his letter Colonel Crawley says:

> On behalf of this depot we cannot allow you to leave Rouen without expressing our intense gratitude to you, and to those kind ladies and gentlemen who have given us such great pleasure on so many occasions. We know that it is you, in conjunction with the highest ladies of the land, who have made these concerts possible, and that it is you personally who have carried out this beneficent scheme. You must have realised yourself the

intense enjoyment that these concerts give to the men, and how readily they respond to the ennobling music and high-class songs with which you entertain them. They have been through hell, and, poor chaps, are soon to undergo it again, and these glimpses of civilisation have had the most ennobling effects on them, and seem to take them out of the drab surroundings here. I think that you know what a grand service you and your artists have rendered them, and I am sure *I* know how grateful we are to you all for this great kindness to us. We only hope that we may have the good fortune to see you personally here again.

At one concert there were about 700 Tommies—500 sitting, and about 200 standing. When I entered the hall, which, owing to the torrid weather, resembled a Turkish bath, I asked the chairman if he would ask the men to remove their tunics. There was a unanimity of modesty among this khaki-clad audience, and the semi-frightened and semi-inquiring glances which went round the hall made me fear that my suggestion might be considered somewhat indelicate, but a burly Inniskilling Dragoon, with an air of righteousness, rose from his seat and said, "Sure, if the girl says it, she means it," and jauntily removed his serge. "There ye are!" he added, and in a twinkling the entire audience were struggling and squirming out of their tunics. Of course, they were very much happier in their familiar army shirts, known as the grey-back.

Once we arrived at a hut to find a long thick queue of men outside, and the hut entirely full. We were just going to start the concert when the colonel addressed the men, and told them that "the chaps outside were going up to the trenches that night," and he wondered if those of the men who were in the hut, and were not immediately for the line, would make room for the ones who were. Every man in the hut seemed to stand up as if it had been drill time, and, turning, they filed out of the building, whilst those outside filed in.

We had a tremendous reception at the Remount Depot, and a letter which I received afterwards settled the question as to whether it was possible to make any charge for the concerts. The adjutant, Captain Ashworth, wrote to me that:

The deafening cheering last night, and the singing of 'He's a jolly good Fellow' perhaps convinced you that, though we haven't suitable words or a song by which appropriately to acknowledge our obligations where a lady is concerned, yet officers and men really felt a great gratitude, not only for the concerts provided under your auspices, but for your own inspiration and leadership in the matter. I thought, however, that it might please you if one tried to express it on paper.

The hut in which you gave the concert last night is the Y.M.C.A. home of two classes of men, namely, cavalrymen *en route* to the Front, and men of the Remount Depot who are here permanently. The latter number nearly 1000. I think that to both classes the concerts have meant much more than would ordinarily be implied by musical performances. They are the expression of a generous feeling of good cheer from their countrymen which comes opportunely to the cavalrymen on the eve of their departure for the Front, and to the Remount men in the weariness and trial of long hours of hard and dangerous work.

I should make this letter too long if I attempted to relate what the Remount men endured last winter, but still I can say that they displayed a marvellous spirit which makes every officer who was here at the time feel how well they deserve the encouragement afforded by your concerts.

We should all be willing to pay to go in, and the place would be just as full, but to pay a *sou* would prick the bubble of that feeling that 'this is done by the people at home, and by the performers for *me*,' which everyone at present has, and which contains all its special significance.

The entertainments themselves have been very high class in performance and tone, whilst your own interest, talents, and gracious presence have ensured the success of the undertaking.

Many people had urged that it was much better to make a charge, and certainly it would have simplified the work; but I am sure that Captain Ashworth was right, and that the concerts, though useful in themselves, would have lost half their value if they had not been coupled with the idea that each note was a loving gift from home and a sign that the people were remembering them and thinking of them. It was this very vital question of finance which made me leave the party after the big concert in the theatre at Havre. General Bruce-Williams, the base *commandant*, took the chair on that occasion, and all the ladies were presented with beautiful bouquets. A delightful speech was made, and I had the joy of replying and expressing the gratitude of the artists.

These performances in the theatres were tremendous events for us. There were a few civilians, very few, and those French; a few ladies; and then tier after tier of khaki, an extraordinary sight from the stage.

The presentation of the bouquets was always made by the men, and on one occasion the colonel was especially asked for three sergeants and a smart private, and it was great fun to hear the "smart private" get roars of applause each time he came on, stood like a board, saluted, presented the bouquet, saluted, turned with a click of the heels, and marched off to the wings. An officer sent the "smart private" on an errand just as the *soprano* began to sing, so her bouquet was presented by some one in mufti, and the "smart private" returned breathless and broken-hearted.

I went straight from the theatre to the boat, very sorry indeed to have to leave the party, which was going on with the tour, but I became convinced that no amount of summer and outdoor games could replace the concerts, and after the letter from Captain Ashworth, obviously something had to be done to ensure their being always a gift and free to the men.

Now getting money always sounds very simple, but I have always found it extremely difficult to accomplish, and returning to London in July, it was quite obvious that none of the ways that I was accustomed to could be used for the purpose, since the summer is notoriously a bad time for indoor entertainments. So I decided to take my courage in both hands and try to write an account of my experiences; and, getting up at four o'clock in the morning so as to ensure some complete quiet, I tried to put an account of my experiences in writing. The Press were good enough to publish these efforts, and the interest of the public was aroused, because every one longed to do all they could to help the men in the war areas, and in a very short time, in response to the articles, although no special appeal was made, I received close upon a thousand pounds.

Chapter 2

In France

There is no doubt that the War Office regarded our work as of importance since they made an exception on our behalf with regard to permits. Few permits at that time were issued for less than three or four months, but we were given short permits for the touring parties. These parties went for four to six weeks. The work was too hard to allow of a longer period; every one was exhausted after the strain of over seventy performances added to the journeys and long hours, although, to simplify the travelling as much as possible, the work was divided up into sections.

The first bases, of course, were Havre and Rouen, not too far apart; then Boulogne, not very accessible from Havre, so Boulogne and Calais became another section for a second party, to which was added Treport and Dieppe. This became too much to handle with one party, so a third party took Amiens, Dieppe, and Le Treport. With the opening up of further bases the number of parties naturally increased, so that there were in all five parties leaving every month, which we called touring parties, because they moved more than the permanent parties who remained four to six months in one base. At the time of the Armistice there were in all twenty-five parties in France.

People thought they might wander a little when in France, but every one was definitely tied down to the area of their work. No one could move to another place without the proper *visées* and the *permis de séjour* it was quite obvious one was in the grip of the military machine. In February 1918 concert parties of seven went on

2nd February for five weeks to Rouen and Paris,
11th   "   "   "   Calais, St. Omer, and Aire.
15th   "   "   "   Abbeville, St. Pol, etc.

25th　"　four　"　Havre and Trouville.

Besides these constantly changing little companies there were permanent parties at Abbeville, Boulogne, two at Havre, two at Rouen, Trouville, Dieppe, Marseilles, Etaples, Cherbourg; there were Repertory Companies in Paris, Rouen, Havre, Abbeville, and Calais, the Single-Handed Entertainers, and the party in Egypt.

Owing to the difficulty in regard to men, in 1917 it was decided to have touring parties composed entirely of women, who went out first in January of that year. This was considered a grave innovation and likely to lead to complications, and only got through because of the impossibility of making any other arrangement. The experiment proved a tremendous success, because the chivalry of every one was immediately aroused at the sight of these "helpless" women; and throughout, touring parties of women only were the most successful, which can be easily understood if one can realise that it was an intense joy, as a man once said to me, "to see a pair of slippers;" and the girls who, at the beginning of the war, always dressed in rather serviceable clothes, soon found out that the brightest colours and the prettiest frocks gave the greatest pleasure to the men, whose love for colour was in some way satisfied. When one of the theatre party was going out, the dressmaker advised a red dress to "cheer the men from the monotony of the guns."

The fees paid on the touring parties varied. Many artists went for nothing; but the lines on which we worked were to make it possible for the artist to go, and the fees were paid not according to the artistic or moneymaking powers of the artist, but rather with a view to meeting the out-of-pocket expenses which would go on at home while they were abroad. The fees ranged from £1-1s. to £7-10s. per week, which was the highest paid. The usual procedure was to pay the artist a cheque for the whole amount on his return from the tour, unless, for convenience, written instructions were given that the cheque was to be paid to a representative. All the artists were billeted, and had to pay for neither travelling expenses nor board and lodging. There was a further expense when Army Regulations issued an order that every one was to be in uniform. All the artists had then to be fitted with Y.M.C.A. uniforms and caps—the only difference between our uniform and the Y.M.C.A. was a slight difference in cut, and each artist wore a concert badge.

The Seventh Concert Party included plays in August 1915. I suppose there is no author who writes more delightful one-act plays than Miss Gertrude Jennings, and it was she who organised this first dramatic party which had immense success. These first plays were *Mother o' Pearl, In the Fog,* and *Five Birds in a Cage.* She had not at that time written her successful three-act plays, such as *The Young Person in Pink,* etc.

There were three musicians who could also take some part in the acting.

I wish a record could be made of the actors who won distinction in the war. There are a great number with the D.S.O, and M.C. A very great number enlisted immediately on the outbreak of war, and I have heard that in proportion to the number in the profession the percentage is as high if not higher than any other. It was for this reason that we had, from the commencement, the greatest difficulty in getting any actors, since most of them were already in the army. Later, we had the help of those who had been invalided out of the army. I was never able to persuade those who were over age to come out and play with us. The only actor of distinction who made the sacrifice of his holiday was Sir John Martin Harvey. I did try very hard to persuade them, but they were not to be enticed to leave. Some were playing in very successful plays, and others were afraid of dropping out or missing some fine opportunity by being abroad.

The actor's position is a somewhat difficult one. With the musicians, they can make arrangements far ahead, and do not require to give so much time before for rehearsals. The actor never knows when he may be losing a job, and always has to give at least a fortnight to three weeks before a production for rehearsals, and he cannot, like the musician, provide a substitute at the last moment. Besides, they are always old-fashioned, and difficult to move in any new direction. I do not suppose any section of the community was more convinced that the woman's place was the home, and though actors have to allow the greater part of a play to be represented by women, they do not like women to represent the profession.

How many years, for instance, have passed before a woman was allowed to have any power in the Actors' Benevolent Fund?—a power so well exercised now by Lady Wyndham. In public events, when there has to be a special performance, the arrangements are made exclusively by the men, and one of the most comic moments to me was when, in 1921, there was a big meeting at Drury Lane, with the Prince of Wales in the Chair, and Lord Haig and Lord Beatty, and all the distinguished actors and managers, when the special appeal was started known as "Warriors' Day." There were men who assured the prince and those great representatives of the navy and the army that the actors and managers, the electricians, the musicians, the stage carpenters, and the Actors' Association would all support this national effort. Though Mrs. Kendal and Ellen Terry were on the stage, it did not occur to any of the organisers that it might have been gracious to have one of them say that the women of the profession would give their services as gladly, as indeed they did, as the men.

Miss Jennings was very fortunate in getting for her plays two most delightful amateurs, Mr. Frank Macey and Mr. Paget Bowman, one a builder and the other a solicitor. Mr. Bowman is now one of the directors of the National Opera Company. His Creator meant him to be an actor, but he chose, or rather, I suppose, fell into the law, where he has had much success. Perhaps these journeys as an actor to France, and later on his directing the musicians at Giro's gradually led him into these new responsibilities, for it was in these associations he first met the singers and musicians with whom he now works.

At that time the newspapers were amusing themselves with girding at the callousness and forgetfulness of the people of England, and comparing us unfavourably with the French nation. Of course, there were soldiers everywhere in France, but there were also civilians in quantities, many of whom seemed to be of military age. I remember the "housemaid" at the hotel in Rouen was a fine, active-looking fellow. The French soldiers were not always as smart or efficient looking as the English, and they looked worn and tired. Their drill is different from ours, and their marching is more for practical use than any demonstration of smartness or show; besides, they went up the line with many odd things slung on their shoulders, frying-pans, etc. There were many widows to be seen, but the general aspect of the towns was very much the same as those of England, only at nights the streets were not darkened, at any rate not to the same extent.

No one was very encouraging about the plays. Concerts were now recognised, but to do plays was a different matter. Cries of alarm rose on every side. There would be no curtain, no footlights, no dressing-rooms, no furniture, perhaps no stage. However, we meant to go, and go we did.

Never was audacity better rewarded. True, all the objections were fulfilled. There were no curtains, footlights, dressing-rooms, or furniture. They dressed in small dark crevices at the side of the stage, their light two guttering candles on a packing-case. They had for stage properties three wooden chairs and a scent-bottle.

In one play scene,—Battersea Park—the chairs stood in a row; in the other play—scene, a drawing-room in Mayfair—the chairs were separated, and represented a settee, a music-stool, and a table. A decanter and a couple of liqueur glasses were supposed to appear in this scene; they took the form of a ginger-beer bottle and two stout china mugs on which was imprinted the legend, "——'s Milk." But what did it matter? What did it matter when they had audiences who thronged the halls, climbed upon benches and on each other's shoulders, pressed in at the doors, looked in at the windows, and laughed and cheered as audiences have never done before?

"Battersea Park" might have come straight from His Majesty's Theatre, "Percy's Drawing-room" from the St. James's—what did the men care? So long as they forgot for an hour "the weariness, the fever, and the fret;" so long as they could laugh and cheer and be happy, they didn't care how much they made believe.

Many of them had come straight from the trenches, where they had been for seven or eight months, others were just getting well after pain and suffering, a few fresh from England, perhaps a little homesick in the strange land. All were glad of the short respite, the plays, and the fine concert which was given in the interval.

They gave two performances every night, often in the same camp, the second audience coming in as soon as the first went out.

One night during the "first house" there was an appalling crash. The men sprang to their feet, but the colonel called out "Sit down!" and they sat silently, all wondering what had happened. The balcony outside had given way, and hundreds of men had fallen through. Luckily it was not high, and the men were so tightly wedged together that no one was hurt. The party were all very anxious till they heard the men were safe, but as the leading man gloomily remarked, "Don't worry. No one will break down balconies to see us in England!"

Another night they played near the Indian Camp. It was a wonderful starlight night, intensely still, and it was strange to see the dark forms of the Indians moving about the tents and standing in silent rows looking through the windows of the hut at the English company. How curious, how mad it must have seemed to them!

The party often gave their first evening performance out of doors. The men liked it better, as it was not so fearfully hot, and they had more room. The strain on the voices was not great, as, luckily, there was no wind. Once, though, a touching moment of the play was rather marred by a talkative donkey, who joined in the dialogue at the top of his voice. The actors tried to ignore him, but he was too eloquent, and a rather pretty love scene ended in helpless laughter from all concerned.

Every afternoon they gave a performance in one of the hospitals. Men whom one would think too ill to open their eyes were carried in on stretchers, and in a few minutes were as cheery as the strongest. They laughed at the plays, they encored the songs as though nothing were the matter. "Gives us something bright to think about, this does," said one poor fellow. Something bright to think about! That was the secret. Wonderful care and kindness they received, everything that love and skill could do was done, but these entertainments from England just gave that little bit of pleasure which cheered and encouraged them.

The perils of the stages in the hospitals were no less than in the huts. They had a stage in one place which, when trodden upon on one side, rose in a sinister manner on the other, and in another place the platform was so small that in order to move they had to take their furniture (always three chairs, remember!) with them. One chair was placed gracefully over the edge of the platform, and the comedian nearly fell off backwards.

Another hospital performance was on an esplanade at a beautiful seaside place. Here the men lay out all day in the sun, and their faces were as brown as berries. The beds were all around them at the performance, and they had to turn in every direction to be certain the patients heard. On this occasion they asked one boy how he liked it, and he said, "Fine! Why, I've paid ninepence and seen worse!"

The first place they played at, No. 1 Stationary Hospital, Rouen, Gertrude Jennings was immensely popular in the title-*rôle* of Mother o' Pearl. She had naturally begun her career as an actress; the writing of plays came later.

I expect one of the most interesting performances they gave was outside the cavalry hut in Rouen, by night. There were about 2000 men able to enjoy the performance, as a splendidly lighted stage had been rigged up by the men with electric footlights. It was a perfect summer evening, with no wind; the front row was seated, men standing behind, and behind them, men standing on water-carts and every kind of box, anything to raise them so that they could see, and behind them all there were the hills that screen Rouen, and behind that again, the dusky skies with a star or two appearing.

They had an overflowing audience at the Engineers' and the Indians' Hut, where there were the white faces in front and the black faces with their glittering eyes behind; Sikhs, Pathans, Gurkhas, and every kind of Indian were in the audiences. So many came to join in the great struggle against the German idea of domination. The dressing-rooms were tents as a rule, bell tents. There was no scenery and of course no furniture. They had to rely always upon the imagination of the audience, and never found that fail. It was quite sufficient to explain that the army blankets represented the corridor of an hotel, or that the same blankets were to convey the impression of the great hall of Macbeth Castle, and immediately the audience understood.

As a general rule our bathroom door was a trestle table top propped up against the back wall, profusely decorated with texts and portraits of the Royal Family. The audience had seen it propped up, and had seen our indefatigable Baritone-"boots," Hudson, pin up *The Bathroom Door* notice. Yet, although everyone must have known that there was not, and could not be, anyone or anything concealed behind it, there was always a breathless hush of expectation when the moment arrived for the door to be opened. That was as it should be, and we congratulated ourselves accordingly. I often wonder if the great attention to detail in the production of plays, the magnificent scenery, the intense realism of the end of the nineteenth century and the beginning of the twentieth, may not have had a tendency to deaden the imagination.

They gave a public performance at the Théâtre des Arts, Rouen, and also in the theatre at Havre. These theatres are both municipal, and belong to the people of the town. The mayor always has his box reserved. The Théâtre des Arts, Rouen, a very old theatre, is one of the largest in France. It is about the size of the old Drury Lane. The big Paris productions have a trial week there as a rule before going up to Paris. To those who love the theatre, the place is particularly interesting as the birthplace of Corneille; his father had charge of the magnificent forests which still surround the beautiful old town.

The French were very considerate and kind about the theatres, but as they had to get leave from the English base *commandant* before they could let their theatre for our performances, sometimes feeling ran a little high.

Some of the notices in the French Press were extremely flattering to our work, and we were always very proud of these French notices, because they are a people who understand acting and the theatre, and their criticism is always founded on very real knowledge. One cannot have a national theatre since the sixteenth century, with all its tradition and influence, and not have a very highly educated appreciation of the theatre as an art. "*Ce fut une manifestation artistique au chef, bien digne du succes, car lui a valu d'interpretation de premier ordre.*" "Remarkable interpretation *de tous les acteurs.*"

There was some difficulty in getting a suitable scene for the lift for *Five Birds in a Cage*, a difficulty made even greater by Miss Jennings' insistence that the word "lift" was "*escalier.*" But in spite of all difficulties the French made a remarkable little scene with two gates and lamps and a centre light. This story always reminds me of the lady who went motoring in France before the war. The motor ran into the parapet of a bridge, and both the bridge and the car were somewhat dilapidated by the contact. This lady was sent on to appeal for help, and after walking some distance she met a Frenchman and explained "*que le motor a crâchez sur le pont.*"

No. 2 Stationary Hospital was almost the first hut, indeed, I think it was the first hut that had curtains, scenery, and footlights. Before the performance the actors showed themselves to the wounded who were lying in beds outside the hut, so that when they could only hear the dialogue they would know what the actors looked like. One of the most amusing efforts of an actor to entertain the men who could not get into the hut was when one of them made up black to amuse the Indian troops.

The tiny stage in the hut of the 27th Division always caused excitement of some kind. Miss Jennings on this occasion, in playing Mother o' Pearl, jumped off the tiny stage and fell heavily. This set everyone off giggling, and anyone who has started laughing in church, knowing that it is against all rules and must not be done, will appreciate the exquisite agony when something starts one laughing during the playing of a play.

No. 8 Stationary Hospital was in a delightful seminary outside the barrier and away from the camps. There was a good stage in the little theatre where the young ladies used to give their performances before the war.

We learnt from the officers who censored the men's letters that they wrote at great length and with great enthusiasm about the plays, and many of the officers said that plays were greatly appreciated and gave the men more to think about than the songs.

The Second Theatre Party went out in March 1916. They were held up for twelve hours at Folkestone and were a little indignant at the delay, but when the *Sussex*, on which they crossed, was torpedoed a fortnight later, and fifty people lost their lives, they understood the reason, and the watchful care which supervised all the traffic on the sea—one of the reasons why we all appreciated the few opportunities we had for entertaining the crews of the trawlers.

This was practically the same party as the first. They took *The Bathroom Door, In the Fog, Mother o' Pearl, The Lady in Black*. They went on the other route this time—Dieppe, Etaples, Calais, Le Treport. Every one then was talking of the big move to come, and all the hospitals were increasing their beds, especially at Etaples.

The party had a variety of experiences with regard to dressing-rooms. Once the men dressed in a large regimental kitchen, with the cooking in full swing; sometimes the coldest of tents, and occasionally in the open air. On 20th March, at the 1st Reserve Canadian Park, they dressed in the open air, with a few villagers admiring them.

During the motor drive into Etaples an incident occurred which must seem very trifling in the telling, but which nevertheless was very moving to them. They were all a little depressed that morning, partly at leaving a neighbourhood where they had been happy and made several friends, and partly at the thought that in a few hours they would have to put grease paint on their faces in broad daylight and assume a gaiety they could not feel. They sat bumping along the road in their motor ambulance, somewhat sad and dejected, and inclined to be cross, when they were held up for some unexplained reason.

Just outside the little French town; and then, as a little breeze whispered in the tops of the pine trees, so a sound crept into their dull ears that set their hearts aflame and their eyes ablaze—the bagpipes! Every fibre of their bodies, every impulse of their souls was awake and teeming with life, as the Cameron Highlanders swung through the street with their pipes and drums. The Frenchmen sat and admired silently, and they, not daring to look at one another for fear of showing the emotion they felt, bit their lips to keep back the tears of pride, and thanked God that they were—what they were.

Several performances on this tour were given in tents, and the cold winds of March made them tremble and shiver, the canvas flapped and banged and the wind roared, but they flapped and banged and roared louder still, and the audience were as enthusiastic as ever. The laughter was so long and loud, and the plays went so wonderfully, that when, in

The Bathroom Door, the spinster, Mary Barton, said "How beautiful!" the other performers might have gone away for the week-end and still have been back in time for the cue!

It was in September 1916 that I went with a theatre party to Havre and Rouen. There had been a great number of requests for Shakespeare, especially from Rouen. I made a mighty effort to secure a cast that could play a whole play of Shakespeare's, but there were no men available. After a great deal of thought and discussion we found that scenes from *Macbeth* could be done with only two men, so our two splendid amateurs who had already made plays possible for us, came to our rescue, and with one professional actor, Ben Field, we made up the cast for *The Twelve Pound Look*, by Sir James Barrie, scenes from *The School for Scandal, The Lonely Soldier*, which was being played at the Coliseum with great success, *The Bathroom Door*, and scenes from *Macbeth*.

I had always longed to play Lady Macbeth from very early days when, as a child in Canada, I sat on the granite rocks under the great pine trees in a forty-two acre pine wood on the banks of the St. Lawrence River, and recited plays to the wild columbines. When a student at the Royal Academy of Music, I was chosen to play Lady Macbeth at one of the students' concerts. In those days there were no schools of acting, and the Royal Academy of Music gave no public performances of plays, and at the students' performances in the academy there was no attempt at scenery and no costumes, although for the performances of scenes from operas the correct dresses were hired for the occasion. The great teacher of singing, Emmanuel Garcia, had encouraged me in my seething ambitions, and told me that I had a future.

It must have been a quaint performance when I played the great part, on the bare platform, dressed in a black grenadine frock. It must have been very raw and very comic, but I certainly was dreadfully in earnest, and his encouragement remained with me all through my career, and I longed always to play the part again. But, alas! I was never thought of, and when I tried to push myself into the very rare productions of *Macbeth*, my suggestion was not acceptable. For was I not the most modern of moderns and living in a time when tragedy was not understood or wanted? And now on the Shakespeare Tercentenary during the Great War, in the last place one would ever have expected, I was to realise my dreams.

We played the letter scene, the scene preceding the murder of Duncan, the murder scene, and the sleepwalking scene. Mr. Theodore Flint arranged plaintive and very beautiful music, which the trio played between the scenes to keep the atmosphere and indicate the change of time and place.

The first performance was in the great big theatre at Rouen, and besides a great khaki audience, there were many Indian officers, French officials, and soldiers in blue in the boxes and the circle. The theatre, of course, was packed. *Macbeth* had the first place on the programme, and could have heard much less than a pin drop, if anything had dropped; the silence was intense.

There is something in the rhythm of Shakespeare, in the splendour and fullness of the language which raises the mind and exalts the spirit, which gets to the soul of every man, whatever his class or education, whether he is a Cockney or comes from the farthest parts of the Empire. In the hour of death, the judgment of man cannot be hypnotised into the belief that murders are trivial things, and that robbery and selfishness are noble. The slipshod sentimentality which tried to make out that the wages of sin is an enviable success, and that there is nothing to hope for from the goodness of man, is useless in the hour of trial. The sight of murder is meant to fill the human soul with horror, and one major said that he had been in many battles since he came out in August 1914, but nothing had given him the cold horror that he had experienced at the murder of Duncan.

I had been nervous of playing Lady Macbeth, because of the attitude of amused contempt which seemed to be felt by every one in England when one mentioned the play—*The Twelve Pound Look*, by Sir James Barrie, was possible, because it had been accepted by the music halls. *The School for Scandal* might also give pleasure, as the costumes were delightful and the humour easily understood—but *Macbeth!* One of the great purveyors of entertainment, when I mentioned the play, said, "What have they done to you?" His powerful position made it possible for him to be candid where others had merely looked their amusement and contempt.

The week following the production of *Macbeth* we played scenes from *The School for Scandal*, and a sergeant, who was kindly helping us with the scenery, came and thanked me for *Macbeth*. He said he thought "it was great." He was so enthusiastic that I was encouraged to ask how the sergeants' mess had liked the play, because, of course, the sergeants in the army are the people who know. I asked for some criticisms overheard which might stir people at home and arouse further interest in the work. He was embarrassed, stroked his neck, massaged his back, scratched his head, examined his boots, and then said hopelessly, "Well, there, Miss, I ain't 'eard no complaints!"

We played the play again at the theatre in Havre, at the Central Y.M.C.A., at the new great Cinema at Rouelles in the Harfleur Valley, and the last performance was at Hangar Q. At Rouelles in the great cinema there were about 1500 men drawn from all ranks, all grades of society, all parts of the Empire, in a place where they were accustomed to the Cinema, and we knew if we lost hold of their attention and interest it would be impossible to regain it. We were all frightened—if we should fail! We held them from start to finish. There was breathless quiet throughout, and the reception at the end was terrific.

The stage was merely curtained with red curtains, and had a soap box covered with red cotton to sit on. We had only the splendid costumes of the period and the plaintive music of the trio to help us. Paget Bowman was splendid as Macbeth, very real in his conception of the cowardly, cruel, ambitious, imaginative man. Mr. Bowman's powerful imagination made the audience see with him the influences that beset Macbeth, and his diction is remarkable, and he has a speed of clear delivery which is most unusual, and tremendously important in the playing of Shakespeare's plays. Here is what he wrote about me:

> Miss Ashwell's Lady Macbeth was truly great. She reached new heights, and it has been a great privilege to me to play in the 'stuff' with this great artist. Had she been less successful as a modern actress, she would have been a great tragedy queen. Her voice actually seems to have developed since we began to rehearse *Macbeth*, and touch new, unaccustomed, and therefore very beautiful, notes.

Of course I am quite conceited enough to believe that it is all true, because all artists feel that they could do very much better things than they are ever able to do. And of course artists are limited by their audiences, and if the audience does not want the best of them, they must bury it away in their hearts. And if, when trying to interpret wonders of the human aching heart, the audience is not interested or moved, the actor must wither at the root. But if one has an audience of terribly alive and responsive humanity, one is able to play better than one ever dreamt of, and all the great subconscious power responds to the demands the audience makes on one.

The last time we played *Macbeth* was at Hangar Q, down at the docks in Havre, where the repairing work is done. Here they repair

200 pairs of boots a day. And here were guncarriages, wheels, harness, watches, machinery of every kind, bicycles, outfits of all sorts. When the king came here he insisted on seeing everything, overstayed his time, and could not be torn away. The men were labourers and mechanics, had no leave, and worked hard. It was almost impossible to find one's way, and no one ever seemed to know the place. I had protested that the place was unsuitable, that the platform was too tiny, and that there was no light, all to no purpose, for Mr. Arthur Reade returned to the attack. He brought the news that the men had especially asked for *Macbeth*, and at last I gave way and promised that we would do our best.

The hut was packed two hours before we were due to arrive, and we were rather late. Dr. Edwards gave a short prologue, written for the occasion, describing the play. The men listened like mice, and the reception of the play itself was too wonderful to describe. In the tiny space at the left-hand side of the platform was concealed the small trio, and those who had to make their entrances or exits from that side of the platform were packed in as well. When I had to change from Lady Macbeth's full robes into the sleep-walking costume, my little maid Lavender and I seemed to be standing on top of the pianist, and it was most embarrassing, but everyone discreetly looked in other directions while I changed, whilst she tried with her very diminutive presence to make herself into a screen. The men presented me with a bouquet for which they had subscribed, and there were cheers, and cheers, and more cheers, the final triumph of this venture of playing one of the greatest of the tragedies.

Although I played once more at a big fair at Nottingham, I always feel that this was my farewell to the stage as an actor, and one could not have made one's farewell under more wonderful circumstances. I am always grateful to Mr. Arthur Reade that he made me play the play under conditions which seemed to be absolutely impossible.

There are all sorts of memories of this tour, so many that one can only mention a few. *The Twelve Pound Look* was always a great success. The audiences were enormous. At the Territorial Hut we gave three performances in one day, and the hut held between fourteen and fifteen hundred men at each performance. Some of the men who found it impossible to get in were so disappointed that we pulled them through the window of the dressing-room at the side of the stage, or rather platform, and they saw the play from there. It was an extraordinary experience to meet a man with the tears running down his face, and when I asked him what had happened, he explained that he had longed so to hear the plays, and there was no room. We had to make a corner for him too.

At the Infantry Hut the crowd was so great that we had to open a door at the back of the stage, and we had the audience all round us. Such an arrangement would not seem to add to the dramatic effect, but the play went as well as ever, though the audience literally surrounded us. Every point was taken, but there was one that puzzled me very much, because it was always greeted with a roar of laughter quite out of proportion, I thought, to the humour of the line. Sir Harry Sims says, "One would have thought I had not been a good husband to you," and Kate replies, "You were a good husband according to your lights, and a moral man and chatty, and quite the philanthropist." After the word "chatty" one had to wait for an incredible time for the laugh to die down. Every one who was in the army knows why!

At No. 2 Stationary Hut we gave a performance on a stage in the open air, with threatening skies overhead. *The Bathroom Door* went through without a shower-bath, but we were about three-parts through *The Twelve Pound Look* when down came the torrential rain. As the whole of the audience was in bed, and no cover could be improvised, they must have returned to their wards in a saturated condition, and the orderlies must have had a lot of bed linen to dry that evening. The men pressed the doors and blocked the windows to get a glimpse of the stage, and any hut where there was a door at the back we had to leave it open so that a few more could stand. One boy down from the trenches cried as he thanked me, and said that we had helped to restore him to life.

It was usually an exciting journey to Etretat when we sat facing each other in the ambulance and were jolted there. We travelled in everything from a Rolls-Royce to a dirty old waggon, and very seldom in a train. Our most hated enemy was a Ford which had been converted into a covered-in van. It was always called "The Meat Safe," for it looked like a meat-safe on wheels. Once when going downhill—and there are some awful hills—swinging and swaying from side to side, someone called it "The Meat Unsafe."

For discomfort, though, it would be hard to beat a springless transport waggon, especially when journeying over cobblestones. But the journey to Etretat, which was included in every concert party's work, was always in a Red Cross Ambulance, which is the most uncomfortable form of conveyance ever invented, if it is used as we had to use it, as a sort of omnibus. We sat along each side facing each other, could not see the scenery, which is beautiful, could not talk because of the jolting—altogether a miserable experience. On the road from Havre to Etretat there was a formidable barrier built across the road, and the French sentries stopped us to make the usual inquiries, and see that we had our passports and *permis de séjour*, and all the rest of it.

Everyone quarrelled at Etretat. There was always a row because by that time everyone's nerves were on edge, and the tour was near the end. The long drive on top of the three performances daily for four weeks had exhausted every one. On this occasion, instead of being out of doors, the concert was in the theatre of the Casino—a fine hall, filled with beds, but with a stage at the far end. We were to give two performances at the Remounts in the evening. It had been decided that I should only play in *The Twelve Pound Look*, but as Grace Ivel had lost her voice, I volunteered to recite to fill up the programme. *The Bathroom Door* ended with the usual joyous applause from the audience, and the Etretat *straffe* at the back.

It did not last long, but it was very funny while it lasted. The indignant hero, wrapped in a bath-gown, speechless with fury, ordering everyone to their rooms which did not exist, and then retiring into a corner to use bad words, and laugh at the whole row. In the middle of this explosion I went on to recite, and was rather put off by the agitation, but was wholly finished by the antics of a very small fox-terrier who came during my recitation up the length of the ward, mounted some steps on to the platform, walked up and sat down in front of me, gazed in my face, turned and had a good look at all the men in the audience, and then turned round again to examine me, and very deliberately and slowly yawned.

Where did all the dogs come from? This one was a darling; but it was against army orders to bring dogs over to the Front, and yet, wherever one went, one was sure to find some delightful dog, and none of them, I am convinced, were born in France.

But the British soldier knows he wants some sort of music even before he has realised he wants a garden and a dog. If he can't have music he must have some sort of cheerful noise, or a noise that will pass for cheerful, even if it be a gramophone or a mouth-organ. We came across a "band" a lonely detachment of motor-drivers had improvised, with cardboard megaphones doing duty as trombones, and an empty petrol tin for a drum. It seems that any privation or hardship is borne more cheerfully than deprivation of amusement, and that the

British Army can stand anything except being bored. The men don't exactly quote Shakespeare's—

Sweet recreation barred, what doth ensue
But moody and dull melancholy,
Kinsman to grim and comfortless despair;
And at her heels a huge infectious troop
Of pale distemperatures and foes to life?

—but they express the same idea in other ways.

Our performance at the Casino was very exciting. Instead of the concert taking place on the stairs, one of the great big halls was the scene of our efforts, and a most attractive stage had been erected at the far end. This stage was covered with flags and had beautiful flowers both as footlights and decorations on the tables which furnished the stage. All went well until we began to walk about upon this platform. As it was made of tables placed but not joined together, the tables leapt apart, and one was in danger of falling between them unless one weighed very carefully the length of one leap from table to table. As no single table remained where it had been originally placed, and as the *prima donna* remarks in *The Bathroom Door,* "*Life was indeed full of pitfalls,*" Ben Field, who played Sir Harry Sims, very nearly did the trap-door act at the end of *The Twelve Pound Look.*

We played scenes from *The School for Scandal* at Forges les Eaux, the horses' hospital. The men had banked up and boarded a good stage about half-way up the meadow, with a ring of flowers for footlights and the Union Jack for a background. The men filled the meadow right back to the road, and along it there was a gallery of motor-lorries, and behind and at the sides a number of French wounded. The trees, also, were full of audience. There were two tents for dressing, but it was not very easy to struggle with a white wig and dresses with big panniers in so small a space. It was a very lovely, sunny day, and the dresses must have looked beautiful. The play certainly went extraordinarily well, and a delightful Tommy came up to me afterwards, and said, "Beg pardon, Miss, but that there old-fashioned scandalous play is great!"

We had a very splendid reception, too, at Rouelles in the Harfleur Valley, but before we began the performance we had an experience which was, I think, the most moving of all the thrilling and moving things which happened on this tour. Nearly a thousand Canadians, in the very pink of training, and fully equipped, were on parade. They were just being dispatched up the line. Colonel Worthington made them sit down on the sloping ground, and as the sun was setting he walked up and down among them and made a tremendously inspiring farewell speech. There were lots of strange oaths and curious expressions, and many references to "God's Own Country in the West." The men obviously loved him. Who did not? They treated him as a friend. They listened in absolute silence while he told them to go through doors instead of windows, not to go on the roof of the train, not to throw away their rations, etc. etc.

Then the *padre*, an ugly man, rather like a prize-fighter, began his address. At first they were restive, but very soon they all turned towards him, listening intently as he prayed *extempore* in a most moving way, facing the dying sun and pouring out in the simplest way what evidently expressed the feeling of the men. Then the men formed up and marched off to the troop trains, headed by the pipes. There are one or two faces I still see; I expect I shall always see them, as they marched away down the valley.

After the performance of *The School for Scandal* in the theatre that night, where Colonel Worthington made a wonderful speech, which took my breath away so completely that I hardly had any with which to make a satisfactory reply, I had a long talk with Mr. Arthur Reade and his brother, St. John. It appeared that they both felt that the most urgent need of the moment was to provide food for thought for the men, and they urged me with intense earnestness to see if it could not be arranged with the War Office to send some lecturers out. They did not especially ask for great educationists, rather for men who could arrest the attention of an audience, and tell them things of interest in a human and interesting way.

They all felt that as the nation to all intents and purposes was there in the war zones under military organisation,' what they read and felt and thought would eventually work out in the life of the Empire; also, that the military training to become an efficient fighting unit made little or no appeal to the brain. And though we were considered a lazy nation, even this dislike of mental effort could be overdone in the arid mental desert in which the men were living. The few men who were thinking at all seemed to be studying Karl Marx and little else, and for all real progress it is necessary to strike a balance. It is just as necessary to build as to destroy, though of course destruction is always the easier.

Lecturers were only granted permits for a period of at least three months, and many invaluable men were thus prevented from going.

On my return to England, Her Highness Princess Helena Victoria was good enough to listen most sympathetically to my expression of their views. Throughout my whole association with Her Highness, I had continually cause to marvel at her understanding, her keen sense of humour, her sense of fair play, and patience. She never spared herself, and sat through endless committees, wisely adjusting extreme differences of opinion; her love of her country, and very real sympathy and understanding of the difficulties of the workers differed greatly from the views of some less distinguished people, to whom paid persons seemed to be in a different category to the voluntary worker. Her sense of humour tided over many a knotty problem, and her generosity of mind enabled her to forgive and forget things which might well have lingered in a less generous mind. My association with her was a long one, and full of the greatest happiness.

On hearing of the new necessity she at once gave the first financial support for this new effort, and thus started the big education scheme of the Y.M.C.A. After many telegrams and telephone messages, Mr. Lloyd George was good enough to see me for a few minutes at the War Office.

The interview was a very short one. He asked me if it was really necessary for me to see him, as his time was more than mortgaged, and people of great importance were waiting. I told him it would only take three minutes, and as quickly as possible explained the situation.

The most remarkable thing about this most remarkable man is his power of vision, of immediately grasping the full import of any situation which immediately touches humanity. I knew at once that he had grasped the situation and would do what he could.

The two points I had to place before him were:—

(1) that though permission had been given through the Y.M.C.A. for lecturers to visit France for three months, that it was not possible for the best men of the country to spare so much time, and that it was very imperative that facilities should be given for lecturers to visit France for a shorter period, say one month, when it would be possible to approach the leading literary and scientific men in England. That it was a very urgent need that first-class thinkers should be able to visit the troops, as it was with the men in France that the future of the Empire lay. That it was a rare and tremendous opportunity which should not be missed.

(2) That after twenty months of work with the Y.M.C.A. at the base camps in France, in which time we had given 2500 concerts and

entertainments, we had also been allowed to send three firing-line parties, composed of men only, to the first and second armies. That I was now getting a great number of requests that these firing-line parties should be resumed, but owing to the fact that all the men had been called up, it was no longer possible to send satisfactory parties composed only of men.

That the parties composed of men and women, so far only allowed to go on the lines of communication, would be grateful of the opportunity of more service to the army. That there was a very great need for our work at such places as Hazebrouck, where there was suitable accommodation, and if the mixed parties could be permitted to visit such places, we would be within easy motor distance of many rest camps where such work as ours would be especially useful. That if permission were granted, we would give special preference to those artists who had already been used for the work in France, and had given proof that they were in every way to be relied on.

I am quite sure, from his letter of 25th October, that he did all that he could to help on these points, but it was not until over a year later that the mixed parties were allowed to go beyond the lines of communication, or that the short permits were issued for the lecturers.

In 1915 the Permanent Parties (called "Permanent" only in contradistinction to the "Touring") were formed for the purpose of doing work which was impossible for the Touring Parties. These permanent parties also got up concerts among the men themselves. They started clubs for them, and in some cases got up orchestras and choirs. The fact of their remaining so long in one place enabled them to get to know something of the possibilities and the talents in each camp, and the relationship between these parties and the troops was naturally of a more intimate and affectionate nature than was possible with the touring parties. The permanent parties usually consisted of four or five girls, accompanist, instrumentalist, singers, and humorist.

The first party was started in December 1915 at Havre, and there were shortly afterwards two permanent parties there. Each party went to the Base, where they were to work for the period of three months. They worked quite apart from the Repertory Companies, which were established at Havre, Rouen, Dieppe, Etaples, Abbeville, and Paris. The Chaplin Trio, which has for so long rejoiced the hearts of the public playing in the orchestra of *The Beggar's Opera*, did tremendous work at Rouen, where they were much loved.

Miss Sara Silvers did unforgettable work, single-handed, at Calais;

she had written music to many of the stirring poems of Fox Smith, and sang these ballads with extraordinary power and picturesque effect. She worked singlehanded for months, and helped the men in hospitals, on the railway lines, before going up to the Front and coming back, with a devotion which gained the love and admiration of almost all who came in touch with her. One of the most successful entertainers we had was Miss Ada Ward, a most delightful lecturer and humorist, who was, very early in the war, prevented from continuing her work in France because her husband was there. (Ada's own story can be read in the second part of this book.)

Incidentally this was another of the obstacles we had to overcome. No artist was allowed to go whose husband was in France. If a singer's husband happened to be in Egypt or Salonica or Malta, all was well, she might go to France. And sometimes when we had made satisfactory arrangements for a special delightful party, all plans would have to be rearranged by the discovery of a husband in France, or that a fine artist was not entirely British, that a forgotten or carefully concealed German ancestor might appear, and then farewell to any prospect of a permit. It was not only the British Government that had to be considered, but also the French, and of course the opportunity for spying was unique if an enemy had succeeded in becoming a member of a concert party.

Amongst the experiences of the permanent parties, here are some which are interesting:

Our first concerts were given in France in the early part of 1913. It is hardly necessary to dwell on the mental state of our men at that time. They had passed that artificial stage of enthusiasm which follows the first shock of war, they had met the enemy, they had contested stubbornly every inch of the ground from Mons, and they realised something of the magnitude of the job which lay before them. Blighty, that little sea-girt isle that springs ever fresh in the vision of her wandering sons, must have seemed very far off in those dark days. Suddenly they were told that on a certain day and a certain hour a concert would be given by a party containing English girls straight out from the Old Country.

Hours before the concert was timed to start, the men poured into the Y.M.C.A. hut in which it was to be held. They at once cleared out the seats, for more men could be got in standing than sitting. They took the windows and doors off their hinges, and a solid wedge of men filled each aperture thus made. Long before the hour fixed for the commencement the hut contained one solid mass of men standing shoulder to shoulder right up to the very edge of the platform, and there they waited, silent and patient, truly a wonderful testimony to the great need of our work. If further proof is needed, it is forthcoming at once in the reception accorded to the first item on the programme. It was 'Annie Laurie,' sung beautifully by the *contralto* of the party. You, who sit at home and listen to your concerts, can have no conception of the effect that simple old song produced. It was too much for those silent men. They had faced hardships of which the full story is not yet written, they had met Death in many ghastly forms, they had put the thought of a short war and a quick peace right out of their minds. Blighty and all it meant to them was far, far ahead in a very dim and unknown future, and to these men it was as though a miracle had been performed. As they listened to the sweet strains of that grand old song, they saw the Old Country in all the glory of its spring-time, they saw their wives, their little ones—Blighty had been brought out to France to them, and they broke down, they sobbed, they cried like little children and thought no shame of it.

From that day to this their enthusiasm has never waned. Wherever we give our concerts we are assured of an audience far exceeding the capacity of the hut in which we are to perform, and an audience which had foregathered probably two hours before our arrival.

The work we are called upon to do in France presents many sides and has many aspects. It is probably only natural that the type of work which appeals to us most is the hospital work. Undoubtedly it is the hardest work from the artist's point of view, as far too many of the men are too ill to give us that demonstrative appreciation which is such a happy and useful feature of our usual concerts. On the other hand we know that the sight of our girls, our music, and our humour are as the very salt of life to these poor pain-wrecked boys. Our hospital concerts seldom last more than an hour, but that hour is sufficient to last them for days—as a pleasant memory, a topic for discussion, and a standard by which they compare concerts in the past and possible concerts in the future.

Throughout the whole of Northern France we have performed at more hospitals than we can conveniently recall, but dwelling on this side of our work brings vividly to mind the picture of one particular hospital where of all the base hospitals in France the need for us was surely most imperative, and where it was our privilege to bring many an hour of forgetfulness to the boys lying there, This particular hospital in appearance was very much like the usual type of temporary hospital one meets with out there. It consisted of about ten long wooden huts, each hut a ward, and a small administrative block.

The whole of these buildings were connected with lengths of duck-boarding to facilitate communication during wet weather, which incidentally turned the whole place into a sea of mud, Flanders mud than which nothing is more mudlike. Not a particularly inviting picture for a hospital, you say. Wait! For the full tale of its undesirability is not yet told. This hospital was rightly famous for a special method of dealing with fractures of the leg and thigh, and it was necessary to erect over each bed an elaborate system of scaffolding, from which the broken limbs were held suspended by an ingenious arrangement of slings, ropes, and pulleys. The wounds were then kept open to admit a frequent irrigation with some special fluid.

Unfortunately, soon after our arrival at this particular base, the Germans decided to embark on a series of night-bombing raids. Night after night, when the weather was clear and the moon bright, and even when there was no moon, the Hun planes came over and bombed us for two, three, four, and even five hours at a stretch. I ask no sympathy for sound people who could take cover, but think, just think what these raids meant to the patients in this particular hospital. Their bones were fractured, in some cases they had just commenced to knit, in others the two ends were lying up against one another ready to give the most intense pain on the slightest movement, and in all cases they lay there helpless, slung up to a scaffolding which vibrated to every explosion around them.

When you realise the enormous concussion of modern bombs you will realise something, and only something, of the intense and awful agony these men endured night after night. There is nobody to blame. The authorities cannot be expected to move their hospitals immediately a base becomes subject to visits from the air. The defences of the area were excellent, but this only tended to aggravate the case, for between the bombs, the vibration caused by the heavy barrage kept the men in a continual agony of pain.

I have spoken to one of these men after a concert, when one of our guns near at hand has fired a practice shot, and the spasm of pain which has contorted his face has told me all I wish to know of what they must endure during raids. To these poor nerve-tried men we were asked to give a concert, and when the full circumstances became known to us, we volunteered to give them one concert per week. For the whole six months we were stationed at this place, we never missed this weekly engagement, and we know not only from the assurances of the staff, but from the faces of the men themselves, that our work proved a wonderful benefit to them.

When a poor stricken man takes your hand in both of his, tries to thank you, breaks down utterly and, turning away, bursts out crying, you can rest content that you have helped him in no small degree to bear the pain, the monotony, and the depression which is his.

Although naturally ninety *per cent.* of our work is on the platform, there is a ten *per cent.* which we perform off the platform, work which does not figure in our official programme, but on the other hand it is work which lies very near to our hearts, and which plays a very big part in helping Tommy to 'Carry on.' It is somewhat difficult to enumerate this work, for it covers the ten minutes after a hospital concert in which we split ourselves up around the ward, and have a word with this man, and a little chat with that.

At the conclusion of a concert a little knot of Tommies will stand a little distance away whilst you are packing up your music, props, etc., and if you smile encouragingly at them, and we always do, they come forward rather self-consciously, and in the most delightful manner possible they claim a war-time acquaintance with you. 'Good evening, Miss, or Sir,' your particular man will say. 'I hope you'll excuse me, but I thought I would like to come and speak to you, because I saw you perform at our camp at Codford last year.' Needless to say, you had never been to Codford in your life, but you are human enough to realise the position. He is lonely, he is aching to talk to somebody straight from Blighty, and his one ambition for the moment is to have a word with one of the artists. Naturally you say it must have been last year you were at Codford, you go to so many places you forget their names, etc., and you chat to him awhile. It is a small thing to you, you cannot measure the joy it is to him.

Occasionally, too, we are invited to attend some social event, and I have in my mind a dance which is held once a week in a particular convalescent depot for the benefit of the men. There were no W.A.A.C.'s anywhere near this particular Base, so the men danced with each other, and the evenings were always a great success. Three of our ladies on one occasion were asked to join the men at this dance, and they readily accepted the invitation. The situation was rich in possibilities, for the men, of whom there were about a thousand dancing, with an equal amount looking on, had not probably danced with a girl for two years or more, and here they were suddenly presented with three girls in dainty frocks and they could dance with them. Recovering from the first shock, one Tommy took his courage in both hands and asked the nearest lady for a dance.

At that moment the Camp Orchestra struck up a waltz, and the lady waited for him to take her in the usual manner and to start, but he seemed stage-struck, and stood with an embarrassed look on his face. Suddenly he blurted out, 'Would you mind taking gentleman?' Poor boy, he had danced as lady so often that he could not take his proper position. A most amusing and yet pathetic incident. The abiding joy of this particular evening was a flirtation waltz; it is hardly necessary to explain that when the music stops partners are changed, and you grab the nearest lady for your next effort.

There being three ladies to a thousand men, the dance resolved itself into three congested groups of hopeful humanity, and in the centre of each group there danced a very hot, a somewhat breathless, and yet a wholly happy girl. Thus do we help always in that one great task of bringing Blighty to the boys, pending that great day when they themselves can return to it.

It is said of the British soldier that whilst in times of success he is full of grumbles, and of foreboding for the future, yet in times of real disaster he rises to heights of cheerful and determined endurance. But there are times when a disaster to a particular regiment or division has unfortunately been so complete and so crushing that it has brought with it a deep feeling of depression. In just such circumstances we were once sent for to give a concert to a large draft of men who were under orders to join their division in the line.

It was at the latter end of March 1918, the time when the Germans were meeting with conspicuous success in their thrust for Amiens. This particular draft had been waiting for their actual movement orders for some days. They were, of course, confined to camp; every detail of their kit was ready and laid out for immediate use; they could not take their clothes off, but lay down and snatched what sleep they could, when they could. They were, in fact, in a state of preparedness to move off if necessary at an hour's notice.

Only men who have been in this position know how wearing, how monotonous, and how nerve-trying it becomes. Nobody seemed to know exactly the reason for the delay; drafts from the camps around them were dispatched with a rapidity which was only warranted by the serious nature of the situation, and yet the orders for this regiment failed to arrive. Suddenly the reason leaked out. Their division had been lost, how or where nobody knew, but it had disappeared, the obvious assumption being that it had either been wiped out or captured. It can be readily imagined that this news flung the whole draft into a state of the deepest depression.

They were not all of them fresh from the Old Country, many of them had served long terms with their division, had probably been wounded, and, having recovered, were only returning to the line under the urgent and imperative need for men. They naturally felt the blow very keenly. They knew their division, regiment by regiment, company by company; they had left many good friends there, and they found it hard to realise that they were all gone, their fate unknown, and that they themselves were to be distributed among other units. To these men we were sent to give a concert, and it must be confessed that at the commencement we found it exceedingly hard work.

We realised, however, that we should probably have no finer opportunity of demonstrating our value to the troops; the whole fabric of our work in France was, as it were, on trial, and we buckled to our job. We succeeded, and it was our great joy and privilege to be the means of restoring those men to something approaching a happy and contented state of mind. There is something wonderfully soothing in the fine old ballads which are so dear to Tommy's heart, there is something inspiring in the strains of such a magnificent violin solo as, say, for example, '*Legende*,' and there is something wholly satisfying in the healthy laughter caused by the lighter side of the programme.

We were giving a concert to an audience of Colonials, a packed house of some eight hundred men. Our elocutionist was in the middle of one of those harrowing pieces that move slowly from one tragedy to another, this particular piece, as it concerned a settler in a virgin country, having a special interest to Colonials. Suddenly all the lights went out and pitch darkness reigned. Without hesitation our artist carried straight on, and not a movement came from the audience. They sat there wrapt in attention, seemingly oblivious to everything save that clear voice which rang out in the darkness and unfolded the story to its bitter end. For fully five minutes by the clock this situation remained, when just before the end of the piece the lights returned as suddenly as they had gone. Had such an incident occurred to a civilian audience, one can safely assume that that recitation would never have been completed.

Occasionally the lights go out not from any defect in the current but from the presence in the neighbourhood of hostile aircraft. On these occasions the interest of the men in watching the demeanour of the ladies is very apparent. I recall one particular occasion when we were sent to give a concert to an outlying camp. The audience consisted of men engaged in quarries in the neighbourhood. On this occasion our performance consisted of three-quarters of an hour's concert, followed by a short play which lasted an equal time. The platform stood at the blind end of the hut, which means that we had no means of communication with anyone except over the footlights. Shortly after the commencement of the play a siren situated close at hand blared out a trumpet note.

Accustomed as we were to alarms and excursions in connection with aircraft, our thoughts flew at once to the possibility of a raid, particularly as we were in an area which is subject to constant visitation. We could hear no sound from the audience, however; naturally, the glare of footlights prevented our seeing them, so we carried on.

Suddenly there was a terrific explosion, undoubtedly a bomb, and one and all we felt conscious of that irritating emptiness which affects the region immediately under the belt in these moments of stress and strain. The initial explosion was quickly followed by shorter and sharper barks, undoubtedly the anti-aircraft guns coming into action. Still no sign from the audience, so we took heart of grace and carried on. In five minutes the raid had developed to such an alarming extent that we could hardly be heard.

I personally began to doubt whether the audience was there at all, and I entertained the unworthy suspicion that they had quietly withdrawn to safety, leaving us to our fate. Fortunately, however, at that particular moment we arrived at a point which had never failed to bring the house down. The house duly descended, so the audience actually was there, thank God for that! At this stage I had got to counting the bombs, having no difficulty in differentiating them from the heavy gun-fire. For exactly fifteen minutes the raid continued.

During the whole of that time our hearts did double duty and our insides were non-existent, but strong in the knowledge that the audience was still there, and apparently unmoved, and that what they could do we must, our morale remained unbroken, and we finished the play with flying colours. I would like to have ended this incident with the story of how we modestly received the congratulations of officers and men on our exceptionally fine spirit under very trying circumstances.

Unfortunately, however, our pride received a most severe blow. There had been no raid at all. It was merely the blasting which occurred twice daily in the nearby quarry. Incidentally it was more than blasting, it was a prize joke they reserved for poor inoffensive concert parties. In this way do we not only entertain the men, but we provide verdant material for the happy attentions of that merry gentleman, the British soldier.

Letters written home from the bases were published with tremendous results; fiddles, concertinas, melodeons, mouth-organs, flutes, gramophones, Jews' harps, all arrived, and some pathetic gifts from the aged folks at home, who had not played these instruments for years, arriving wornout like their owners, but none the less real gifts of love. When the bagpipes arrived at the hut of the 27th Division, the Scottish hut, the excitement was intense. The news flew through the division that a beautiful set of war pipes had arrived that morning, and every true Scotsman's heart rejoiced. New pipes have to be syruped, and there was a rush to the Y.M.C.A. canteen for a can of syrup for this new war baby.

A piper from the Royal Scots came at once, and made weird sounds as he coaxed the syrup through the "innards" of the bagpipes, and then walked up and down, up and down, while every one listened anxiously while he tuned them up. By the evening the bagpipes seemed ready for the fray, and the piper headed the concert party, and out from behind the counter they swept through an avenue of hundreds of kilties, led by the piper skirling away with "The Cock o' the North." They marched down the avenue, and the men followed behind, and they went up the long hut into the other hut where they usually had services, on to the platform there. They nearly all went mad.

It was a truly Celtic evening, with hundreds of Scotsmen who were off up the line the next day. When they were told their favourite fairy-tales about Cuhulain and the Scottish Giant, they played the old joke of going out of the hall when they were told that all those who did not believe in fairies must leave at once, but they popped in again to show that they were not quite serious about it, for of course all of them do!

There is an incomplete report of the work done in the Abbeville area by the second concert party—there were two resident parties there besides the Repertory Company. This report covers the days from 12th August to 29th December. They gave 280 concerts, covering an area of 150 square miles. Of these concerts, 170 were given in the ordinary huts round about the town, and 35 were given in the hut on the railway lines to the men passing to and fro from the line.

The transport difficulty at that time was very acute, and many times the small party had to travel, even on very cold nights, in an army transport waggon.

They gave fifty concerts in the hospitals round Abbeville and also at Amiens. They carried a portable piano which they took into the wards, and gave short concerts to the men who were unable to leave their beds. Ten concerts were given at the Summer Rest Camp, Cayeux, about fifteen miles on the coast, and ten at the big Antiaircraft Depot, five at Army Training Schools, six to Cavalry Divisions who were resting, and fifty concerts were given in and around Amiens.

The party also visited Forest Labour Companies, Prisoners of War Companies, Convalescent Depots, and Antiaircraft Sections, where the men are hardly ever allowed out of the camps. They gave concerts also to the Chinese in the Chinese Labour Depots, the Chinese showing very keen appreciation of the instrumental and vocal music. They even tried to join in the choruses.

Whilst this work was going on, the No. 1 Concert Party was doing similar work, and the touring parties were visiting Abbeville every month for a fortnight, giving three concerts a day.

There were a very large number of letters from the C.O.'s of the camps visited, testifying to the number of concerts given, and the benefit which the troops derived from them. They were unanimous in their opinion that the concerts of the kind that we were giving had a very great effect in maintaining the morale of the men.

Whether in the base, where the monotony of the life tends to undermine their effectiveness, or in fighting divisions, where the roughness and hardness of their lot tends to produce a state of mind in which nothing seems worth while.

CHAPTER 3

Malta, Egypt, and Palestine

In 1916 we seemed to be spreading widely in all directions; the number of visiting parties was increased from two to four and even five in a month. Permanent concert parties and repertory companies were established in the different bases. More parties were asked for, for the firing line, and we began the arrangements for sending artists to Malta and Egypt, with the possibility of Salonica.

The first concert party for Malta left on 12th February in the *Caledonia*. The party was sent at the suggestion of Lady Methuen, and Lady Chesterfield sent a donation of £200. Malta, as well as being a Naval Base, was a great hospital for the wounded from Salonica and from Egypt.

The party were met on the quay by Mr. Wheeler of the Y.M.C.A. They were very kindly received by both Lord and Lady Methuen and Admiral and Lady Limpus.

The usual day's work was a concert at three at a nearby hospital, and another at seven at one farther away. The island is roughly eighteen miles by ten, and was dotted with hospitals and camps, some being quite remote. Occasionally three concerts were managed in a day, but they found it rather too much, as the usual practice was for each artist to sing four songs consecutively, and do it twice in the show. Every Wednesday they had a special performance at the Australian Hall, built by the Anzacs as a thank-offering for kindness received, and capable of holding fifteen hundred men at a pinch. Thursdays were always reserved for Lady Limpus, the wife of Admiral Sir Arthur Limpus, for her hospital across the harbour.

They were able to give a very delightful concert in the ballroom at Government House, and a big public concert in the Opera House. Not only did they give a concert on a troop-ship to over two thousand men, but also to the men who had been saved from the *Minneapolis* and the Simla. The men on the Simla had been all night in open boats and had lost everything, and the concert seemed to cheer them up enormously. This party went from Malta to Taranto, and from there, at the invitation of the Admirals of the Fleet, gave concerts on board some of the battleships.

In a letter from a commander in charge of the net-drifters, he speaks of the thousand men concerned in the vital work of subduing the great menace of the German submarines. There were eighty boats with a personnel of eight hundred men, and a staff working on shore numbering over a hundred, to which must be added numerous officers, bringing the total close to a thousand all told. Of course, most of their time was spent at sea, and they were not actual service men but mainly fishermen and peaceful British citizens—

> All very homely people who have volunteered to do their bit for their King and Country and for their families they love so much and have left behind. The little ray of sunshine brought to us by your party during the last week has again brought us in touch with those we love in dear old England, and we are very grateful to you. Your party deserves the greatest praise. Besides the very hard work they put in daily, we who are fighting the submarines in this district know the enormous risks they run by being torpedoed in the merchant vessels in which they make their various passages. Also, at present they are in the war zone, and subject to bombardment from sea and air. Truly they do their big bit for the same cause.

San Angelo and the canteen they repeatedly visited, and the enthusiastic reception they got from the bluejackets there made them accept with alacrity the invitation they received to go to Italy and sing to the sailors of the Adriatic Fleet at their Bases. They left Italy on 12th May by a Fleet Messenger, and *en route* caught sight of an enemy submarine about two miles astern.

> Nothing happened, however, as we were a very fast ship. I asked a petty officer why we did not fire on her, and he replied, 'Wot, them pore h'Austrians, sir? They didn't want to fight, sir, and think of their wives and families—'sides, she's out o' range.'

In a letter from Lord Methuen, regretting the party going away from Malta, he says:

Nothing was too much for them. Two, or even three concerts a day, lasting sometimes three hours. They enjoyed making everyone happy, and no people were ever more successful.

He asks if it is possible to send another party, and speaks of the tremendous need of Malta, where there were sixty thousand patients in the hospitals.

Lady Limpus wrote that she knew I should like to hear one more testimony of the enormous amount of pleasure given to every one, soldiers and sailors and those civilians who were privileged to hear them also.

They were most kind in giving me one day a week regularly all the time they were here for our navy and those military hospitals which are over on our side. It was inspiriting to hear the welcome given to them after having once heard them. The men were never tired of hearing them. The poor, weary faces, worn with pain and shock, brighten up, and they forget their troubles to sing the choruses or listen spellbound to the 'cello or laugh heartily over some comic touch. Thank you very much indeed from the admiral and myself—and I may say we speak for all the naval people here—for sending us so charming a concert party.

There was a very touching tribute, which came to me later on, in the shape of a delightful letter from a poor woman living in the north of London, who wrote to say that her boy was one of the seamen who had been three years away from home. He described the concert party so enthusiastically, and he ended up by saying if his mother had any money to spare, would she send me half a crown as a recognition of the delightful evening he had spent. His mother sent me the half-crown in the hope that it would help to provide more happiness for those at sea.

Another delightful recognition on the part of the men was after the party had given three concerts on His Majesty's ship *Prince of Wales*, and Commander Kettlewell very kindly sent me a programme, painted on board the ship, which the ship's company begged that I would accept. The programme is delightfully got up, and is that of a concert not given by the party, but by the men on board, who played a sketch called *Backing a Winner*, and sang songs, "Watching the People pop in," and "Hot Mince Pies." It was a complete surprise for the concert party, who were put comfortably in armchairs whilst the men of the ship entertained them.

There was a hope that the party might have gone to Mudros, but by April 1916 it was cleared of all huts that were not actually being occupied, and it did not seem possible to make the necessary arrangements.

The navy showed its appreciation in a very practical manner by bringing the artists home free of charge in a transport, which was a very great delight to the party, and also gave them a good rest. They had the honour of being fellow-passengers on the transport with six hundred naval ratings, and the voyage was not the least enjoyable part of the tour, as the evenings spent in singing and dancing on the lower deck will never be forgotten. One bluejacket, on hearing Miss Leon play the 'cello divinely, removed his pipe from his mouth and said to his "raggy," "Blime, when Miss Leon plays the 'cello, I kin see our blinkin' bandsmen's eyes standin' out o' their bloomin' 'eads like 'at pegs"

They were away altogether twenty-one weeks, visiting Malta, Taranto, and Brindisi.

The other two parties that went to Malta until it was evacuated as a hospital base, went as Red Cross parties, as the Red Cross, recognising the great value of the work, undertook the financial responsibility. Of the visit of the third party a very interesting record was kept, and the account which follows is taken from a diary written at the time by one of the musicians.

They went in January 1917, stopping on the way at Marseilles for two vivid days. Unfortunately no berths had been booked, but by this time the companies were so well-known that the stewardess, who was quite an old friend, got hot-water bottles and rugs to comfort the little party till they were well on their way, when they were packed in somehow for the night. Up to their landing in Paris they were the "Lena Ashwell Concert Party," but from Paris onwards they became "Red Cross."

There was some difficulty in getting food in Paris, and the company had to do with two apples and a little bit of cheese. The cold was bitter in January 1917 in Paris, and there were no fires and no buses, and dreadful tales of the weary waiting in queues and the fight for coal; there were no potatoes and no sugar. The gas was cut off at certain hours, and if the electricity exceeded a certain limited amount, it, too, was cut off. There was no heat in the carriages, and the snow was lying thick upon all the country, and it was a comfort to be going south, where, though there was a nip in the air, there was warmth in the sunshine.

Marseilles, which is the third city in France, with its million inhabitants, was very remote from the war. They heard no guns and saw no wounded, so they merely cheered the foreign legions who marched through their streets, and returned to their revolutionary discussions. The *cafés* were packed every night; no one was safe after dark. There was an average of one assassination per night. Life in Marseilles is cheap. One can get rid of an enemy for five *francs*, and ten *francs* is a fancy price. One of our Tommies was killed one day for sticking up for a woman.

Marseilles is a noisy town. The church bells jangle, the trams go thundering past and clang, the crowds shriek and quarrel and talk shrilly all day, and most of the night motors hoot and wares are cried. It is a city that never sleeps.

The first concert is at the Stationary Hospital out at Musso, where the gardens are a jumble of mimosa, plane, cactus, firs, every green thing a darker green than ours against a turquoise sky; there are the white houses of the rich, principally Greeks. The *château* (a hospital) is rich in stone balconies, and stands in the middle of black firs. The doors and windows are doubled with wire to keep out the sand and the flies.

We enter the hospital through an avenue of firs, and on either side are long stretches of tents on the clean sand. The cases are mostly enteric, breakdown, small-pox, skin diseases, and the convalescents are many. Marseilles was the oldest Y.M.C.A. war centre, and it was the Indian troops who were the first to institute it. This information was given by the head worker, Dr. Dutta, a Bengali.

At the docks a transport arrives with hundreds of Annamites, the Cochin-Chinese. They are tiny little men in badly fitting cotton khaki. They have Mongol faces, shocks of straight black hair, and smiles showing shocking teeth; a funny little crowd drawn here for labour in the docks and ammunition. They have their own N.C.O.'s and French officers.

The next concert is at Hangar 8, and the ride takes us along the docks, giving a wonderful view of busy wharves and unspeakable slums, of *Zouaves* crowding on to their transport, and of our Tommies sitting by the roadside cheerily responding to our waving hands. We see the *Caledonia*, now in dock with a hole in her hold, but reported officially "sunk"—the same boat that the party travelled on in Febru-

71

ary 1916. Here they have cargoes of hides, which, when damp, make noisome scents. I believe the *Caledonia* had many on board, but there was nothing "whiffy" as we passed. There was difficulty in getting at Hangar 8. Passports are asked for, but at last we were taken into the Holy of holies, past a transport full of our men who have been there for hours and will go three hours' journey before the transport knows its destination. In spite of these precautions, spies find out everything.

The next concert is at Carcassone. We are some time finding the way, and get out of the motor-bus to walk up a steep hill with a most perfect view of the bay and mountains. After another climb we find a platform and piano are placed on a slope in a camp of white tents. The men are tightly packed, looking like a monstrous photographic group, and sit or stand on the rising ground; further groups on hillocks and impromptu stands testify to their interests. As we go through the long programme, the hills receive the sunset glow, and the daylight dies, and some of the men have been in their places since two o'clock.

An officer in the Flying Corps sits next to me at high tea. He has been in the infantry and twice wounded. Someone suggests he should have a V.C., and he answers, "No, a very different sort of cross." He and eleven friends had dined the night before leaving Salisbury Plain, and had pledged themselves to meet again after the war. The eleventh had died in his arms at Loos, and almost his last words were, "No dinner for me, old chap!"

The journey home on the tram after the last concert, illuminated by lanterns, candles, and other portable lights, is not a comfortable experience. At each stop more Tommies crowd on, and by the time we reach the town they are on the roof, clinging to the steps, even standing on the couplings and holding on to both cars in most dangerous positions. They all take it perfectly naturally, but an Indian was killed last week by dropping between the cars and having both legs wrenched off.

At the Indian Camp next night the adjutant waxes indignant over the "Swine" that went on and left him to his fate, and the matron speaks with great indignation of a Frenchman and woman who watched him without attempting to help. Two Tommies gave all the first-aid they could, and tied up the arteries, but the poor mutilated lad clung to the matron, crying, "Me better dead; plenty of brothers, father; better not live now!" When the wood is gathered for the funeral pyre, and the ashes are scattered into the sea, the matron, who loves the Indians, remarks, "So clean."

When we were busy packing to go on board the *Mongolia*, which was coaling, an officer regaled us with solemn warnings of the horrors of the Mediterranean, which was "sown with mines—submarines and mine-sweepers are powerless—liners going down every dawn—the Germans are having their own way with our boats, and will have the world's commerce as soon as peace is declared." At last, thoroughly cheered by this extreme pessimism, we are towed out with our attendant coal barges, to make room for the *Wooltah*, and we lie amid stream till the morning, seeing a French transport off.

Lifeboat drill is a great excitement. A hooter sounds the alarm. The crew get on deck and take their special places. The passengers go for their boats—ours is No. 8. The boat is supposed to be out of order, and we rush for No. 7, in accordance with orders. As this drill entails having warm clothing on, and everything necessary for shipwreck, we pass an arduous morning. The second day we are rushed on deck before completely dressed.

When we sight Malta, which looks a little sand-coloured island after the wonderful coast we have passed, the ship begins the usual zigzag. A doctor tells us of the delights of Malta, the forts built and named after the various Grand Masters, the harbour that the Turks swam nightly during a two years' engagement with the British; we see the church where the Knights of Malta lie buried, the Arabic domes that crown the Sliema side, terrace after terrace of white houses, archways showing streets of steps, here and there a tiny bush, and over all the glare of sunlight and the bright blue sky. As we are landed in tiny boats, it seems ridiculously like Earl's Court or a dress rehearsal of some opera.

The Imperial Hotel is built in a square, the garden being enclosed. Lemons, oranges, bananas, and strawberries grow all together, and a lovely purple creeper climbs over the white, arched passages. In the streets are flocks of goats, driven from door to door and milked on the premises. The carriages have canopies and white seats, and the horses, shaking bells. The drivers all carry flywhisks. Beggars are everywhere. Priests are everywhere. The large black silk hoods, stiffened on one side, serve as either umbrellas or sunshades to the peasant women. The women of Malta have worn black ever since the Saracens owned the island and ill-treated the women.

Coal is £7 a ton. The army get it for £2-10s.

On Monday morning there is a loud explosion which shakes the hotel, which, like all the other buildings, has stone walls and a flat roof.

From the roof can be seen flames and smoke coming from Valetta Harbour. We hear that a French boat has been blown up. The flames go shooting up through the black smoke, and, later, there is another explosion as she is torpedoed to sink her. We heard afterwards that if she had not been torpedoed in time, she would have blown up Valetta in the explosion. There were thirty-three deaths and many injuries.

The residences of the Knights of Malta are still known as *auberges*, but are completely shorn of their inside glory, and used as Army and Navy Stores, Manchester Houses, etc., though outside they still have coats of arms which proclaim their historic past. Government House was the headquarters of the Grand Masters of old.

The first big concert is in Australian Hall, with two thousand Tommies present, and it is very clear they have had no music for some time.

At the huge Naval Hospital there are white pathways under pergolas and beds of green, tufty plants. We have a dark audience, for the uniforms and strong footlights leave us gazing into dark space. However, ringing appreciation comes from the shade, and we get a voluntary cheer from them as they depart. The moon is nearly at the full, and the gardens are surely Babylon or Nineveh, were it not for the distant piano and the one-fingered rendering of "The only Girl in the World."

Anyway, we descend to the Arabian Nights, for the harbour is glistening with starlight, and even the houses and mosques look pink and fairylike, the home of glittering beauty and romance.

Next morning the concert is on the other side of the island, and we skirt the coast, the white camps, the deep blue sea, and the sun-kissed rocks, making such a vivid picture impossible to realise. There are no birds, no rabbits, no trees. One lonely palm stands on the Salini Salt Works. We work round the corner into St. Paul's Bay, where the apostle was wrecked.

In the Convalescent Camp there are upwards of six thousand men, and the first concert is in a tent. The sides are open, and the audience overflows endlessly between the two lovely bays.

There is a rapturous audience next day at the Floriana Hospital. They laugh themselves hoarse.

Next day there is a great festival. At St. Paul's Cathedral the floor is strewn with evergreens, and all the silver altars are uncovered. Candlesticks, images, and vases glitter against the purple hangings. It is the day on which St. Paul was shipwrecked. If he were to be landed here again, I wonder what he would say to the glitter and magnificence, the fat priests, and the ragged peasants who put their savings into this pomp. When the Pope visited Malta last, he said one of the churches was too rich, and fined them £2000, which they paid right away.

There are many officers from Salonica, who all tell the same tale of its difficulties and dangers, and the awful climate. They paint its drawbacks and inhabitants graphically; the cosmopolitan life, the fever, and the loneliness. Dr. Pick, who is on a boat running between Malta and Mudros once in three months, describes Salonica as "the last thing in Hades." How our men loathe it! They laugh heartily when we ask about Salonica. Some of them have been to France, and all of them prefer it. ———'s tales of Salonica are on a par with the rest: spies, disease, discomfort. Conversation often turned on the horrors of Salonica and the advantages of France. As a whole our men long for active service, and even prefer the trenches to the monotonous waiting whilst fever and air-raids may come to deal death. We heard later of a big air-raid there, and how the wretches had bombed the hospitals.

We go to Valetta Hospital, which is five hundred years old, with great rooms unsupported with pillars—the rooms are the largest in the world, and certainly the dimmest. We see the great arched roofs over the stairs, and glimpses of the courtyard and the sea.

We have a great run to Melleha, where we give two concerts in tents. Here the peasants are of different speech and of fine physique though they never eat meat. The houses are almost bare of furniture, and fuel is so scarce that an outside fire serves for many houses. There is, therefore, little cooking, and the meals are mostly bread from the one bakery in the village, and fruit. There is very little typhoid as they live such an out-of-door life. The women do much of the field work. We see a little patch of ground only half a yard square, which is carefully planted with peas, beans, and tomatoes, growing under what appears to us hopeless conditions. Each patch has to be carefully walled round, for the great enemy is the wind. There is a little shrine in the rock which the women must pass returning home, where there is a collection-box, and opposite to it a cleft large enough to hold the little bunches of flowers which they sometimes put there.

In this camp the men were mostly suffering from fever and chest diseases, but there were 1400 happy faces in spite of their unhappy diagnosis. In a large hospital over the Chapel of Bones we gave a concert in a large wine-cellar filled with surgical cases. A man who was operated on for appendicitis at ten o'clock in the morning insisted on coming to the afternoon concert.

We gave a concert at Fort Wardia, a high peak overlooking St. Paul's Bay. Next day was a day of forts, in Tarpa, and indeed the whole of the north, including Gozo. There are about forty-five men in charge of barbed-wire defences and two 12-inch guns. The concert-room is rigged up in a combined church and dining-room, which is their principal building. They are unused to concerts, so remote from civilisation are they. It takes three weeks to save up for a trip to Valetta. Their nearest recreation is in a tea-room in St. Paul's village, which we see far below us. The concert is considered to be a great success, but it is difficult to make the men laugh heartily.

The next is at Fort Madeleina, nearer home; after many narrow roads and perilous climbs, the car glides over a moat, the sentry smiles, and we arrive at a tiny courtyard. We alight, and go down a steep tunnel, to find an audience of 140 men in a deep cutting roofed with canvas. They are easy to please, and love the programme.

The next concert is in the Valetta gymnasium, where we find a crowd of men standing outside. There are no seats to be had. It makes one miserable to leave so many outside, but the place is already packed, and the mystery is, how they will ever be able to get out!

In the old city, Notabele, there is the cathedral where Publius, Prince of the island, was converted by St. Paul, and became the first Bishop of Malta. He is buried in the cathedral, but the Arabs and the earthquakes have entirely demolished the old building, and the new one is very handsome, glittering with silver, good paintings, and quaint marbles, one quite unique, in *lapis lazuli,* brought by the Phoenicians from Siberia.

Once, in France, I had a long talk with a *padre* who was distracted at the difficulty of finding suitable addresses for the men. He seemed very surprised when I suggested that a very lively description of St. Paul's adventures might be found quite thrilling, especially as some of the men might have been in Malta, possibly at Mudros, and many of the troops from Australia and New Zealand might have caught sight of some of the places that he visited. I do not suppose many modern travellers had as exciting and interesting sea experiences as that great traveller. I suppose the bother really is that in trying to be properly respectful to great religious teachers, we generally succeed in making them inhuman and entirely divorced from real life.

We were given a special blue permit to approach H.M.H.S. *Karapara,* the most wonderful hospital ship in the world: ninety beds in one ward, and smaller wards and beds tucked away in almost impossible places, cupboards and lockers in no one's way, sliding doors, air and light for every one, stores of blankets, clothes, rugs, instruments, tins, crockery, brooms, sponges, linen, splints, an X-ray room, an operating theatre, lifts, and even one wheezy harmonium, with a hymn-book in readiness.

The sisters tell us the great danger is from the Greeks, who hate us. They say that Malta is sown with Greek spies. We heard the same story in Marseilles. There also they regard the Greeks as their greatest danger.

We see the *Royal George* leave the harbour, and also have a view of Hassim's Cave in the rocks, and the line where the German submarines attack us each night. Grain has just come to the island, and yet two French transports have been sunk in St. Paul's Bay only last week. One had 1200 survivors, and the other only 200. On the first boat were the Cochin-China and Singalese troops; 600 of them refused to leave the ship. It was six o'clock in the morning, and many of them were asleep; and the officers who went round waking the men were all lost, and the captain went down.

We have considerable trouble at giving the concert in the Naval Canteen, for the first gate of the quay will not allow us to pass, nor will they allow us to telephone, or telephone themselves, to headquarters to find out if we should have access to the dockyard. The door is firmly shut; even though we see the sailors passing to the concert, we are firmly locked out. We drive round to another gate, but this is barred, and though we knock and shout there is no response. Another reckless drive through the old and dirty part of the town to the south gate, where we are again refused admittance, then we are directed to another gate. Another drive through dirty streets, narrow and dim, where the gaping inhabitants throw dirty papers into the car; up steep *culs-de-sac*, down sheer hills, attended by a crowd of dirty children, we arrive finally at the last gate.

Again we are refused, but a naval officer coming out realises the situation and returns to plead our cause, so at last we gain admittance to the dockyard. We glide in and out of bales of goods, over narrow bridges, round cranes and donkey engines, through all sorts of perilous tunnels and narrow tracks. We see, or ought not to see, submarines in dry dock, huge furnaces, stacks of shells. In this hidden corner, which no one suspects or can see from the outside, there is an immense dockyard employing 12,000 men.

On arrival at the Naval Canteen we are somewhat roughly told that we are late! Once the concert begins we forget all the irritation, for there is a great sight from the platform of the way the audience bare their heads for the king, and the great sound they make when singing brought one's heart into one's mouth.

On another visit to the docks we see the poor old *Renown* with her torpedo hole, just getting mended. There are still the old arched docks where the Grand Masters kept their galleys, and where the names still show *San Giovanni, San Cattornia*. There are steep ladders, too, where machinists are making flags, and up still steeper ladders there are machines driven by machinery, stitching sailcloth; there are furnaces where bolts, rivets, and hooks are being beaten whilst the sparks fly from their red-hot paid in twenty minutes each week. We see guns all cased and waiting to be shipped, and going up more steps we see the propellers for seaplanes being made. When we are having tea at the admiral's house, we hear that Bagdad has fallen.

Later we give a concert in the Trawlers' Tent. This brave little crowd represents our safety, and keeps the food supply of the island still intact. They rescue our shipwrecked sailors and sweep the sea for mines.

The O.C. says in his speech, after the second concert, that we are a much pleasanter remedy than a large dose of quinine, and infinitely more efficacious.

There is a large hospital near the wharf at Cottonera, consequently most of the worst cases seem to find their way there. Just round the corner is an internment camp where, though it is of course a secret, the men from the *Emden* are interned. They seem to have a very pleasant time, clean uniforms, and nothing to do. The Emdenites received letters about the beginning of the German submarine warfare and became tremendously "cocky." According to them the war was to end by our being thoroughly crushed; they were going to triumph since we were going to starve. Their arrogance knew no bounds. The submarines have been doing their worst for months now, and England still carries on, so the Huns are filled with melancholy and depression, and no longer strut and brag.

If Italy had not joined the Allies, the position of Malta would have been desperate; as it is, we are almost isolated. U-boats come round, mines are laid so near in that the Grand Harbour has to be swept daily. The little forts round the island which we visit, watch the seas night and day. The spies who are responsible for the sinking of the French transports in St. Paul's Bay have been tracked down and shot. An Austrian spy, posing as a Frenchwoman, and making it her business to worm into French secrets, has been caught and sent for internment to England. Boats are erratic. Each mail has to run the gauntlet. It is possible that sea traffic will be stopped for two weeks to track the U-boats to their lairs.

No one is to leave the island, no one allowed to land. Women and children may leave in May, after which no chance till October. We hear of hospital ships torpedoed in home waters, and the sound of that is frightful enough, but here we get the poor wrecked crews, and see them driven through in the ambulance cars. We see many of them when we go round the wards, and speak to those who have been at the concerts. At the Naval Hospital there were many coloured patients from torpedoed boats. They looked like blots of ink among the audience.

We gave a public concert at the Theatre Royal on 28th March 1917, at 8.30, and a ripping concert at Spinola, where, as the tents had been blown down, we gave the concert in Don Manoel's Cave, with just the light of swinging lanterns. The cave was made in 1725, and there is only one air-shaft. We had got rather used to the wind, even in Australian Hall, where there were about 15,000 men, bound, poor dears, for Salonica; but the gale grew so terrific that the concerts had to be countermanded, as all the tents blew down.

We are told by the matron that the men have been saying to all the newcomers how good the concert party is. I had a delightful letter from a corporal in the engineers, in which he says:

> How much the sick and wounded think of you and your con-cert party at Malta! I was in hospital there, and was present at four concerts, which I think were a bigger success each time; and each artist gave four encores, which must have been very hard work, and each concert was packed with about 1200 men, and it would have made you feel happy to hear the praise you got. Some remarks were, 'Why, it was worth half a dollar,' and 'I say, chum, it's worth being queer,' and 'I say, she must be a grand sport,' etc.

Of newcomers there is no lack. The boats are getting torpedoed, and the survivors reach us smashed and maimed. There is also a fresh batch from Salonica as a result of the air-raid. . . . The sea is getting more and more risky; the Japanese destroyers have just arrived and hope to sweep the waves clean. . . . As we cross the harbour we some-times see the mine-sweepers and mine-layers returning. We have seen

79

their nets and ammunition at close quarters. . . . Food is getting scarce. The fiat has gone forth that the hospitals must go to relieve the food and water pressure. Twenty thousand men are to be moved in secrecy, but boats can only come and go through great danger. . . . A Taranto boat will not take more than three women a voyage, sailings are uncertain, traffic nearly suspended.

The concerts go on as usual, and at Valetta Hospital we again visit the largest room in the world with no support to the roof, which is of chestnut. Among the 300 bed-cases there are many sufferers from the Salonica air raid, the biggest on record, and also from the two torpedoed transports. One man I spoke to was in the water for two hours and had given up all hope, then said his prayers, and was saved. The next boy "jumped" on to the destroyer. Both legs are hurt. They are tended by a walking case with both hands bandaged. He came down the ropes. Another has lost both legs in the air-raid. . . . Everyone is on the move now, and coming to say goodbye. St. Andrew, David, Spinoli, and Bavière fold their tents, and the bare hills remain. . . . Our epitaph is spoken at the military farewell concert at the Australian Hall:

You have made them like good music. When first you came the boys were all for songs with choruses, but they know better now.

A Specimen Programme

Handel's "Largo."
Adagio from Concerto in G minor from Mendelssohn.
"She alone charmeth my Sadness," by Gounod.
Violin Solo, "Romance," by Svendsen.
Prelude and Allegro, by Pugnami Kreisler.
Aria from *Tosca*, by Puccini.
"*Una Boce Poco Fa,*" by Rossini.

We gave the first sacred concert given on the island on Good Friday, The songs were "Nazareth," by Gounod; "Jerusalem," by Mendelssohn; "Honour and Arms," by Handel; recitative and duet, "What have I to do with Thee?" from Handel's *Elijah*.

We are to leave on a very small and very dirty Italian boat plying to Marsala, and do the journey in sixteen hours. Soldiers, children, crew, and passengers are one jumble, the decks are filthy, and there is not a seat. The steward creeps in during the night from time to time and tries to close the porthole; we keep it open. But our voyage is not to Marsala; two boats were torpedoed yesterday on that route, so we are to land at Syracuse.

In his minute to the Director of Medical Services, in March 1916, Lord Methuen wrote

It is not easy for me to express in simple words my debt of gratitude to all who have worked with me in doing one's best to help the 60,300 patients who have been in our hospitals since they were started last May. From a few hundred beds we rose to nearly 20,000, and could within a month have accommodated 25,000. From the letters from patients which I have seen, and from the remarks made to me in the hospitals, I think that in no English hospitals could the patients have received abler treatment, or had greater care bestowed on them. But whilst recognising the good work performed by all those connected with the hospitals, I must emphasise the great help given by philanthropic associations, the members of the Ladies' Committee of the Order of St. John and the British Red Cross, the local talent and the people in Malta, including the generosity of the Marchesa Scicluna and the 'Casino Maltese.' I attribute the orderly conduct of the patients in a great measure to the concerts and other amusements so admirably organised in the different hospitals and camps.

The first party that visited Malta and returned on the transport, after a short rest, was reconstituted and left on 30th September 1916 for Egypt. They intended to be in Egypt a few months and visit Malta on their way home. Permission had been obtained for them to go to Salonica and Mudros, but the submarine menace altered all the plans. They did not visit either Salonica or Mudros, or make the return visit to Malta, for they were not allowed to go by sea until they returned home in 1918, after the Armistice, having been away two years.

They were delayed tremendously at the start by the ports being closed owing to the submarine menace, but finally reached Havre just in time, by making a frantic dash, to catch the Paris train, the whole anxiety being whether it was possible to arrive in Marseilles in time to get the boat on which the passages were booked for Alexandria. The party just managed to scramble on to the boat at Marseilles, and they had the usual "zigging" wobble to Alexandria. This party was under the direction of Mr. Theodore Flint, who, you will remember, commenced work in France, took the first party to Malta, and was now to continue his pioneer work by this new adventure in Egypt.

Mr. Siegfried Sassoon has given me permission to quote his poem, (in the war poems of Siegfried Sassoon), as it describes so delightfully our concert party:

They are gathering round . . .
Out of the twilight, over the grey-blue sand
Shoals of low-jargoning men drift inward to the sound,
The jangle and throb of a piano . . . tum-ti-tum . . .
Drawn by a lamp they come
Out of the glimmering lines of their tents, over the shuffling sand.

O, sing us the songs, the songs of our own land,
You warbling ladies in white.
Dimness conceals the hunger in our faces,
This wall of faces risen out of the night,
These eyes that keep their memories of the places
So long beyond their sight.

Jaded and gay, the ladies sing; and the chap in brown
Tilts his grey hat; jaunty and lean and pale,
He rattles the keys . . . some actor-bloke from town . . . '
'God send you home'; and then 'long, long trail',
'I hear you calling me;' and 'Dixieland' . . .
Sing slowly . . . now the chorus . . . one by one.
We hear them, drink them; till the concert's done.
Silent I watch the shadowy mass of soldiers stand.
Si'ent they drift away over the glimmering sand.

His description of Mr. Flint is so vivid—"the chap in brown . . . jaunty and lean and pale." He was rejected from the army on medical grounds, but the work he did was fairly strenuous for a delicate man. We reckoned at the end of the visit of the Eighth Party to France, that he had played 24,800 songs and pieces, making an average of about fifty a day!

The following account is from letters and diaries:

It is hardly possible to believe that we could be a greater success than we were in France, but we are. The concerts are glorious, and the men so enthusiastic that we are having a perfectly wonderful time. This last week we have given concerts at the camps and hospitals, one every night, and each concert lasting two hours and a quarter. Last night we gave our first public concert at the Alhambra. Every seat was sold forty-eight hours after the booking started. The whole of Alexandria was there, and they turned away not hundreds but thousands. We have done a lot of hospital concerts and the Red Cross are fearfully pleased.

Tonight we have just given a concert on board ship to 1500 men. No guests were asked, so as to leave all the room for the men. It was very exciting, and we were all so delighted. Before we leave Alexandria we are all to be vaccinated, and dine with the High Commissioner, and do all sorts of exciting things. Everybody was very kind to us in Alexandria, and we were very sorry to leave. It was a great wrench when we left on Monday for Cairo.

On the way we got off the train and gave a concert to an Irish regiment. They were nearly all old men, dear things, and they thoroughly enjoyed the music. At first they were very dull, but at the end of the concert they were yelling and cheering their joy. They hadn't heard a note of music since the beginning of the war. It gave me a lump in my throat. Cairo, of course, is a most wonderful place, full of mosques and mosquitoes. Last night we were taken to see the Pyramids. I can't describe to you what the Sphinx looks like in the moonlight—magnificent, mysterious, mystic. It made me feel terribly sad, but we had a camel ride to cheer us all up. I wonder if the Sphinx knows when the war will be over.

This letter I received from Dublin in February 1917 shows the impression made upon the audience:

I saw a programme of the lovely concert your party gave to the old Irish Regiment at Tinta; and if the cheers of the old men and officers brought a lump into your throat, perhaps you will be gratified to know that your beautiful singing brought tears of joy and thanks to the eyes of both officers and men. My brother was one of those officers, and wrote home saying he can never forget how everyone yelled with delight, and how affected they all were hearing such music almost in the desert. The fortnight's tour in the Fayoum district was glorious, entertaining the men in the Western Desert. Many had not had a concert for ages. We were told that we were going to rough it, and this is how we did it. At one place the general turned out of his headquarters for us, and left us in possession of a bungalow, four ripping bedrooms, one for each of the girls, and a little mess. There were floral table decorations which they sent for to Luxor, miles away, especially for us, *and*, last but not least, a real, live bathroom with a bath made of white enamel stuff, and heaps of hot water! We lived in the lap of luxury, and rode camels.

At another place they erected a little reed hut especially for us girls. It was square and brown, just like the little 'Mother house' in *Peter Pan*, only we had not a top hat to let the smoke out of! We had beautiful spring-mattress beds from the hospital and mosquito nets. Every one is so awfully kind to us. My hair keeps up beautifully, and is acquiring quite a noble contour. I look most grown-up and womanly. The concerts created the most intense excitement, as for so long the men have been cut off from civilisation. There is the usual report to us that crime in the camps has dropped. We have just returned to Cairo—after three wonderful days in the Fayoum. We travelled each day, and had to get up really early. Once the train started at 3.45 a.m. I suppose that is the part that is roughing it.

We had a glorious trip through Bedouin villages where they had never seen white women, and we saw many huts where horses, dogs, chickens, men, and women lived happily all together! We bumped along over the tracks—there aren't any roads—through orange groves and palm groves, and once we slept in a wooden hut right in the middle of the camp, and we were literally almost killed with kindness.

After we had given two concerts to 1500 men each, they gave us a concert, so that we could have a rest. It was so good and so funny. They have an orchestra composed of wind instruments in the way of combs, reeds, and a tom-tom; it sounded jolly good. The conductor was the *padre*. They had a good deal of talent there, too. One man gave a mouth-organ solo, and another Tommy, dressed in baggy trousers with a red nose, fixed me with his eye, and informed me that he was 'Burlington Bertie from Bow.' We had a ripping stage when we were in the Fayoum, with very strong footlights that seemed to attract all the insect life in the world in the way of mosquitoes and moths, even a huge locust flopped against the back-cloth, much to our consternation.

At Assyut we were invited to a Coptic wedding. When we arrived the whole house was illuminated outside with coloured lights and flags, and a native band played weird national airs, mixed up with 'Tipperary.' We were ushered into a kind of drawing-room upholstered in bright red. There were heaps of Egyptians, who all bowed low and said, '*Saida, Saida,*' which means 'Greeting.'

After sitting there in rows and rows for ages, one of the English guests hinted to the bridegroom that it was about time we got a move on! The bridegroom didn't seem to mind at all, and just smiled all over and said, 'Oh yes; shall we have the banquet in five minutes?' We thought that would be a very good plan, and all went into a huge kind of marquee where two large tables groaned beneath all kinds of viands. There were no chairs, and only one knife, fork and spoon and plate for each person. There was nothing to serve from the dishes with, so if you wanted anything you just took it with your fingers and fork.

We gave a concert at the hospital in Cairo last night, and one night we went to Gara; there were 2000 men there, and we gave a most wonderful concert. A platform was erected for us in the open. We had two great big electric lights for illumination, and the men sat on the sand in a huge semicircle—wave upon wave of them—and the stars were all out overhead, and everything was very, very still, except for the music we were making. I sometimes have to remind myself that this is not all a dream.

We have been to Luxor. We had a day and a half there, and it was so wonderful. We saw Karnak and Luxor temples, and the tombs of the Kings of Thebes, and did thirteen miles on donkeys. The next day we got up at 5.30 a.m., and did a twelve hours' train journey and got to Shusha, where we gave a concert the same night. At Shusha and Gara we rode camels, the most supercilious and cynical brutes. When they get up you think you are coming off; they oscillate their necks so that they can bite your calves if they feel that way, and look down their noses at you and open their mouths, exposing terrifying yellow teeth, and say, 'Wuff, wuff, wuff.'

We are staying in Cairo now for about three weeks, and have our Opera House concert tomorrow night. There is not a seat to be had, which is good, but sad in a way for I am asked right and left by people for seats, and they are impossible to get. Then we go off to the Canal zone for December. We have to do all our own washing, and have bought an iron, the pride of the party. I do wish you could see . . . ironing his own shantung suits. If he had not been a musician he would have been 'some laundryman, as they say!

There is a certain zone forbidden for any woman—or anybody else, as far as that goes—to go. If you could realise what a wonderful thing it is to get permission to go to this zone, you would be as proud as we are. It just shows what a real help the music is to people, and how they are simply hungry for it. Only one white woman has ever put foot in this zone. This zone is the Suez Canal, the whole of which was fortified. In December 1916 the party stayed here six weeks, making Ismailia their headquarters, giving concerts from there to all the surrounding camps, and to those on the other side of the Canal, in huts or in the open air, and occasionally in a hangar, and sometimes motoring very great distances.

Ismailia is a very beautiful place just by the Canal, and very near a great salt lake. There are lots of palm trees covered with coloured creepers. The party received, also, a very special permission to cross the Canal, which was lined with camps. When they crossed the Canal they went to Moses' Well, which is mentioned in Exodus, and described as the place where there were "four score and ten palm trees." The palm trees are still there, only there are many more. At Moasca, where a new division arrived which had been for many, many months in the desert, they gave three out-of-door concerts to about 14,000 men. A very good description of a concert was written for an Australian paper:

That evening we had a farewell sight of the 'Boys,' and never shall any of us forget it. The Lena Ashwell Concert Party were to be there. We were conducted for over a mile across the dark sands to the very centre of the camp—a remote light being our guiding star. The whole event was a beautiful allegory. There was our Guiding Star of Bethlehem in the distance. The night was very dark; the burden of the war rested heavily on our hearts, as we were soon to say goodbye to these 'Boys.'
We passed near the wet canteen, and that was the saddest sight to us that day . . . but the star shone steadily ahead—guiding to what was pure. The darkness grew less, we walked into a soft light, and the full glory of the scene burst upon us. There was a small, elevated stage over which our star shone brilliantly. A slim young girl stood singing (it sounded like a Christmas carol), and a vast sea of five thousand rapt faces listened to the ethereal

music. It was all so reminiscent of that wonderful night two thousand years ago, that I felt strongly inclined to go down on my knees on the cold sand and worship. But in a moment the spell was broken (or the song ended, and wild clapping, whistling, and shouts of 'Encore' rent the solemn darkness).

Our escorts said it was perilously near our train time, and the station was not near. The sea of faces, cup-shaped, because rows of standing men ten and twelve deep surrounded the seated thousands in the centre, was rippling with laughter over comic recitations being given. We started to move away, but oh! that silvery, ethereal voice stopped us. It was only 'The Broken Doll,' but every word fell like a crystal jewel on the hushed audience. The desert silence and darkness surrounded the guiding star and its adorers once more, and we went softly away. Suddenly five thousand voices broke into rapturous singing like a stupendous choir. (It was only the chorus of the song.) It shook our very souls with its music in that dark, war-troubled desert of a world.

We left them singing, and the music of every 'Boy's' love and sacrifice shall continue to sound through all ages to come.

In a letter from the 24th Stationary Hospital:

I cannot tell you how I enjoyed the concert. I have only been out here seven months, and these three hours have been the happiest I have spent since I left home, but what the enjoyment must have been to the lads who have been eighteen, twenty, twenty-two, and even twenty-six months out here, God only knows! Not only have we enjoyed the concert, but it has also done us good by lifting our thoughts upwards. . . . When in the Canal zone, I don't suppose the party will be allowed to go up farther, and I am sorry for those who will not have an opportunity of hearing them. The camp and all the patients in our 800-bed hospital, and all the patients that could go were sent in field ambulances and the consequences risked, for it would be a very long time before we got a treat like this again.

How I wish you could have seen the faces of the audience, intense at times, or full of smiles, or at other times heard the hearty laughter. I wish I could draw a decent pen picture and show you the huge hangar filled with at least 2500 men and officers sitting on forms or on the platform or on the ground.

In one corner were the patients in their hospital clothes, some with heads bandaged, others with arms in slings, and looking utterly wearied from long-borne fatigue on outpost duty far away in the desert.

In front there were several rows of officers, and then behind, rows upon rows of men. Every window was filled with faces, every crack was filled with an eye gazing in, every available space was filled with men. There were Scottish, Irish, Welsh, English, Australians from the Southern Hemisphere, Egyptian officers and interpreters, who were working under us in war against the Turk, and we all came away with a unanimous opinion—it was the finest concert we had had for ages.

The party did go farther up the Canal, for railway carriages were placed at their disposal.

In a delightful letter from Brigadier-General Hoare, he says:

They gave two concerts in the open air, as we are practically camped on the desert, and have no suitable building for a concert. I cannot tell you what a great treat these concerts were to me and my men. . . . They also sang to the sick in hospital here, and left amid the regrets of us all, but the memory of their visit will last a very long time."

And in another letter:

Your concert will long be remembered by us all, and I meant what I said from my heart when I hoped that your names would be handed down to history as having helped in no small way to achieve the great purpose of our lives.

On Christmas Day they joined a choir of soldiers and sang carols in the different wards of the hospital. The sun was shining and the sky was very blue, and they stood in the open air to sing. In the evening they gave their concert to about 2000 Australians in the open air. The evening was very cold, and the concert not nearly as cheery, because the men were very solemn, having had a tremendous Christmas dinner.

Ismailia is full of generals, and there is also an admiral.

We shall be in this district until 1st January, and then have been given permission to go up the line to Romani, a place which we captured only a few weeks ago. We are having a most wonderful time, absolutely a royal programme all along—motors and launches at our disposal, and there are always most wonderful audiences to sing and play to. Sometimes there are as many as four or five thousand men who have forgotten the sound of anything less compromising than a cannon, and who have forgotten what a white woman looks like.

At one place in the desert the Royal Engineers laid telephone wires so that the troops ten miles farther on could have a share of the concert.

On New Year's Day, 1917, the concert party was at Ismailia, and gave a concert in the old cinema, very kindly lent by the C.O. of the hospital.

From Kantara, which was the Military Base, the party also received special permits for Mohomidir, which had not long been taken from the enemy. It was a wonderful experience. Special trains were run from outlying posts to bring the men in to hear the concert.

We went to and from the concert by camels, having travelled up *via* Kantara to Mohomidir, and gave a concert in the disused aerodrome, which holds about 2500 men. The weather had been pretty wild and a great deal of rain had fallen, which isn't very usual here. The concert was a pretty difficult one, as the piano was a minor-third down, and Mr. Flint had to transpose everything up as he went along, which wasn't easy, and two of the girls sat one on each side pushing up the notes as they stuck! The wretched thing, after all this attention, would hardly speak at all.

After the visit to Mohomidir they made their headquarters at Suez, and amongst other places went to El Chat. There had been an unusual amount of rain in the hills, and towards the end of the concert they had the unusual experience of the results of a cloud-burst.

Just as we finished the *Water Melon,* we heard a commotion outside, and an order was given to put out all lights. We, of course, thought of raids, but soon the order was countermanded, and to our surprise a torrent of water poured into the tent. In no less than three minutes it was up to the stage, and we quickly sang 'God save the King,' with the general up to his knees in water. Then they put a table for us to walk to an ambulance, on which we were to be taken through the water to the general mess on the bank. It started off, loaded up with eight or ten of us inside. All went merrily for about 200 yards, when, with a dip, the bonnet of the car disappeared, and we were left at a standstill, with the car at an angle of 45 degrees. But we were rescued from our plight, and carried to safety. We found out afterwards that the car had gone into a trench, and we were only saved from utter ruin by barbed-wire entanglements. I supped in a blanket for a skirt, and military boots, and we were none the less merry for our adventure. It was a narrow escape.

The men, also, had a very "close shave," since, to give more height, after the tents were pitched, the sand was cleared out, so that the level within the tents was two or three feet below the level of the desert. The flood came suddenly, and at night. In the ordinary course, if the men had been in bed, they might, many of them, have been drowned.

By the end of January, when the company returned to Cairo, they had covered the Canal from end to end, giving concerts at hospitals and camps. In February they were back in Ismailia, and gave several special concerts to the 42nd Division, which was on its way to France. It was then that they gave concerts to the biggest audiences of the war:

Thursday, there were 3800 men, the next concert there were 4000 men, and on Saturday, 6000.

I received a letter which said:

We are one and all sorry that the Lena Ashwell Party are leaving us. They have given us a glimpse of home out here on the desert. Singing their choruses has moved the sand from our throats and given us new life. We feel we are not forgotten; we thank them, and wish them God-speed and the best of luck whenever the troops call to them for a message from home.

The letter from General Dobell was especially gratifying. In it he said:

They have given concerts at all posts where it was in any way possible to allow them to go, and the fact that the ordinary rules were waived, and special permission granted them to travel where no civilians in any circumstances had previously been allowed to go, will make it clear to you how high a value we attach to their entertainments. We were all very sorry when the members of the party departed a few days ago. . . . I would take this opportunity of thanking you from myself, and on behalf of all the troops of the Eastern Force, E.E.F., for the great trouble you have taken in the organisation of these concert parties, and at the same time would venture to congratulate you on your wonderful success. I can only assure you that your efforts in this respect have been most highly appreciated, and have been most beneficial in every way to the troops.

During the summer, as the heat made it impossible to continue the concert work, the party ran, or undertook the managing of a Y.M.C.A. hut at Aboukir for about eight months, giving only a few concerts. After a rest there, they went on with the concerts.

Early in 1918 the party were desperately anxious to return to England, but it was absolutely impossible. They had found the work very exhausting, and the heat was especially trying the shade temperature was sometimes up to 116 degrees. They, however, decided to carry on until 1st July, in the hopes that they might get permission to go on with the army into Palestine. When the *soprano* and the violinist left the party to get married, the work that was hard with the complete party was especially trying now that the little company was reduced to four, so that in July, when they were at El Arish, about half-way between the Canal and Jerusalem, but still in Sinai, they had great difficulty in carrying on the work, but managed to keep each concert to over two hours. From El Arish they gave a series of concerts in the open air to audiences ranging from three to four thousand.

They then received a telegram from the General of Lines of Communication, giving permission for them to visit Bela and Gaza, and later on to go to Jaffa and Jerusalem. It was a tremendous excitement to leave the yellow glare of the sands of Egypt and the changing blue shadowed sand-dunes of the desert for the undulating slopes of Palestine, wild, mountainous, rugged, and cultivated, such a contrast to the miles of sand they had been living in. Although the concert work was much harder for the little party of four, there was a great advantage in getting the smaller number, since they were able to go to so many more places; a car for four people is always easier to obtain.

They were too late to see the country one carpet of flowers blue irises, scarlet peonies, and yellow flowers—but there were many wonderful coloured butterflies, and millions of grasshoppers, some with large scarlet wings.

Their first stop was at Bela, where they stayed for a week, and where there were no Englishwomen except the sisters of the hospitals, and beyond Gaza there were no more even of these. From Bela onwards the whole countryside was scarred with trenches, barbed-wire entanglements, and many isolated graves. At Gaza (famous for the exploits of Samson) they also stayed for a week, and saw the battlefield by the sea. The place was called Umbrella Hill, and was captured, lost, and recaptured many, many times, and innumerable lives were lost over it. They saw the stretch of sand cut by trenches, thick with shells, bombs, and war implements, and a long line of sand-bagged graves.

At Lud, the burial-place of our patron saint, St. George, they were within a few miles of the line, and got quite accustomed to the booming of the guns. During the concerts the guns carried on, but the noise did not disturb them, and they grew as accustomed to the din as the firingline parties in France. The heat at Lud was tremendous, and as the tents were pitched in an olive grove, they got very little breeze; but they had a full-sized bath, which was a great luxury in camp life.

From Lud they went to Jaffa, and on their way they gave a concert at G.H.Q., and General Allenby was very pleased. From Jaffa they gave concerts to the surrounding camps, and at last they got permission to go to Jerusalem. They travelled by car from Lud. The traffic of motor-lorries and ambulance convoys from the Jericho road had covered everything with dust; all the olive trees were white, and looked as if they were covered with hoarfrost. The road winds up and up through the Judean hills, and as one nears the summit the olive trees look like little plants down in the valleys below. The road descends towards Jerusalem abruptly in a series of hairpin bends.

They stayed at an hotel within the city walls by the Jaffa Gate. They saw the last great Allenby "stunt" from Jaffa.

Everybody knew when it would be. You could feel war in the air. I could hardly sleep all night for thinking of it, and at 4.30 in the morning the guns began to thunder. We all climbed on to the highest part of the roof and watched the battle from afar, like the people of Troy or Ancient Rome. It was a wonderful sight. The noise was deafening, guns boomed and shells crashed, shrapnel went ripping through the air and looked like lighted matches thrown about. The flash of the guns and star shells and Very lights lit up the whole sky, and silhouetted palm trees and houses against the sky. It was very cold. As it grew lighter we heard the droning of propellers, and a formation of our aeroplanes came in sight. They were off to bomb the Turks!

They stayed in Jerusalem some weeks, the idea being that they should go from there to places quite near the firing line, and give concerts, motoring back after. Most of the concerts were given out of doors, the evenings being absolutely still and hot. All the party were much occupied in reading the Bible, and found it so tremendously interesting to see the brook that David got the stone from with which he killed Goliath, and the place where St. Peter lived, called Lydda. Whilst at Jerusalem they gave concerts on the Mount of Olives, and at a monastery overlooking Bethlehem, where there was an audience composed almost entirely of New Zealanders. Another "very special one" was given:

> For the Governor of Jerusalem (Colonel Storrs)—a wonderful mixture in the audience. Priests of all nations, Shylocks by the dozen, a real German married to an American, and an Austrian, as well as generals of our army, and sisters of the Red Cross, about 300 in all! If we could have given songs in about fifty languages it would have been all very well, but only knowing 'I love you' in six languages does not help much. Still, the 'Dear Old Rag-Picker' went like anything, and some of the Holy Fathers behaved 'no-how.'

They gave a concert in a German hospital, which is now the British Headquarters, but which was built by the *Kaiser* on the Mount of Olives. On the ceiling of the chapel is painted a picture of the *Kaiser* and his wife, surrounded by disciples and saints. In the courtyard is his statue in the dress of a Crusader. "What a dreadful thing it is to have no sense of humour" It is rather wonderful to stand on the Mount of Olives, which is nearly 3000 feet above sea-level, and look down over the Jordan Valley. The Dead Sea is 1000 feet below, and some of our fellows are hard at it in the frightful heat.

In August they gave a concert at Solomon's Pools. No one seems to know if these huge reservoirs were used only for the irrigation of the king's gardens or for Pontius Pilate's water-supply at Jerusalem.

The advance was so tremendous that naturally the concerts came to an end for a time, and as all the Y.M.C.A. were wanted for various things, the party took the places of the Y.M.C.A. Two of them ran the Y.M.C.A. Jaffa Hotel, one ran a hostel for one of the divisions, and the other the men's Y.M.C.A. The hotel was for officers only, the servants being Armenians, Syrians, Egyptians, about twenty in all. They had as many as eighty officers dining, and worked very hard, and though they did not give concerts themselves, they helped the men to get up singsongs, and had a choir, and so on.

They stayed until after the Armistice was signed, and then went down to Egypt, giving concerts on the way. They had to wait some time for a boat. The last concert they gave in Egypt was at a camp at the base of the Pyramids.

CHAPTER 4

Raising the Money

It was obvious that it would undermine the self-supporting basis on which all recreation must be organised if we used the theatres for free performances. The takings of the great number of performances in public buildings in France were kept, and administered by the Y.M.C.A., for expenses in connection with the performances, and also used towards the expense of billeting the artists—no small item when so many professionals were at work in France.

Miss Rosemary Rees, in charge of the Repertory Company in Rouen, showed by her accounts that £800 was taken by the theatre representations there during the months she managed the repertory. Other bases took less, as there were no large theatres available, and the public performances were not so many. The sum of £100,000 was raised to pay for the entertainments. The only time money was charged for admittance to any of the entertainments was when we were using a theatre, or in small places where there was no theatre, when we made use of the cinema of the town for the purpose of giving a special performance, when the public were admitted.

All the entertainments in the camps, hospitals, and wherever given in co-operation with the Y.M.C.A. for the army were free of charge, the entire point being to make the army feel that every note of music, or every word of a play, was, as it were, a loving message from those at home who were thinking of them and trying to send them some happiness. It would have been quite simple to have made a charge and to have made the effort self-supporting, and, possibly, a commercial proposition, as was later done in England by the Army Canteen Board, who started their work in England, in 1917, principally under the direction of Mr. Basil Dean.

There was one unfortunate moment when, without my knowledge—for I was never informed, much less consulted charges—were made by the Y.M.C.A.; but that was after the Armistice, when I think there was considerable anxiety as to the financial situation.

The whole of this large sum of £100,000 was raised by the theatre—in fact, the whole of the organisation was carried on by members of my profession.

The first performance given for the purpose of raising money was at the Coliseum on 25th March 1915, when £1500 was raised. Their Majesties Queen Mary and Queen Alexandra were present, also her Royal Highness Princess Mary, Princess Victoria, Princess Helena Victoria, and Princess Alexander of Teck.

I was playing at the time in *Fanny's First Play* at the Kingsway, but managed to organise the *matinée* with the help of Mr. Croxton, the delightful manager of the Coliseum. But for the immense help given us by Sir Oswald Stoll, I do not know how we should have managed. He was good enough on more than one occasion to allow us to take all the proceeds of the Coliseum over and above the daily expenses.

After my return from France in June, articles and letters to the Press realised about £1000; but my efforts were somewhat hampered by illness, as I had to have an operation which laid me up for about six weeks, and I was able to get the help of Miss Olga Hartley, whose journalistic experience during the great Suffrage Campaign made her an invaluable help to our cause, until we closed up the work in 1919, when she had time to write that delightful novel, *Ann*.

As she undertook the press work, I was able to go on searching for artists, and arranging the parties which were needed for France, and it was very delightful to be lying in bed feeling one was thoroughly virtuous in doing so.

As one of the founders of the Three Arts Club, I had a great hope that clubs could be founded in all the provincial towns, so that artists, when travelling, would have decent accommodation and an opportunity of some kind of social intercourse with the artists of the town which they were visiting. The life of a travelling artist is a very lonely one, and the accommodation in many of our towns is, to say the least of it, unsatisfactory; and it seemed to me that, as many of the artists who were living in the provinces would be called on to help in the work of entertainment with the armies abroad, co-operation with the Three Arts Club would be valuable.

When I was invited to undertake the work in France, I therefore took it up to the Three Arts Club. In the storm and stress of those days, disagreements and misunderstandings grew up, which in days of peace might have been avoided. After a few months it seemed better to organise the work independently. I resigned as Governor and withdrew from the Club, and with the consent of Her Highness, and the Ladies' Auxiliary Committee of the Y.M.C.A., carried on the work from the Kingsway Theatre and my own home, and afterwards at 44 South Molton Street.

Early in October "business as usual" had to take a front place, and I produced *Iris Intervenes*, followed by *The Starlight Express*, at the Kingsway Theatre. Early in February I arranged to go on tour with Iris Intervenes, and was so able to hold meetings on behalf of the work at Eastbourne, Hastings, Nottingham, Folkestone, Birmingham, Newcastle, Manchester, Edinburgh, and Glasgow.

At this time I was pursued by Zeppelins. The night before the production of *Iris Intervenes*, there was the big Zeppelin raid which did so much damage to the Kingsway. On the tour I hardly went anywhere without being preceded by a raid, or having one during the week. As soon as the tour was arranged for in the Midlands, and shortly before it began, there was a big raid over the whole of the midland counties. Travelling to Newcastle on the Sunday, the train was stopped outside Durham, where we spent the night in the dark, arriving at Newcastle at 5.30 Monday morning. The Germans had dropped leaflets all over the place to inform the population of Newcastle that they were returning, and would return until they had razed Newcastle to the ground.

When the curtain went up on Monday night, the audience consisted of two St. John's Ambulance men and two nurses, all of them in uniform, with stretchers in the background, I suppose for the benefit of the company and those attached to the theatre, there being no one else in view. Four nights that week there were air-raids. All the trams and trains stopped, all lights were put out, and the populace walked up and down outside the station hotel in the dark, singing comic songs and jeering derisively, and shouting cat-calls at every dropping bomb in the neighbourhood. The noise was deafening.

The only air-raid Edinburgh had took place a few days before we were due there. A Zeppelin visited the city and dropped bombs all round the Castle, doing a good deal of damage. The airmen at East Fortune had no bombs, but went up all the same with dummy bombs. There was a great deal of excitement, as it was said that the guns had just been removed from Arthur's Seat to Hull.

The only air-raid or warning of a raid that Glasgow ever had was on the second night of our playing there.

Nottingham gave us a good deal of help, including the gift of a car from Mr. Dennis Bailey, which was used for many months in the firing line.

At Edinburgh the Lord Provost did not sympathise with our work, and did not allow us to hold any meetings. Dear old man, he loved his country, and told me that he did not approve of the English coming up to Scotland and taking money from Scotland for the English. He was very uneasy when I told him that I was Scotch, and furthermore, Edinburgh, by all the laws of the land, since when a woman marries she becomes of the same nation as her husband, even if she cannot speak the language. He said that Edinburgh was going to send a Scottish concert party to the Scottish troops, and nearly died with horror when I told him that there were no Scottish troops in France. There was an Imperial Army, and he would not be allowed to know exactly the position of the Scottish regiments!

In Glasgow a delightful committee of real enthusiasts was formed and a meeting held at the house of the late Mrs. Ogilvie Matheson. Lady Cargill was the chairman, and that most generous-minded of men, Mr. Dunn, the honorary secretary. Every effort was made by them to form a committee which would represent Scotland, including Edinburgh; but Edinburgh refused to be beguiled, and, I am afraid, remained angry, at any rate unsympathetic, to the end. I suppose, for the same reason that the army enjoyed the "Hymn of Hate," and, to the great confusion of the German prisoners, invited them to sing it, I must confess to having enjoyed the attacks which were made on me at this time. In an article in a Scotch paper headed, "Scandalous Insult to Scotland," I am referred to as a:

Theatrical damsel of a very aggressive type . . . who comes on the stage alone and pirouettes as an English heroine, who has at last subdued Scotland and placed it under her heel.

I fancy, at the back of it all, there was a little musical jealousy, though, of course, I am a Fellow of the Royal Academy of Music, a musical degree which helped me enormously throughout the work.

The Glasgow Committee, which had hoped to represent the whole of Scotland, were good enough to work in cooperation with us, and we were thus able to send a great number of musicians from Scotland, and a special firing-line party, the account of which is in another place in this book.

When the tour finished, we had been able to secure a great deal of financial support, and also, at the different places, I was able, through the kindness of the musicians, to meet many of the local artists, and secure their help.

In the autumn of 1915 we were able to arrange with Mrs. Leyel to organise the raising of the funds. At first the office was in my back drawing-room, and I still am able to gaze almost with tears on the spilt ink in the middle of the carpet; but the work soon outgrew the back half of a drawing-room, and that part of the work was moved to 101 New Bond Street, which was lent to us, and of course we quickly outgrew that too, but there we had to remain. Mrs. Leyel has the courage of an Arctic explorer, and the persistence that most human beings lose when they are four years old. The word "impossible" means nothing to her. She pursues her way with a ruthless cheerfulness which sees only the object to be achieved.

At first the work was more or less stereotyped. There were meetings arranged, and concerts were given in different provincial towns as far apart as Wales and Yorkshire, Eastbourne and Bath. For the purpose of raising money, organisers worked in the different areas to create interest and secure support for the meetings at which I spoke, and audiences for the concerts at which the artists gave their services.

There was a second Coliseum *matinée*, and flag days with medallions instead of flags. There were Lavender Days, when for weeks the office was more like the inside of a lavender haystack than anything else. Lavender was collected from gardens all over the country. Sometimes it was green and arrived steaming and mildewy at the office, which was literally up to its neck in lavender.

When the public became weary of charity *matinées*, Mrs. Leyel felt that the only way to make a really successful bid for support was to make the attraction so great, and the effort so original, that the public would willingly pay for the tickets for the sake of being present, and the Chelsea *matinée* really created a sensation. The Chelsea Music Hall, instead of a fashionable theatre, combined with the daring of invading Chelsea with a revue that joked with and cheeked its artistic idols and heroes, appealed to the public's sense of humour. It was a brilliant artistic and financial success.

The programme of the Chelsea matinee stated that the revue was written by far too many people, under the disability of far too large a committee. There was not one committee, there were five. The Writers' Committee actually was responsible for writing the revue. Mr. Nigel Playfair was the moving spirit, and his methods were exhilarating. First of all, he asked one celebrated dramatist to write the revue. The dramatist was good enough to consent. But when Mr. Playfair saw the rough draft, he calmly laid it aside, and requested a second famous dramatist to undertake the writing of it. This endeavour, too, failed to satisfy him.

This went on for a considerable time; in fact, all the dramatists and literary stars of London would have been tried and rejected, had not Mr. E. V. Lucas been persuaded to lend his quiet and mightily efficient aid to put an end to this state of things, which seemed likely to wind up with bloodshed or at least with wounded feelings. There were shades of Whistler, Rossetti, Swinburne, and all the Chelsea celebrities, written by Monckton Hoffe. It was delicious to hear dear Ellen Terry's remarks, and wonderful to think she had known them all. Special music was written by some of the leading composers. There was a ballet in which Gerald du Maurier and Fay Compton danced divinely to Edward Elgar's music, and the programme itself was a *tour de force*.

Financially it was a success as all the seats were sold beforehand at fancy prices, and artistically because it really was a perfect revue, full of wit and beauty, and the audience enjoyed it immensely. The Chelsea revue was encored, and another revue, which included some of the funniest scenes, was given at the Lyric in the following June, called *Ellen Terry's Bouquet.*

Although both matinees were so successful, the work grew so rapidly that it was obvious that we needed a much larger sum, and in the autumn of 1917 we decided to risk the expense and have a bazaar in the Albert Hall. Mrs. Level was afraid that, unless something unconventional were evolved, a big bazaar would be dull. All sorts of ideas were forthcoming. One suggestion led to another, and some one, who surely ought to have known better, murmured the word "Tombola" to Mrs. Level, and the thing was done. It was quite wonderful how quickly the general public grasped that the new, strange word meant "lottery," and it was more than merciful that the authorities, whose business it is not to permit even the most innocent gamble, had no inkling of the true meaning of the mystic word.

Mr. Plank designed a delightful coloured picture poster, and it occurred to Mrs. Level that pillar-boxes formed admirable posting stations, and one morning London woke to find nearly every pillar-box in the West End surrounded with this delightful picture of the "Petticoat Lane Tombola." The government evidently said:

This tip I to myself will take.
It shall be mine, and I will make
This new idea mine own,

—for afterwards pillar-boxes were strictly reserved for government posters. Advertising at that time was full of difficulties, so new ideas had constantly to be resorted to. The proprietors and contractors of the Hyde Park Hotel, Piccadilly, kindly lent the site of the skeleton framework, but the advertising firms found it was impossible to get timber at any cost, therefore it was impossible to erect a hoarding. Mrs. Leyel solved that difficulty in a few days. She bought up cheaply a supply of strong Italian cloth, found a cheap line of different sized iron hoops, and had the iron hoops covered with the Italian cloth, on which were painted the ten prizes. These were easily erected on the steel frame, and made a striking and effective advertisement. So when we were told by envious people that we must have spent thousands on advertising, we were able to smile contentedly, because the cost was infinitesimal. As a result of the splendid publicity, the "Petticoat Lane Tombola" grew and grew and grew.

Miss Elizabeth Asquith (now Princess Bibesco) was Chairman of the Committee of Stall Holders, and worked indefatigably with the rest of her committee, collecting prizes for the Tombola and gifts for the stalls. Everybody was wonderfully kind, and the list of prizes given was really marvellous, headed by the Baroness d'Erlanger's gift of a freehold piece of land on the Chiltern Hills.

The more it was advertised, the more prizes were given. I think all the biggest shops in London contributed generously.

The demand for tickets was enormous, and the greater the demand, the greater the difficulty of dealing with it. The Bond Street office was not large enough to hold an adequate clerical staff, and, to add to the difficulties, the special worker Mrs. Leyel had secured to take charge of the staff dealing with the tickets was frightened of air-raids, and whenever there was a threat of an evening raid, which was fairly frequent, she began to show her terror about six o'clock, and insisted upon going home, quite regardless of the fact that there were oceans of applications still to be dealt with.

At one moment, as it was impossible for the office to hold more workers during the day, Mrs. Leyel arranged for double shifts, and a night staff to work when the day staff left. The theory was a sound one, but proved impossible to work, as the Government offices had swallowed up vast quantities of capable workers, and it was impossible to put unknown and untrained people on to this work, which necessitated meticulous care in dealing with every ticket and the large sums of loose money.

When the night staff came on duty, it was found to consist solely and entirely of volunteers from among those who had been working their hardest all day—Mrs. Leyel herself, Miss Elizabeth Asquith, Miss Olga Hartley, and two or three others. They tried it for two or three nights, working until the wee small hours of the morning, and then I returned from Yorkshire—Liverpool—I forget exactly where, and peremptorily and emphatically put a stop to the experiment which would have ended in the complete collapse of the office.

The emergency was tided over somehow, and we gradually evolved a very efficient, trained staff, and though, of course, the work had to be done at high pressure, it was carried through.

The prizes were certainly the oddest mixture: a bathroom with porcelain bath, beautiful dresses from the leading London dressmakers, a pedigree turkey, pedigree puppies; but quite the most thrilling and imposing gift, I think, was a real, live pedigree bull. We were very grateful, and the bull was a great success, but it was indeed almost the "last straw" to the harassed office. At first there was unmitigated delight to have so splendid and original a gift to advertise, but when the telegrams began to arrive as to the weight and health of the bull, and there were details to arrange for its being properly met and looked after before being shown at the Hall, we had some anxious moments. It was a little perplexing to know where it was to be put when it arrived. There was no room for it in the office, and nobody could think of any solution until Messrs. Tattersall consented to stake the steer, in other words, put up the bull and its escort.

There were carpets and furniture, hats and fur coats, pianos and pictures, and, at one moment when we were given a perambulator, it was suggested that we should apply to the Foundling Hospital for a baby to put into it.

The bazaar lasted for three days, and was opened by the Queen of the Costers, who drove round in her coster cart, but, as a matter of accuracy, it is disappointing to narrate, it was opened a few minutes before by Mrs. Asquith, who insisted upon bringing in the bull and opening the fair. There was a vast crowd, and the bazaar was a tremendous success.

The city which gave me the most help and encouragement was the wonderful city of Liverpool. Dr. Utting was the Lord Mayor, known as the khaki Lord Mayor, because, having a right to wear khaki, he never appeared except in uniform. Sir Archibald Salvage, the Lord Mayor, and his secretary, Mr. Percy Corkhill, were amazingly kind and generous to me. The Lord Mayor made the entertainment work the object of his special fund, and they arranged for me a real campaign for raising money. In three days I spoke twenty-two times, and each time I spoke was introduced by the Lord Mayor himself, or Sir Archibald, whilst Mr. Corkhill poured advice, helpful suggestions, and flattering praise into my ears.

I spoke, and collections were taken on the Exchanges, the Docks, and other places where business people congregate, as well as in every place of entertainment in that great city. The last of the twenty-two, I was literally finished, and had no recollection of what I said. It was in the music hall in the north end of the city, where the poorest of the workers live, and the audience gave me the largest amount in proportion to its size of any that I spoke to. When it was all over, Sir Archibald almost persuaded me that I might be able to live through a General Election Campaign. I returned later to receive at a reception at the Mansion House the gift from the City of Liverpool, and the cheque was the magnificent sum of £6070. This was not all, for we were able to open a branch office there for the sale of tombola tickets, with the result that the fund was the richer by another £1000.

There are some moments in life when friendly help is of untold importance, and I shall never forget these three kind and generous men and the help they rendered me.

When the time came for the drawing for the tombola prizes, it was difficult to decide how it should be done. Small numbered tickets were printed to correspond with the tickets sold, but the problem was to find some means of mixing up the tickets properly. At last somebody suggested that the best instrument to use was a churn. We tried to beg or borrow a churn from dairy manufacturers, but discovered that no churn would hold all the tickets. Our thoughts then turned from milk to beer, and finally we borrowed an enormous barrel from a kindly brewery. Messrs. Tattersall kindly lent their room for the occasion, and we got a number of boy scouts to come and roll the barrel about so as to mix the numbers. Lord Jellicoe, Sir Arthur Stanley, and Mr. E.V. Lucas came to preside over what we have since reason to suppose was a highly illegal proceeding. Some of us had qualms during the afternoon, and when a large policeman appeared at the glass door, we thought he had come to arrest Lord Jellicoe, who was drawing the winning numbers out of the barrel. However, it turned out that the policeman was a ticket holder, who came to see if he had won a prize.

Wales was especially generous in supporting the work. After a meeting at the Cardiff Mansion House, I was invited to speak on the Cardiff Docks Exchange. I felt cold and tongue-tied with nervousness when escorted into the gallery of the Exchange, and saw the busy crowds of men on the floor below. A bell was rung, and I was introduced to the members of the Exchange, and then from the gallery made my appeal, which appeared to me especially flat and uninteresting. I could not feel in any way in touch with the audience, speaking from so lofty a position above their heads, and no one was more astonished than I when, descending to the floor of the Exchange, over £1500 was rapidly handed to me.

Swansea vied with Cardiff in its generosity, but perhaps the most thrilling moment was when, going up one of the valleys, the managers stopped the works for half an hour to allow me to address the men and women. On one occasion, in one of the biggest works, I addressed an enormous number, and at the end of my address there was a long silence in which I could really have wept with despair at losing such an opportunity. I was quite convinced that I had failed to make them see what was happening in France, when quite spontaneously the whole audience broke into the National Welsh Hymn, "Land of our Fathers," singing most beautifully in Welsh; and then, with an exquisite courtesy which moved me almost as much as the wonderful sound of their singing, they sang our National Anthem, "God save the King." And this was in the heart of a district devoted to the leadership of the I.L.P.

Every time I went to Wales I heard artists, and we had most invaluable help from the musicians in the different parts of Wales.

There were meetings at Leeds, Sheffield, Wakefield, York, Doncaster, Hull, Harrogate, Barnsley, Huddersfield, and other towns. We were not as successful in interesting Manchester as we were in Liverpool. We were unfortunate enough to come up against one of the leading musicians, who made many damaging statements with regard to our work, which, owing to the kindness of the Lord Mayor, we were able most substantially to refute by the documentary evidence of the office. Perhaps the misunderstanding arose through our holding a diametrically opposite point of view with regard to the work to that of this distinguished musician. We were not concerned with the artist who was suffering from economic reasons, and to find him a job which would tide him over the crisis, for our object was to find the very best artists who would, for an out-of-pocket expense fee, undertake the work in the war areas.

At any rate, though we had to refuse the help of a few artists who were quite unsuitable, we were able in Manchester to secure a number of very experienced and talented people who were invaluable in our work. The number of these artists was great enough to more than use the generous donation from that great city. It is a very common human failing to have one's prejudices, and so one can quite understand though not excuse him for declining to be present at the meeting at the Mansion House, when he could have aired all his criticism, and perhaps have been converted to our cause.

The auditions which were held everywhere were arranged by the people in the town, and generally either representative musicians or leading members of the city were present; one was then able to know something about the artists.

The first requisite, of course, was a good artist, but one had always to consider suitability for the work, which required a certain amount of stability of character, and also a desire to be of use, and sometimes one would choose a rather less efficient artist really because of the atmosphere which the singer or player created. In some ways selecting a party can be compared to making up a bouquet of flowers, or selecting a number of colours which would not interfere with each other, and the most successful parties were those in which there was a great differentiation but equally great harmony. Sometimes one would put in a singer principally for the fragrance of goodness and sweetness of character.

I remember once in France a Y.M.C.A. leader complained to me about a certain party. He considered them too attractive, and he explained that every man in the audience must have wanted to kiss a certain young artist, who always gave me the impression of a wild rose in spring. He then drew up a party which met with his idea, that no member of it should have awakened such a reprehensible desire, and his party, I must frankly confess, selected out of the different parties he had seen, would have been rather a chilly affair. I always have felt that the audience should love the artists, and the appeal to beauty and goodness should be so great that the longing to kiss one of them need not necessarily be an ignoble thing at all—indeed, to kiss something may represent the highest form of worship. One can kiss a cross as the symbol of the greatest wonder and miracle of Love.

Sometimes at an audition one could enjoy oneself, but generally it was a very great strain, because one's decision as to suitability and artistic value had to be made very quickly, and it is, indeed, I feel, something to be proud of that in dealing with six hundred people, in spite of the tremendous temptations and difficulties of our work, we were let down in only three or four cases. Though I feel a great admiration for the goodness of human beings, I think this fact was partially, if not entirely, due to the admirable help of the other office, where Miss Dorothy Dundas presided over all the arrangements for the parties, the passports, travelling, the settling of innumerable disputes and difficulties. At this little room, at 44 South Molton Street, was the office for the disposal of the funds.

Miss Dundas was an actress, and when she first came to me in 1915, declared that she could not possibly undertake the work, as she knew neither shorthand nor typewriting, and was the last person fitted for such a job. I explained that I did not want a typist nor a shorthand writer, but I did want a well-balanced brain and a sense of humour; and I was very lucky when she agreed to come, because I do not know of any one who could have carried out an extremely difficult piece of work with the faithfulness, tact, and wisdom which she displayed throughout. She always managed to soothe people down, and persuade them to be thoroughly reasonable; and I am sure she saved me from many a libel action, for whenever I had an explosion of wrath, and expressed my heated feelings in a letter, she would solemnly write it down without expressing any opinion, and, returning next day after all the other work was done, would say, "You know that letter you wrote yesterday? Would you like to look at it? Because if you really want to send it—" And then, of course, it found its way to the paper-basket.

Mr. Bernard Cowtan was the honorary treasurer of the Y.M.C.A. Ladies' Auxiliary Committee, and all our accounts passed through his hands. He was always most delightful and helpful and thorough in his work of supervising all our expenditure. He was very surprised at the efficient way the office was run, and often praised us for the way the accounts were kept by the very able accountant, Miss Borrough, who, in spite of miserably bad health and much suffering, never failed to be at her place and keep us all straight on the important matters of detail.

There were some amusing incidents at the auditions. On one occasion, when a feeble-looking youth was playing the violin very indifferently, I decided that he ought to have a chance of going, as he evidently had been refused when he had volunteered, and was trying to play the violin in order to go out and do some job for the army. So I asked him most sympathetically if he would like to go to France, deciding that on this occasion artistic suitability might be waived in view of the desire for self-sacrifice. He looked at me vaguely, and said, "Oh, I shouldn't like to go where there's any fighting!" I decided it was better to stick to one's principles and not let sentimentality interfere.

On another occasion there was a very smart woman, extremely well dressed, accompanied by a beautiful Chow dog. Whilst the violin was being played and the singers were singing, this delightful person remained quite quiet, not uttering one sound of protest, but when his mistress got up to sing, which she could not do, he sat right in front of her and howled his protest, and the higher she went, the louder he howled, and the duet was excruciatingly funny. If only they could have repeated it and gone to France together, it would have been a wonderful turn, but it was quite unintentional, and she was the only person at the audition whose self-confidence was such that she asked "what clothes she would need for France."

On one occasion there was a very fine *soprano* who was abnormally stout. She had a rather wandering eye, which made me feel uncertain of her suitability, but when there was a great demand for singers I felt that her voice was so good that it might be safe to count on her abnormal size as a make-weight to the levity of mind. So off she went, and though I was very angry, I could not help laughing when I was asked to withdraw her, as she would sit on the officers' knees in the public restaurants. I cannot imagine now how this was done. It must have been a combined effort on the part of the officers, as no one knee could have stood the strain. Anyway, back she came, and all went well.

Of course it was impossible to prevent a certain amount of romance, and many of the artists became engaged in France and have married since.

CHAPTER 5

Back in France

On every visit to France there was a change in the aspect of the scene, and a still greater change in the men. In early 1915 there were the men who had fought the great retreat—grave, steadfast men; then there were the laughing, jolly first drafts of Kitchener's Army. In June 1915 the laugh had gone, and there was a smile which made one wonder. At the bases the only paper that the men had to read was the Paris edition of the Daily Mail, and that paper repeated day by day a grave warning that we had no ammunition, that there were no shells, and that the men we were sending to fight for us were quite helpless in face of the overwhelming superiority of the German resources. It may have been necessary at home, but I often wondered if the writers realised what it must have been for the army to read day by day this statement of the position of affairs, and nothing else.

Anyway, the English only cry and grumble when they are really successful. It is good manners not to rub in one's superiority, and it is dreadfully bad manners to show any feeling of depression when things are going badly. So the smile was there, on every man's face, though it was rather wistful. Nothing seemed to depress the irresistible spirits of Tommy Atkins, that strange soul who mystified friends and enemies by charging machineguns, shouting, "Front rows, 6d."

In 1916 the last of Kitchener's Army landed, and there seemed a gradual growth of the feeling that the war was habitual, and that nothing could end it. Organisation was at its height, and human kindliness was not quite so simple or so ordinary. The French were not quite so full of the appreciation of the English; America was the overwhelmingly popular figure. I crossed with the first contingent of American R.A.M.C. and nurses, who landed at Boulogne on their way to study the Imperial hospitals in the North of France. The French gave them an overwhelming reception. They were overjoyed to see them at last landing on their shores. The American Army landed farther south, at Brest.

It was a great disappointment that we were not officially allowed to help the American Y.M.C.A. Their leading administrator had been working with the British Y.M.C.A., and it would have seemed that there might easily have been useful co-operation. I made several offers, but was always refused. But in spite of the official refusal, the parties at Abbeville, Paris, and Amiens were requisitioned on many occasions to give concerts for the Americans.

America had great schemes for the organisation of magnificent entertainments, but there were obstacles which prevented much of their work materialising. Firstly, the German submarines prevented the easy transport of women, and both concert parties and play needed their help; secondly, it is not possible to organise on a large scale, and more or less nationally, work which has been considered of no national importance. America is worse even than England with regard to its outlook on recreation.

Early in 1918 the impression was very vivid that the war was the great one which was to see the beginning of the end of the world. Certainly all nations seemed to be represented in France; all races, all colours, all portions of the earth had sent their men to take a part in the great struggle. The French had their black troops from Africa, the Cochin Chinese, and other races. There were Portuguese, Italians, Belgians, with the Imperial troops, which included English, Scotch, Welsh, Irish, Canadian, Australian, New Zealand, South African, and Indian troops. The Japanese naval uniform was very much in evidence in the ports. There were thousands of Kaffirs and Chinese, and, I have no doubt, other races working at the bases and on the lines of communication, passing through which were an increasing number of khaki-clad women.

The first women that I saw were the telegraphists, but towards the end of the war they seemed to be everywhere, and surely it speaks well for the progress of civilisation and the increase of chivalry amongst men that so many women could pass so freely and safely.

In March 1918 there was such complete organisation and apparent stagnation that it seemed the war could never end, but had become a deadly habit of mankind. At Candas Aerodrome I unwisely made the remark that I wondered how long it would be before the human race realised that war was no solution of differences; that you might kill a man because you did not agree with him, but in killing him, what you disagreed about might easily remain, ideas were not so easily disposed of; and that it was possible that some day the human race might attempt the experiment of *"overcoming evil with good."* The whole mess fell upon me with the argument that war was the great means of bringing out what was finest and best in man. It is a pitiful tale that men keep on telling each other.

It was at Candas that the little party played a triple bill, and I recited between the plays. The immense hangar was a sea of mud, and the dressing accommodation behind the stage had to be seen to be believed. The mud was so deep that there were duck-boards to walk on, and there were only two or three chairs as furniture, balanced on the boards.

An aerodrome always makes me think of an old sewing woman we had who, when aeroplanes first were used before the war, was asked what she thought of them. She said, "The h'earth and the sea are h'enough for h'us. We've no right to h'interfere with the h'air."

It was curious at that great aerodrome to hear the experiences of the C.O. He said that when the Press was filled with the continual praise of the German Fokker engine—pointing out that no English airman had a chance against these superior machines—one boy after another would go up with grim, set lips, convinced of failure, and would fail. It was a terribly trying time to live through, but when the news flashed through the aerodrome that an English pilot in single combat had sent a Fokker crashing to the ground, there was a complete change—every face was alight with the possibility of success; there was no more crashing. Their tails were up.

Crossing in May 1916, there was a little fluttering old lady dressed in black, very agitated, and crying silently when she felt unnoticed, a crumpled telegram in her hand, evidently a relative of some soldier desperately wounded.

Perhaps the finest bit of work that the Y.M.C.A. carried out during the war was their work in connection with the relatives of the wounded. Crossing to Boulogne in May 1916, there were many of them on the boat. A telegram from the War Office was sufficient for travelling on the railway. The Y.M.C.A. were everywhere on the watch to guide these people, who, some of them, came from small villages, far from the big cities. Many were quite unused to travelling, having never before been away from their village, some could not read, and all would have been confused and helpless but for the Y.M.C.A.

Near the hospitals they established hostels where the relatives were greeted by friendly people, who, on their arrival, telephoned to the hospital to inquire and give them the latest news of their people, and then fed them and tucked them away in comfortably furnished cubicles. I was met by Mr. M'Cowan, the head of the Y.M.C.A. in France, at the docks in Boulogne, and we had a car full of relatives to deposit at the different camps in Boulogne and Etaples. We dropped my little old lady at her camp, seeing her welcomed in the hostel by a charming and kindly woman. The people who undertook this work were extremely understanding, and when the relatives were too late, or when their particular warrior Joined the great company of those who had finished the fight, they took the relatives up to the cemeteries, and brought them flowers to lay on the graves, helping them all through the tragic days.

No one could ever forget the fields of crosses at Etaples, who saw them as I did through the masses of moving troops, through the little gaps in the hills the fields bristling with little white crosses, so small and so white, right down to the sea. They are buried with their faces towards England. Where a funeral was still in progress, there were the Union Jack pall and the white robes of the *padre*. The members of the parties generally talked to the relatives if they looked lonely and desolate in the hotels. When the hospitals were in or near the large towns the Y.M.C.A. did not build hostels, but billeted everyone in the hotels. There was one typical old soldier at Rouen. It was obvious in all his movements and manner that he was an ex-private. He explained that he had three sons; one was a prisoner of war in Germany, the youngest had not yet been drafted out, and the second was dangerously wounded in hospital.

Every day the artists inquired, and the news was none too good, and the lonely soldier was very melancholy. One morning they found him combing his hair carefully with a pocket comb, and scrutinising his appearance in a small looking-glass that hung in the hotel entrance. He was looking very spruce and smart, and turned round in the most cheery way to ask if he looked smart enough for the funeral. It was experiences like this that made one understand the driver of the Y.M.C.A. car whose special duty it was to look after the relatives. One day he was looking very woebegone, and told me what a sad day it had been. He was still whisking away tears that would come. A relative had arrived too late to see his son, but he said: "But I sez, 'Look how lucky you are.'" I looked very surprised. "Yes, lucky, I sez.

'You knows wheres he's buried, and in a week or two I'll send you a snapshot of the grave.'"

There are degrees of sorrow: my little maid, like many others, never learnt where or how her brother was killed, and no one knows his resting-place, and the old soldier knew that his boy had done his bit, and knew where he was buried.

It was a bitterly cold night, and I was very thankful when we had located all our relatives and found shelter at the nicest of all the hostels, Les Iris, at Le Touquet.

The crossing was in brilliant sunshine, but we had two destroyers to escort us, and a silver sausage flying machine took us half-way across the Channel, when we were met by the golden sausage of the French. These flying machines from a height could see a great depth below the water, and could spot the approach of any submarine. The boat was packed with khaki, gold hats, staff hat, New Zealand felts, and the Australian *sombrero*. Some of the officers were carrying whips, many of them swords, and everybody was having a miserable time, embarrassed by lifebelts. The misery of a lifebelt on top of a fur coat cannot really be described. Every time I crossed I was amused at the sentries on deck who always started in a most businesslike manner and quickly succumbed to sea-sickness. The anguished expression of their faces when trying to keep up the dignity of the sentry whilst suffering from the horrors of a disturbed "little Mary" was comic. It was never a long struggle.

All the visits that I made to France after I played *Macbeth* I was alone, going for the purpose of visiting the different Bases, to see the parties and arrange differences, for naturally there were a great number of difficulties and dissensions which some one had to smooth out. In all these early journeys I was met by Mr. M'Cowan, who motored me to all the bases, and was a most delightful and kind escort, and who either took me himself to the different huts at which I recited sometimes at five or six in the evening, three or four poems in each hut, with a little speech as well; when he could not go with me himself he handed me over to the leader of the base, who carried me round on the same mission.

I look back with regret that any difference of opinion should have altered the pleasant relationship of that early time. The difficulties which ended in somewhat strained relations between us were based on the desire of Mr. M'Cowan and the Y.M.C.A. to make the entertainments Y.M.C.A. I am not usually very obstinate, because my natural instinct, when a disagreement arises, is to "clear out" as soon as possible; but on this point I insisted, that all the entertainments should remain "Lena Ashwell." The arguments were most reasonable from the Y.M.C.A. point of view, that an organisation was bigger than a name, that the Y.M.C.A. could include every method of helping mankind, and so on.

I had every sympathy with them, but my whole object from the beginning had been the demonstrating that the arts were essentially and vitally necessary to human beings, as necessary as the Red Cross, and I could not see why the professional musician or actor should be submerged in the Y.M.C.A. organisation; one would not expect surgeons or nurses or doctors to be called Y.M.C.A., and I always considered my name merely as a label to signify that all the people concerned in the work were professionals. Undoubtedly the entertainment work became extremely powerful, and to a non-professional it must have seemed very pig-headed to insist upon the professional standing, but then Christian organisations have not been treated with the indifference and contempt that the music and drama of this country have suffered under.

Of these visits in 1916 I have many vivid recollections—Le Triage at Abbeville, the hut on the railway lines; passing over the level crossing, we would often have to stop while the transports rolled through, thirty to forty men and eight horses in each van, and guns following. The station had originally two railway lines, but now had, I should think, at least twenty, such was the traffic that passed there to the Front. The audience was always on the move, perpetually, either going up the line or coming down. When they were going up, none of them knew where they were going, and very often the men had been on the train for thirty-six hours with no food or rest.

At Abbeville, too, I saw the hospital barges which were splendidly fitted up for the purpose of bringing the men straight from the Front to the coast. A concert was just beginning when we arrived, and as I sat on the platform with the others, there was the constant sound of the trains passing outside; the soprano sang a song with the refrain of the cuckoo, and above these sounds, a nightingale poured out its heart in the wood.

Then there was the night in Calais when I heard the party of men—Walter Hyde, Charles Tree, Arthur Fagge, Nelson Jackson, and Percy Sharman, who were just on their way to the firing line. It was wonderful to hear the joy that these fine artists gave to the men of the

Remounts, who were packed tightly in the hut.

There was rather a good story of a man who had lost his horse, and, as it was rather a large thing to lose, had to be reported to the C.O. When the C.O. expostulated and said, "You might lose a small thing, but of course you can't *lose* a horse. What have you done with it?" the man said, "Well, it was dark when I come in last night, and I anchored the horse with a bit o' string, and when I come in the morning, there he was—*gone!*"

It was at that camp that, going by in the morning, I saw an old Scottish Pastor sweeping out the hut. He explained that he had come out to teach the men, but he was grateful for all they had taught him, and he felt he did not even sweep as well as he wanted to. He was a dear old man.

There was another *padre*, whose name was Hardy, who had the greatest difficulty in getting over to France or up the line because of his age. But before he was killed at the Front he had a V.C., D.S.O., and M.C. The night before he left the Base for the firing line, and so realised his ambition, he came to a concert. The tenor was singing "Ike Walton's Prayer." After the song was sung the *padre* left the hut. When the concert was over he came round and apologised to the tenor for leaving, but said that he wanted to keep the memory of the song to help him when he was in the line, and he was afraid that if he remained to hear the other songs the memory that he wanted might be obliterated. As he thanked the singer the tears were running down his face. He often wrote afterwards, and it was a very great sorrow when the tenor heard of his loss.

Then there was the visit to Les Attaques, the amazing camp where, as in Havre, the trains came down filled with the *débris* of the battlefields, which was sorted and distributed, and where thousands of watches were mended, boots repaired, bicycles practically remade, and all the miracles of a repairing workshop. It was a funny sensation to go into the hut, and be the only woman, and be cheered and cheered and cheered, after I had spoken and recited three or four poems, just because I had been able to send the men something which gave them a few hours' happiness. It was in Calais that we first heard the news of the Battle of Jutland, and the first whisper I got was in one of the repairing workshops. The report was worded in such a way that it was not for a considerable time that it was realised as a victory. It was amazing the way silence fell on everybody and the heart was taken out of everyone. For the English, it seemed that the skies might fall before any defeat might happen to the navy.

It was not a very happy morning, for with the news of the battle there was also news that there had been a terrific air-raid on London and enormous damage had been done. To add to one's depression— no letters!

One of the entertainers, a delightful and most amusing man, though certainly a snob as some other distinguished Englishmen, met me in the street, and inquired if I had heard of the terrible air-raid. I said I had, and he said, "Tell me, is anyone of importance killed?" which gave one a humorous idea of the manner in which he would graduate the value of life according to position and caste.

In July 1917 the concert party were exceptionally fine, and not far from Cinder City in the Havre Docks I dropped in to hear the concert at which Carrie Tubb was singing. Of course the men adored her, with her beautiful voice, joyous manner, splendid vitality, and all-pervading good humour. She was a joy to be with; she never minded when or where she sang, and never wanted to be treated differently from others less gifted and well known, but just joyfully gave her best for the love of helping to kill care and grief of heart.

From this camp all the supplies sent up the line and all the requests from the different battalions were attended to—an indescribable medley of large and small things—everything from pontoons to screws. Much of the store was kept in boxes open in the front, piled high on top of each other—a makeshift arrangement very easily put together, and, I suppose, quite adequate. We always say that the English are no good at organising, but it always appeared that this camp, at any rate, piled with stores, was a miracle of efficiency.

The hangars were, of course, among the railway lines, and every truck had a list of goods required fastened inside the door, with the number of the battalion, but no one knew the exact position they were being sent to.

It was always immensely interesting to watch the fate of different artists in France. There were, of course, no advertisements, no news-paper criticisms, nothing to tell the men by whom they should be impressed. There was no possibility of a star entrance, or any trick by which it was possible to establish one's position as an artist. There were no lighting effects, no friends to direct appreciation, no decorations to enhance the appearance. The artists all sat in a row, rather like the old-fashioned Nigger Minstrels, and the leader of the party, or more often the officer who was taking the chair at the concert, would merely announce that Miss So-and-so would sing a certain song, and the singer advanced and sang. An unreal reputation just collapsed.

At Abbeville there was a delightful party, including John Harrison, under the direction of Mr. Charles Tree. They gave a public concert in the little cinema at Abbeville, and in the programme there were a number of classical items, including songs of Mozart. At supper afterwards there was a lengthy discussion on the merits of the programme, and a colonel urged the advisability of a higher standard, and expressed a wish to be allowed to choose a programme. With the interest of the work very much at heart, I naturally asked him to give me some new ideas, and he immediately mentioned "The Perfect Day," "The Old-Fashioned Town," "Donegal," "Roses in Picardy." Apparently everybody had a different idea as to the meaning of the word "classic." One Y.M.C.A. leader, in a long letter, urged the necessity for a high standard of classical music, and begged me to send immediately the Fisk Trio. They were the noted coloured singers of negro melodies.

It was necessary, of course, in our work to strike a balance, not only that the men might individually hear something that they liked and understood at a concert, but there are singers who can sing classical music, and there are also singers who are quite valuable in a different way, but are quite incapable of adequately performing the greater works. There are singers who are quite delightful in "The Perfect Day," who become a misery to themselves and the audience when they attempt *Madame Butterfly* or *La Tosca*.

Now there are critics who would have everybody sit on the mountain-tops and insist only on the singing of the great works, however ineffectual the artist; but with us it was wiser to encourage the artists to do the work that was natural to them, for the audience knew with a horrible certainty when the performer was going beyond his powers. And so our parties sometimes did the lightest of light work, quite good of its kind, but not to be confused with the word "classic." But that the general level of our work was sound is shown by the following letters:

...Your last 'Home Party' was here on the 16th; some 1800 men listened to it. One and all were full of the pleasure it gave them. To me it was a real treat. The whole tone of your entertainment, the class of music, and the entire absence of vulgarity are a liberal education to the men. After forty years' service, I feel convinced that that is what is sadly wanted for our men—and sometimes for others! Everything should be done to elevate them and alter their tastes.

Would like to thank you for your music, it's good to hear *good music*; one gets very sick of the piffle of the camp, and God's greatest gift is so refreshing and uplifting.

Looking around, one can see that we men are lower than when we enlisted, mainly because we are shut off from all refining influences, and are unable to get away from the filthiness of conversation in the huts, and we have to be so very careful to try and always look for the gems in life, which seem so few and far between. Might I offer you a word of advice: don't in any-wise lower the tone of your music. I know there are hundreds like myself, who hunger for the riches which your great gift can supply, and it's so helpful.

I drove from hearing Carrie Tubb and her party, Charles Tree and his, down to Boulogne, where Gervase Elwes was taking care of a very brilliant party: Dilys Jones, Adelaide Rhind, F. Kiddle. Norah Blaney and Gwen Farrar began their friendship, which has resulted in their partnership, in the music halls; but at these concerts Gwen Farrar played the cello with very real and exceptional talent. The concerts were brilliant, and I do not believe any one was more loved by the audience than that fine artist, Gervase Elwes. He sang his usual repertory, and had to respond with encore after encore. Finally, at the big rest camp outside Boulogne, he accompanied himself on the piano, and sang a quaint little funny song as his fifth encore.

It was not only his singing which made Gervase Elwes such a power, it was his radiating goodness. He made every one feel that there was a splendour in simple goodness, and his singing was the expression of the beauty of his character. He introduced each singer, but it was not until I asked him to tell the men who he was, that he ever thought of himself. After my pleading with him, he used to say, "I am going to sing, 'Where'er she walks,'" and then, in a very amused, shy voice, "and I am asked to say that my name is Gervase Elwes." His reception was especially interesting to me, because I had so many times heard people say that the army would not understand his songs or appreciate his fine work. It was supposed by these critics to be above their heads.

We gave an extra concert on Sunday, at Equihen, near Boulogne, as the requests were so urgent, and the men at this rest camp were returning immediately to the line. As a rule we rested on Sunday, or followed the tradition of the touring artist and spent part of the day travelling. This Sunday was terrifically hot; the tent was a very large one, and though the sides were all open, the men made a dense wall round, and were packed tight under the canvas, so that the heat was suffocating. The platform was so filled with men that there was not much room for us. Behind us the men were crowded, and I was puzzled all through the beginning of the concert at their restlessness, because generally the stillness was intense. I wondered vaguely what was wrong, and why we failed to grip their attention. About halfway through, after I had recited "St. George of England," and "Little Trawlers," and a few Elizabethan love lyrics by way of encores, and had just sat down, there was an expectant hush, and a sergeant, literally shaking from head to foot, stepped into the middle of the platform. He apologised to me for the interruption, and read out the following letter:

3rd Army Rest Camp,
A.P.O. S.31, B.E.F., France,
17th June 1917.

Madam, In the name and on behalf of the N.C.O.'s and men of the divisions of the 3rd Army, who have the good fortune to be at this Rest Camp at this time, we beg to express to you our deep appreciation of the concerts to which today and on a previous occasion the members of your party have been good enough to entertain us.

They have brought to us recollections and suggestions of "dear old Blighty." We confess that we would rather listen for ever to their melodies than go back to the horrid Orchestra of War, but they have helped us to realise again that we are fighting for the Empire, Home and Beauty, and for all they mean in the life of mankind, and therefore we shall go back from our rest to our work with firmer will and sterner purpose to pursue our struggle to a victorious end, and secure for the world a just and enduring peace.

We are aware that not only this concert party but many others have come, under your auspices, to hearten and brighten the lot of His Majesty's troops. You have been, and are, the fairy-godmother of us all, and we are proud and grateful to be able to look you in the face today, and to say from full hearts, "Madam, we thank you."

May we respectfully request you and each member of your party who is here today to accept a small souvenir as an expression, although utterly inadequate, of the deep gratitude of over 1500 soldiers of the King.—We are, Madam, yours very gratefully,

The Boys of 15 Divisions of the 3rd Army.

He then presented each member of the party with a souvenir spoon.

The cheers which followed shook my heart and scattered my senses. Gervase Elwes whispered to me, "This is exquisite agony." An expression of love like this should be acknowledged in a joyous manner, as it was meant to give happiness, but when one is shaking with emotion and battling with tears, it is a desperate affair to try to control oneself and speak articulately. Some critics have said that my enunciation was bad, that I was inaudible and monotonous, and I have differed with them silently, but on this occasion all these criticisms were true.

From Boulogne I went to Dunkirk, and on the way saw the armies on the move, masses of men marching in the dust and heat. It was then I discovered how many different colours there are in khaki. Going through Dunkirk to Bergues late in the evening, I found myself in a tent which seemed in the darkness to be far away from everything and everybody. I stood on a table and recited all the poems that I knew, and as I recited, more and more men came in and sat down anywhere on the ground around me. I did not know that I knew so many poems, but wished with all my heart that I had learnt many more, as the audience grew and grew, and they sat silently round like hungry children. It was a quaint, gentle, peaceful evening, and curious that on that night I should have been nearer to the firing line than at any other moment. It was just behind Ypres, and it was rather amusing when the driver told me with a grin, that it was "just as well that we *had lost our way.*"

On one of my solitary journeys I was again up the Harfleur Valley, and though there was a service going on in the Y.M.C.A. hut, in Camp 20, Colonel Worthington was anxious that I should speak to the men, and the *padre*, without a moment's hesitation, stopped the service and told the men that I had something to say. The hut was adorned with maple leaves, and the rafters were hung with flags, and the men kept crowding in while I was speaking and reciting. When the colonel began to speak, there was a packed crowd of Canadians. He spoke kindly of me, and of the concerts, then of the cause for which they were fighting, and finding no words with which to express himself adequately, he burst into Henry V.'s speech to his soldiers, "*Once more into the breach, dear friends.*"

It was a curious and illuminating link in human experience to hear that speech in the mouth of a Canadian addressing those English-speaking men who had come in their thousands from a land unknown, undreamt of, in the time of William Shakespeare, and to realise, furthermore, that the words were being said on the very spot where Henry V. was camped, and may very well have addressed his soldiers.

Down at the Bakeries at Havre the men sometimes worked from seven in the morning until two the following morning, and at one concert quite a number of men got up and went out, their places being filled up at once from the queue outside. We found out the reason afterwards. There were 700 men and 800 horses starting up the line in two hours. After the supper at the officers' mess, we came out into the darkness and mud to find the roads all blocked with horses covered with white blankets, the men standing stiff and coated at their heads. There were rows and rows of guncarriages farther on, the horses harnessed to them, and the men sitting there waiting in extraordinary silence; not a word, even the horses seemed exceptionally still.

We passed through the silent lines. Two of the party addressed the men, but got no reply. They did not realise that no soldier may speak on duty. The motor took some time to start, and we seemed to stand there ages in the darkness, surrounded by that quiet throng. The men on the carriages were still and erect; the only noise seemed to be when a soldier walked round a horse and pulled a rope or stroked the horse's head.

"Bakeries" was the hut I loved least, somehow, in France. In the first years of the war the atmosphere was always difficult, the men seemed to have bad manners, everything was uncomfortable, somehow. But on one visit, Mr. Reade asked me to go there, and I begged to be let off, because I was so unutterably tired; but he seemed to have a very special reason for my going, so at last, groaning in spirit, I went. The atmosphere had absolutely changed. The hut had become a charming, bright, and happy place. There was a special little room for silent prayer. The manners of the men were delightful; it was as if a curse had been lifted from the hut. Mr. Reade had especially wanted me to see this hut because of the reason of the change. A little Scotswoman, widowed in the war, had waved her wand of love and understanding, and all the men seemed to love the hut and her. Goodness, what miracles love and understanding can perform!

Not far from Dunkirk there was a hut in the midst of drifting sand, an oasis in the midst of surrounding discomfort. Amongst the surrounding camps were the large ones of the Chinese *coolies*, surrounded with wire. They once broke camp in their terror of the air-raids, poor things. The hut was run by two Scottish girls, most charming, both of them, and they spoke with great warmth of the few concerts we had been able to send them. Dunkirk was attacked from sea as well as by air, and we had few opportunities of visiting them. They told me of the visit of the Divisional Concert Party, and spoke with regret of the coarseness of the entertainment given. They had sat in front of the audience, and after a time withdrew, not showing any critical distaste, because they felt that if the men were enjoying the jokes, they had great need of laughter and amusement. The next morning many of the men apologised to them, and said that they were ashamed that it should be thought that they really liked the ugliness of such fun.

A concert at a German prisoners' camp to the guards and engineers, about sixteen miles from Etaples, proved full of excitement. There were 870 Huns, very happy and comfortable. It was difficult to find the camp. There were streams of khaki on the roadside, but no one seemed to know where the camp was. Finally we arrived at a farmyard, and we were told that some one in a barn might know the way. We were hailed from the lower darkness and led through a filthy farmyard, following the swinging lanterns over a sea of deep sand. It is astonishing to find sand so far inland, but, after all, Montreuil, G.H.Q., was once a seaport.

The 870 Huns lived in comfortable huts surrounded by barbed wire. Our men lived under canvas, and the officers' quarters were in railway trucks; having crossed the railway line, and then passed over a bridge, we found the hut, which was a dining-hall that had been converted into a concert room. There were vases of flowers on the platform, and stable lamps in a row in the front for footlights, and on the piano, tin cans filled with sand had tallow candles stuck in them.

A lot of new huts were put up at Etaples and at Camiers, which the parties had the honour of opening. In these new huts there were furnished stages and painted scenery and stencilled curtains, with charming paintings. There were footlights and headlights, and it was always amusing to watch the faces of the different men who had done this work. One gazed with ecstasy on the painted panels, another at the stencilling, and others looked lovingly from one electric bulb to the other, they were naturally so delighted with what had been accomplished.

There were thousands upon thousands of Anzacs, who pressed against the walls of the hut until they positively bent, and there was a free fight as the party entered. Some of them pushed their way in a second time, because they wanted to hear the first items again, and the first items are always the serious part of the programme.

> I have seen New Zealanders enjoying themselves often enough before, but have not seen anywhere an audience more thoroughly happy than these were! All the small party always gave one the impression that the evening was a pleasure for them, and entered into everything with such a swing that it made one fairly take a breath of home, and go away feeling ready for anything!
>
> The good such work amongst us has done and is doing is hard to estimate, but I fear your reward for starting the movement and infusing such life into it will be small indeed. Be that as it may, those who are fortunate enough to get back to our own far-away shores will treasure amongst their most happy memories those rollicking songs and singers, both grave and gay, who formed the parties that bear your name.

The Australian Camp might be in the desert of Sahara in a thunderstorm as one plodded over mud and snow, and there were cries of "Mind the trench!" and a flashlight showed a large ditch at one's feet. The hut held 1300 men, but the windows were white with faces, and from the rafters dangled many long legs. They were a very good audience, but rather disconcerting, as they do not laugh as much as the other troops, but make strange noises, whistle and "coo-ee" and cheer.

The different dominions gave different cries. The English always gave three cheers; the South Africans, when really stirred, always gave a Zulu war-cry; the New Zealanders, their thrilling and inspiring Maori war-cry:

> Leader: *Kemate! Kemate!* (It is death! It is death!)
> Chorus: *Kaora! Kaora!* (It is life! It is life!)
> *Tenei te tangata puhuru huru.* (This is the strong or hairy man.)
> *Nga nga i tikei mai whiti te ra.* (Who brought us from the Rising Sun.)
> *Hupane!* (Eyes left!)

Kaupane! (Eyes right!)
Hupane! Kaupane! Whiti te ra. (Eyes left! Eyes right! Look to the Rising Sun.)

The Australians gave their "coo-ee," and the Canadians their "Razzle dazzle, razzle dazzle, zis boom pah! Canada Canada, Ra! Ra! Ra!"

On one occasion in a hospital there was a very amusing Australian; his face was much tied up for neuralgia, but as the concert progressed, one wrap after another was discarded, and finally his mouth was open, and great shouts and guffaws came from it. He had been wounded three times, but his appetite was historic. For one meal he managed to dispose of six tins of sardines and twelve eggs!

Our chauffeur at Etaples had lost part of his hand, and after he had been dismissed from the B.E.F. as medically unfit, he joined the 11th Fighting Corps, and was again wounded at Verdun and discharged. He said Verdun was only saved by a miracle, as at one time they were driven into a three-mile line, shelled on both sides by the enemy. The Germans could have taken Verdun. How many miracles there were from the retreat of Mons to the time of the Armistice, which was signed at Mons!

At one mess there was an Australian officer who gave a curious description of "No Man's Land." A German officer led a handful of men to retake one of the trenches. He could not take it, but tried bravely.

I'd had this hand damaged, and it was just beginning to tell on me. We got the best of it, and when I got out in the open, instead of killing him, I was too far gone to touch him. I stood opposite him, swaying to and fro, and he swayed too. Then I saw that his left shoulder was all blown away, and we just steadied ourselves and shook hands. We supported each other to the nearest lines—fortunately they were English!

In June 1917 I was taken to the Marne battlefield, which is about twenty miles from Paris, about the same distance as Bromley or Maidenhead. Many of the graves in the fields or by the roadside were marked with small white crosses, and in the fields, whether there were a number or only one, there was a little railing of wood around the graves, and in the sea of ripening corn they looked like strange islands. In all the villages there were signs of the battle and marks of shot upon the walls, the broken roofs, the damaged churches. On the top of the high plateau there was a small walled graveyard in a position that commanded a wide view of the open country and the straight, white roads, bare of hedges and trees, entirely unlike our English country.

In the wall made of cement and rubble which surrounded this tiny graveyard, with its memorial wreaths and crosses covered with glass upon the graves, the French soldiers had made holes through which to put their rifles, and, in the long hours whilst they waited for the enemy, had scribbled their names underneath the holes, and each man was buried in the place where he had written his name. In spite of the beauty of the country, it took one's breath away as one imagined and felt the fear that must have filled those men at the first battle of the Marne, when they saw that tremendous grey army surging down upon them. We crossed a bridge which had been blown up by the French to prevent the German advance.

We used to be a good deal chaffed on the subject of the submarine menace. There was a good deal of danger, and on almost every crossing some one or other felt, if going through the mine-fields, that the Germans were after them at last. But on one occasion there was no doubt of the danger of the crossing.

It was on 8th January 1918, there were German submarines especially anxious to get Mr. Lloyd George, who was crossing about that time. The packet was packed so closely that no one could move; there was natural resentment, therefore, when one of the crew forced his way through the crowded deck on to the bridge; but his breathless announcement, "Periscope on the starboard bow, sir!" was distinctly audible.

Almost as he spoke the boat cut strange figures, and darted to and fro in short runs. It was impossible to move on the deck, and before anyone had time to think what the words meant, two torpedoes glided past. They rolled through the water like a strip of carpet rapidly unfolding. The third came on the other side of the boat. There was no panic. Everyone was jammed too tightly to move, and hardly anyone had realised what had happened. There was only one woman crying, and she was a Belgian, with a tiny baby.

There were many experiences whilst travelling which were strange and sometimes difficult to cope with. There had been a muddle about berths when a party was going to Havre, and the artists were packed in anywhere. One musician was tucked into a cabin with a stranger who said, "You won't mind my little boy being in here? He's only a very little boy." As in wartime everyone wished to be as sympathetic and obliging as possible, she complied without much alacrity. She came down to go to bed rather late, having tried to sit it out on deck, and was getting on fairly well in spite of the roughness, when the head of a boy of quite fifteen years old leant over the top berth, and in tones of thrilled excitement said, "Mamma, the lydy's tykin' off 'er stys!"

The accommodation in the huts was not always very comfortable, and when the rain poured through the roof the artists had to use umbrellas. There was something comic as well as grotesque in lying apparently comfortable in bed under an umbrella, but if one curls up small enough it is quite a good way of keeping dry. There were sometimes leaders of the huts who were deeply prejudiced against all artists, and sometimes prejudice makes people rather cruel. If one feels very superior to another human being, it is apt to produce an almost inhuman indifference to their comfort. The most prejudiced of Puritans was to be found on Salisbury Plain. When the concert party was there on one occasion, they literally wept for hunger.

A dinner of one sardine on toast does not make for a good performance, and that sardine, with a few biscuits, was all that was obtainable from the leader. He was the man who was finally cornered by a very diminutive violinist, who told him that the sheets on the bed were dirty. He tried to put her off by contradicting, but she was persistent, and forced him to come with her to look at the bed she was to sleep in. They were both quivering with rage as they stood over it and she laid back the bedclothes. He looked at her very indignantly and said, "Oh, I can easily explain that. We had all the convalescents to tea yesterday, and there were not enough tablecloths to go round. That isn't dirt; it's nothing but honey and jam." Only a sense of humour can save one on these occasions.

CHAPTER 6

The Firing Line

During the whole of 1915 we received letters from all ranks of the army in the trenches, saying: "We hear of concerts at the base camps. Do send some up here; we have not any." But it was not until we had given close upon 2000 concerts on the lines of communication that we received permission to respond to these many urgent requests to send a concert party into the firing line itself. Of course the party was to consist of men only, and these men had to be over military age or rejected for the army as medically unfit.

There were in all nine Firing Line Parties, the first going up in January 1916 to the northern part of France and Belgium, to Bailleul, Poperinghe, Locre, etc.

There was a certain amount of excitement and interest in seeing a civilian. It is a curious thing that men would feel they were somehow in touch with civilisation again in just stroking a sleeve of a coat which was not khaki. They were deluged by requests to give concerts, as of course the troops were always changing, and what is one tiny little party of four men amongst the thousands who were in the front line?

When with the Second Army Corps on St. Valentine's Day, 1916, there was so much to be done that they stayed a few days longer before going to the First Army.

It is impossible to convey in a letter what these concerts mean to the men. We are deluged with requests to give concerts, and they all want us to stay months instead of weeks. You see, the men are always changing. It is very fortunate that there is a large place here which holds about seven hundred men. We were very near a heavy bombardment the other day, which continued the whole day. It is astonishing how quickly one gets used to the sound of the guns. In between two concerts we walked up the hill and had a wonderful view of the line. The nearest we have been to the front line is a mile or a little over.

The nine parties at different times gave their entertainments to the different armies, but there never were more than two parties out at the same time, for we soon found that the conditions were impossible; most of those who were medically rejected, especially when the age-limit was raised and age was added to the disability of bad health, could not remain fit for work under the very trying conditions.

We had the car presented by Mr. Dennis Bailey from Nottingham, and bought two small pianos which were easy to transport. One was called "Little Peter," of course because it could not grow up; and the other was nicknamed "Wee Donal" by the Scottish party. He had no pedals, so was supplied with a fearful contraption constructed with "a window pulley, two boot laces, a block of wood with a swivel, an armature supplied with a nice penny hook, and two gimlets with which to attach it to the floor. It had a Heath-Robinson appearance, and excited unseemly mirth."

The concerts were often given in the open, punctuated by 9.2 guns, with one or two aeroplanes coming over the platform, which was two empty packing-cases of unequal height. Whilst the aeroplanes were being happily shelled, the party carried on. The big guns were firing directly over the concert, so the party were literally performing under fire.

Here is a description of a concert in June 1916:

It was a great experience. Our concert last night took place in a small glade in the open at the foot of an important hill, and the nearest trenches were about a mile from our performance. Our audience consisted of Yorkshire Tommies, who are daily in the actual firing line—a splendid set of lads in their new steel helmets. A lot of them were going on duty immediately after our show. The concert was going splendidly, and Charles Tree was singing, 'O no, John! no, John! no, John!' Precisely on the last note a 9.2, about one hundred yards behind us, spoke, and over our heads. Lord! What a crash! I am proud to say not one of us so much as blinked. It sent the Tommies into torrents of laughter and cheers.

I had the next turn, so opened up by saying that 'they had

missed the last performer, and I hoped they'd miss me.' (More laughter.) My turn was punctuated by a 9.2 and a few of his gentlemen friends, lesser men but more noisy, as is usual, of a six-inch pattern, so I said in Liverpool style, 'Oh, shut up! You're spoiling the show,' which brought down the house!

Then two aeroplanes came almost overhead, and the rest of my stunt was further punctuated with German shells bursting all round. But I stuck it, and got a huge encore, which came off in a torrent of shrieking shell-fire. It was absolutely ripping. I've never enjoyed anything so much.

On our homeward journey we called in at a camp where we were to give two concerts the same evening. When we arrived, a *padre* was holding a service, and was praying *extempore*. It was a beautiful prayer, and the kneeling soldiers in the dim light made a most touching scene. I can stand shell-fire, but this picture knocked my end in completely, and I had to retire to hide my emotion.

My school friend sent four of her sons over from Toronto, one of whom was killed. The third son, who was twice wounded, wrote in December 1916:

We had one of your concert parties last night, and, Lena dear, it was wonderful, such a treat as we seldom get out here. I wish you could have been there. It was held in the Y.M.C.A. Cinema Hall, which is in an old brewery, and which is used as a disrobing room for the divisional baths. It was bitterly cold, and the poor performers were absolutely blue in spite of an oil stove, which they hugged when they were not doing a 'stunt.' This in no way interfered with the spirit of the party, and they certainly put their whole hearts into it. I wish you could have heard the way the coughs and sniffles died away when the tenor sang 'Somewhere a Voice is Calling' in his beautiful clear voice, and the violinist held them in the same way.

There is no doubt about it that music means more than can be realised, even to men who have never troubled about it before, when it comes under these circumstances as a beautiful thought from home. I am positive that every man that was in that hall— and there must have been five or six hundred of them—left feeling that life really was worth living and the war worth winning facts which we are sometimes apt to lose sight of amid all the rottenness and discomfort and fed-up-ness of life out here. It sums up to be more than the entertainment of the men for a couple of hours and the forgetting of weariness and discomforts, though this in itself makes it worth while. It acts as a tonic and uplift to us, which does not wear off in a hurry, and I am convinced that it was not only my own 'bucked-up' feeling which today made the men seem to be much more alive and happy than they were yesterday. I suppose you have heard all this before.

He was a company commander.

Another concert was given in a barn on the roadside. To reach it the artists, with "Little Peter," travelled twenty-five miles on a transport waggon—not an ideal conveyance over rough roads, especially when "Little Peter" worked loose and went bumping about on his own. There was some difficulty in finding the barn, the night was so dark, and of course it is unhealthy to show lights so near the enemy line. The platform, however, was lighted by two acetylene lamps, and in the straw of the barn was crowded the audience—lines upon lines of faces looming out of the dim light, on the floor and up in the eaves. How they got there or what they were supported on, or how they were going to get down again, was a mystery to the performers; but the audience did not only consist of soldiers—there were also rats, and they were obviously musical rats, for they came out and ran along the beams, and seemed to enjoy the concert in a most whole-hearted way. The audience were entirely friendly to them. "They're our little bed-fellows," they exclaimed in chorus, when a fat but agile specimen started a star turn in a prominent position right in front of the platform. The following letter is from a member of the audience:

In June 1916, in a great tent, bedecked with coloured, shaded electric lights, we found 2000 men and officers assembled— among them a general and a Scottish earl. A blue haze from at least a thousand cigarettes and pipes was rising to the roof, an incense from all the blends and brands of all the tobaccos of the British Empire, Egypt, and America, filled the air. Every seat in the great tent was occupied, and there was a fringe of standing men at the sides. A film filled in a few minutes. Then an elderly, grey-headed man appeared; he was the pianist of the concert party, and briefly and amusingly he gave us an inkling of what was in store for us.

There was in addition a violinist, a tenor, a baritone, and a comic man. These five formed what was called 'The Lena Ashwell Firing-Line Concert Party.' Similar concert parties, arranged by Miss Lena Ashwell, and supported by generous donors, have been touring behind the lines in France and Flanders. This particular company had actually given a concert well within range of the German guns. The violinist played well, the tenor sang delightfully, the baritone almost brought down the tent, especially with a famous West Country song in dialect, and the funny man was really funny, and sang and told stories till the tent was rocking and filled with jolly laughter.

There was no woman's voice in that entertainment, and all who listened were warriors who had been in, or were about to go into, the trenches. Their strong, determined faces, and their big frames, gave no indication of any degeneracy in the British race. There were officers and men from almost every part of our great Empire, and even Britons from neutral countries still farther afield.

Sometimes when the hut was crowded the men made distracted efforts to get something of the concert. Sometimes they climbed on the roof and tore off the slates, making holes through which they could see and hear. Sometimes they took the sides off the barn, but on one occasion, when the concert was in a tent, and there were men left outside, a strange-looking thing was seen, apparently hanging on the canvas wall inside the tent, which, after a long scrutiny, was seen to be a somewhat large and very red ear. One brilliant genius had evidently discovered that he could hear better when he had made a hole and stuck his ear through.

By way of precaution in the danger zone, the artists were provided with gas helmets. Mercifully they were never required to use them, but the reality of the danger was brought home on more than one occasion. One welcome was, "There may not be a very large audience today. You see, we had a shell through the roof yesterday!"

Perhaps the most complete record of a firing-line party was that of the Scottish party, as one of the entertainers happened also to be a journalist, and was able to give some vivid descriptions of the experiences. They also were in France for Christmas 1916. Their first concert was in the canteen at the Gard du Nord, where the Tommies were wolfing buns and drinking tea. It was a bit noisy, but they did their best to shout through it, and got a great reception, especially from the Scots in the audience.

At St. Pol, which was then the headquarters of the Third Army, they were directed through a town in pitch darkness to their headquarters. They were all very much struck by the cleanliness of the town, "owing to the fact that the Tommies are excellent scavengers and have such fine ideas of cleanliness." A bombardment was going on, and the heavies were engaged, and in the churchyard were the graves of Highlanders, Black Watch, and Gordons, as well as some Germans.

Their guide while with the First Army was a lecturer who had travelled round the world, and was up in the front line giving lectures with limelight views of Siberia, America Today, the Discovery of the North Pole, etc. He was an old campaigner, and had lots of humour (Mr. Starmer).

They travelled about in a London bus, which was put at their disposal by the military, and of course into the bus was packed "Wee Donal." On the way they passed thousands of troops, guns, ammunition, cars, and supplies—one continuous stream of war material. At Sombrin they found a large hut packed with men who had been waiting for more than an hour, and who were much amused when "Wee Donal" was carried through the audience, with the party marching behind looking rather like a funeral party.

It rained every day, and the mud grew thicker and thicker, and walking along the roads with an endless stream of transport waggons was wearisome work. Once, splashing through some awful mud, they arrived to find the hut packed, and at least a thousand outside, so they gave two shows, the first consisting of Scottish, Australian, and South African troops, the second lot of Canadian and English—all of Kitchener's First Army, the heroes of Ian Hay's *First Hundred Thousand*. (Republished by Leonaur in one edition entitled *Doing Our Bit* which also includes his other book *All In It*.) There were some officers who had come down from the trenches, about three miles away, especially to hear the concert, and were going straight back.

On New Year's Day they met the Motor Transport men, and accepted an invitation to "jump up and see our drawing-room." The transport service is not all peaches and plumcake and the leisurely life. Ask the drivers and hear the retort, "Is it what? Not 'arf." Most of them are English, and Cockney at that—ex-London motor-bus men, or taxi drivers, equal to taking the fine risks in traffic, and nonchalantly measuring distances between wheel hubs to the breadth of a hair.

They live in their waggons in France, cook their meals in them, wash, dress, and arrange their neckties in them, so to speak. They sleep on the iron-girded floor below the mottled tarpaulin cover, with the stars overhead winking at them through the chinks, or the rain dripping in when the weather is wet—as it mostly is these months. They seldom leave their waggon. If, when in a hot corner, a shell catches it in the midriff, they go west with the debris. That does happen sometimes, but one hears little of it where the merry waggoners gather. They talk of clutches, gearboxes, carburettors, back axles, magnetos, and tool-kits lost and "found." When a tool-kit is lost another has always to be "found." That is *kismet*. There are invariably searchers on the prowl. The merry waggoner sleeps with one eye only half closed.

The distinction of the "four-tonners" is their crests. Convoys have each their own. There are the Martells or Three Stars; the Trumps, bearing, as the case may be, the Ace of Hearts, Diamonds, Spades, or Clubs; the BonBon Boxes, with shells painted on their panels; the Down Unders, with Kangaroo couchant; the Jocks, with Scottish Lion Rampant or Thistle proudly waving; and the Huntsmen, with the Little Red Fox. It would take the brain of a super-Holt schooling to figure out the numbers of waggons and the variety of their identification marks. To hint at a seven-figure total, however, would not be an extravagant estimate, but figures are elusive, and it is broad impressions of the immensity of the Motor Transport service that remain.

Motor-waggons flank the main roads in lines at all the principal centres, the lines extending for miles. They are packed in villages, squares, and open spaces, and crowd the cross-country bypaths. The marvel is that the Boche artillery can shoot without hitting them. Certainly in the immediate danger-zone in the daytime he couldn't, but that zone is not, as a rule, an open thoroughfare for the merry waggoner between dawning and dusk. He drives there mostly after dark, carrying no lights, and seeing none to guide him other than the star shells soaring up ahead.

"I tell yer 'ow it is," said 'Erbert of Putney to me the other day—"I tell yer 'ow it is when you get well forward, an' one o' these 'ere blinkin' magnesiums goes fizzin' and fuzzin' into the firmament. You feels somehow as if yer bloomin' waggon was twice as big as the dome o' St. Paul's, an' not anythink like so far off neither."

'Erbert and his mate, Bill, are typical of their class. "There's one or two of what yer might call gentlemen drivers in these 'ere parts," 'Erbert confided in me later, "but I 'aven't met the man as could drive through the traffic round 'ere, give as good as he gets, and remain exactly what you might call a gentleman. It's humanly impossible, that's what it is." Candidly, I think 'Erbert's opinion is not lightly to be set aside. I drove with him for three days. He nursed me free of a spell of bumping sickness—a malady common to all novices at the motor game out yonder—and in a moment of expansion he told me the story of his life. He had her picture framed inside his waggon. He had tacked a sprig of mistletoe above it. I wonder what for? Oh, 'Erbert!

Pictorial and photographic embellishment of waggon interiors is usual. It is a homely touch, varied occasionally by the evidence of the acquirement of a Parisian taste, but that by the way. The merry waggoners are a fine lot. Those who drive the old London buses are deemed lucky by their fellows. The buses mean life and travel *de luxe* when compared with the life and travel in the four-tonners that maybe carry shells today, stores tomorrow, mud to be emptied elsewhere, road metal for the turnpike, a concert party for the Divisional entertainment centre, or fodder for the horses. But there is one thing the lads always seem to carry, and that's a light heart!

On the way up to give a concert to the front line they passed streams of traffic, ammunition, guns, waggons of provender, droves of horses, infantry trudging back to the trenches in the mud from their so-called rest. When they came within two miles of the line the exposed roads were screened, and they were congratulating themselves on how well they were getting on, and how easy it was to get up to the Front, when all at once they were challenged by a sentry and ordered to stop.

"Who are you and where are you bound for?"

They told him who they were, and that they were making for Bailleulmont, and showed their military passes.

"Well," he said, "if the Lena Ashwell Party attempts to go farther in this old bus, there will be no party. *Fritz* is shelling the road, and the bus would be a fine target."

He told them to walk a hundred yards apart, and he would send on the bus when it was dark, and they started off in twos to walk the mile and a half to Bailleulmont. Shells were bursting in a wood half a mile away, and they had their first taste of direct shell-fire. Everywhere aeroplanes were gliding about like birds, and the noise was terrific. They passed German trenches and dug-outs from which the Germans had been chased, and, just before entering the town, they saw the ruins of what had once been a part of Bailleulmont.

There they were met by an officer, who had not expected them under such conditions. Their billets were very primitive, one being a kind of cellar with only two rough wire beds in it, with no pillows or blankets. They were told that during the last concert on Christmas Eve the town was shelled, and as they were being told this cheery news there was a great shrieking of shells overhead and a tremendous explosion. There were about eight shells, and then *Fritz* stopped, but neither the concert hall nor any of the men who were hanging about in hundreds were damaged. While they were giving the first concert that evening in a packed hut to the men just out of the trenches, there were a thousand waiting outside for nearly an hour and a half in the mud and snow; in spite of three days' "sloshing," and having just come out of the trenches, they were determined to get into the second concert rather than be resting in their billets.

Our guns were in a wood quite close, and made a great deal more noise than "Wee Donal," who could only be heard very occasionally. In the middle of one of the songs a "Jack Johnson" sailed over the hut dangerously near the roof, and went off with a bang nearly a hundred yards away. The men only looked at each other, but never made a move. I expect if they had shown any signs of alarm, the concert might have come to an abrupt finish. It was very dark that night, and the gun flashes and the star shells seemed right over them, and they were able to see the surrounding country for miles. They were taken to see the Boche trenches, which were only a thousand yards away. The guns kept up an incessant roar all night, but not even the big, well-fed rats in the not-at-all attractive cellar could keep them awake.

Lucheaux, which was the headquarters of the 7th Army Corps, was a fine old town famous for its old *châteaux*, and in one of them they were shown the damage done by the English cannon-balls some six hundred years ago. In all the northern part of France—Creçy, Gravelines, Dunkirk—there are records of our many disagreements with the French. Why do people always quarrel with their neighbours?

On one point of the tour the London bus deserted the party, and a "bloomin' old motor-waggon, with no springs to speak of," took its place. The artists were lucky to have boxes to sit on, but "Wee Donal" did not know his head from his heels, and was pitched upside down several times, and there was great difficulty in bringing him round again.

At Bernaville they were on the Somme, and on the Sunday gave a concert to a tremendous crowd in the largest aerodrome in France;

and although the great audience showed little enthusiasm over the singing of the solos from the *Messiah*, they seemed to enjoy them, though not too enthusiastic, but in the second half of the programme, which was secular, the rafters fairly shook.

At Asheaux, about a mile and a half from the line, there was a tremendous bombardment going on, shells shrieking overhead incessantly and the noise deafening. There were ammunition dumps only a few yards behind. The concussion of the guns was so great that they could not hear themselves speak. Gun flashes and the German star shells were dazzling. Asheaux was one of the most awful places. They ploughed about in seas of mud. A large and heavy baritone walked over the duck-boards and almost sank out of sight. The others had great difficulty in pulling him out of the mud back to safety, but he was distraught that one of his loved goloshes had not come up with his foot. However, it was dark and could not be found. Next day an orderly presented the enormous golosh on a plate, saying to the officer that "one of the ladies of the party must have dropped her slipper!!

Some of the Y.M.C.A. huts were shattered by the shells. One got fourteen bits of shrapnel through its roof less than a week before the party visited it.

There was a Gordon Highlander wearing the Military Cross who attracted their attention, and they were still more interested when told that he had taken a hundred prisoners single-handed. "They widna fecht, an' a just bagged the crood!" he said.

At Senlis they were to give a Scottish concert at four o'clock, but at three o'clock word was sent along that the barn was packed out, so they started at three. There were about twelve hundred packed into every corner of the barn.

At Albert, which was most of it in ruins and the few civilians that were left going from pillar to post in daily dread of another bombardment, the Madonna on the top of the cathedral spire looked very pathetic. The French believed that when she fell the war would finish.

They gave two concerts that evening, an obligate to the programmes being furnished by guns in position within bow-shot of the concert centre. Thunderous and insistent, they never ceased fire for longer than three minutes. Surely the most imperious obligate ever known! To the sound of the guns was added the scream of the shells as they passed by overhead. "Comforting thought that they were ours, and going in the right direction. Fervent hope that none might be marked 'R.S.V.P.'"

Between the shows some young officers came to them with the announcement that their mission was important. Could they escort the concert party to their mess before the next show? There was plenty of time. Were there any ladies in the party? But in any case, could not the invitation to supper be accepted? They were immediately nicknamed by the party, "The Three Musketeers."

These Musketeers did all their own cooking, and there was a wonderful sweet, which was nicknamed the "War Trifle," which looked like petroleum jelly and shaving soap well mixed, though it tasted all right. They finished up with a slice of cake from a home parcel.

"Tommy" and "Jack" make a grand audience, and when you have lads like the Three Musketeers clamorous for encores, the men determined on no refusal, and the Staff officers coming down from the high altar of headquarters among the boys, cheery as any of them— well, let it rain outside, let the tide of mud flow onward and upward, let the guns roar, let all thought of the water-logged trenches—left two hours ago on the arrival of the relief contingent—let all these things slide. "Another song, please! Let's have 'If you were the only Girl in the World.' Give us 'The Floral Dance.' Come away, fiddler, another Scotch reel. Let it rip! . . . Give them three cheers, boys—Hip, hip, hooray!" And while they cheer, I'm blest if the eyes of two of the concert party are not brimming with tenderness. It took all like that by turns.

They supped with these Three Musketeers after the second concert. The banqueting hall was an upper scullery with apertures, that had once been windows, covered over with sacking that sagged sadly and flapped in the wind. There was no door to the regal apartment. It had been removed and made to serve for a table; it was placed on two empty wooden cases and covered with an army blanket—you had to be careful of the knob when passing plates along. For light there were carriage candles on a toffee tin. The heating appliances were no less excellent. A biscuit box, in which holes had been punched with a bayonet, was filled with charcoal, and, smoking furiously, was brought in, carried round, and taken out again, until such time as it had decided to glow. Frequent inquiries were made as to how it was progressing, but it did not emerge again that night. Possibly the orderlies were nursing it in the byre below.

At Engelebelmar they were right in front of our guns, and a stone's-throw from the brick heaps—all that remained of Thiepval and Beaumont Hamel. At the Church of St. Michael all was quiet; a shell had caught the corner of the roof the previous day. Inside the church the pews were piled high in the apse, and an enormous mug and half a sandwich were on the book-board of the pulpit. Soldiers' equipment hung all round the walls, the altar bare except for a corporal, who stood on the steps with his sleeves rolled up, polishing his belt and smoking a cigarette. Men lay sleeping in various corners, others writing letters or reading.

From there they passed right through between our guns, all blazing away, to Toutencourt, which was about five miles behind the line. Many times, when near the line during a concert, the wounded would be brought in on stretchers and treated whilst the concert was going on.

One party at Brai, when amongst the Canadians, were a thousand yards from the line. The major was an ex-mayor of Toronto, and made a splendid speech, expressing the determination of the Canadians to win at any cost. There were only five of the original forty officers of the 58th Battalion.

I have referred a good deal to the Canadians, more perhaps than to the other Imperial troops, because when one is brought up in a country, all the memories of one's childhood link up with the later events and make a deep impression upon one's mind. I was at school in Toronto, and we were able, I think, to do more entertaining in the north of France and Flanders amongst the Guards and Canadians. But I think that all Canadians felt that the English generosity in giving the credit always to the Byng Boys, the Australians, and New Zealanders was sometimes a little over-generous. Everyone knew that it was the men of this little island who were the finest example of how to "stick it," and many Colonials during the war got through that impersonal mask which so often chills the expansive Colonial when landing on these shores, and began to understand and love them.

Lord Cavan came with his staff to one of the concerts, which pleased the party very much.

The Scottish party had rather a trying time in a miserable transport lorry, when they were all knocked out by the petrol fumes, and a tenor had to be taken to hospital at Doullens; so they were able to have a good rest the first they had had for three weeks—in a comfortable hotel, where they actually got fresh beef for dinner, which was a great treat. The Y.M.C.A. hut in Doullens was once the Fruit Bazaar, a huge place and very draughty, but a great source of comfort to the men, who thronged it day and night. There were long queues waiting to be served with coffee, buns, and "fags," and dozens sat reading, and there were also rows of men writing letters home, and the musical ones bumped the life out of the poor old piano, which had already seen its best days.

It is quite impossible to imagine what the men would have done without the Y.M.C.A. huts, and their tea and coffee, buns and cigarettes, notepaper, pens, ink, stamps, and often kindly advice and help from the workers in the huts. These huts were all over the war areas.

The last two concerts of this party were given at St. Pol, and General Allenby, who was then with the Third Army, with his staff, attended the second concert. After "Auld Lang Syne," in which all the audience joined, the general made a great speech, "and we came in for some very flattering compliments. 'Top-hole show' seemed to be a very favourite remark, from the general downwards. He seemed very interested in the places we had visited and in hearing of our experiences, and said we had seen more of the war than he." When General Allenby was transferred to Egypt he was equally sympathetic and considerate to the party, who followed behind when he captured *the* city.

This very last concert was the fortieth, and they must have performed to about forty thousand men. They were all dreadfully sorry to come home, but the continuous strain of such work does tell on all artists after four weeks, and we found that whether in the front line or at the base, four weeks was the limit of endurance for the artists, who travelled long distances, and gave two, and very often three, concerts in the day.

I had several most delightful letters, one from the general officer commanding the 33rd Division, who in his letter said:

Their performance was delightful, and much appreciated by all ranks, who are deeply grateful to you and to them for their kindness. I enclose a cheque for ten guineas from the Divisional Funds, which the G.O.C. hopes you will accept and disburse for the benefit of some charity in which you are interested.

And in a letter from the officer commanding the 37th Infantry Brigade:

The men were only just out of the trenches, and General Cator cannot tell Miss Lena Ashwell how much it means to them to have a jolly evening and something that takes their minds away from the dreary routine of trench warfare. He thinks their only regret was that Miss Lena Ashwell was not there in person, but he knows how grateful they are to her. They love to feel they are not forgotten.

In 1917, when the Y.M.C.A. were permitted to send lecturers on short permits, Sir John Martin Harvey spent his short holiday in France, and wrote to me to say that:

It has been one of the most memorable incidents of my life, and I cannot tell you how grateful I am to you for making it possible. My only regret is that whilst it gives any enjoyment to those splendid fellows out there, I could not stay longer. . . .

The last firing-line party went at the end of February 1917. We could not continue this part of the work owing to the impossibility of getting men. There were no longer any men over age or seemingly anyone medically unfit!! But in January 1918 we received from G.H.Q. permission to extend our work along the line of St. Pol, St. Omer, and Montdidier, and the mixed parties of men and women, from January 1918, visited St. Omer, St. Pol, and Aire.

When we found it impossible to make up concert parties of men, and had not yet received permission for the mixed parties, or those composed of women only, to go farther up the line, we were fortunate to find a few single-handed entertainers. These men were able to get about more easily, and able to give an hour's programme on their own. Further, a man travelling alone can give his show when and where he sees his opportunity, but it was not altogether an amusement to undertake a trip to the rear of the line. One, a ventriloquist and teller of stories, had many experiences. As he was in civilian garb, men would often halt at the roadside to stare at him and question each other as to how he could have come there, and sometimes call out jesting offers to purchase his garments.

He gave altogether thirty-six performances, of an hour and a half each. They were given in all sorts of places and at all manner of times: in a disused Tobacco Factory to an audience consisting of infantry out of the first line of trenches, which was succeeded by an audience of transport men who had just left their ammunition lorries; a munition works, which for months had attracted the attention of the German bomber, was filled with an enthusiastic crowd; and casualty clearing stations were cordial in their thanks and applause.

Some miles back from the line there was an isolated detachment set to guard a Prisoners' Camp, who clamoured vigorously for two performances, so that every man should have a share of amusement, and not only the lucky ones who happened to be off duty on the day the entertainer turned up. Two miles from the front line, a hut, which was called the "Hôtel Cecil," was shortly afterwards blown to pieces, and many of the inhabitants of Vielle Chappelle were killed.

His oddest experience was giving an entertainment to Portuguese soldiers. Of course, as he spoke no Portuguese, and they understood no English, the programme had to be varied to meet the situation, and he met the difficulty with card and other tricks, and a selection of imitations, not of the mannerisms of actors of the London stage, but the more familiar tones of the gramophone, aeroplane, the cock heralding the dawn, etc. He says that they "laughed like a lot of babies," at his imitations of horses. So great was his success with the Portuguese Tommies that he was asked to repeat the entertainment to a second audience of men of the same nationality. Perhaps none of the many entertainments of the tour were better worth giving than these, for the comparatively small Portuguese Army must have had very few opportunities of amusement.

At the end of a hard day's travelling, he arrived at a makeshift officers' club—being directed thereto as the only place where dinner might be obtainable. Dinner was obtainable, and the miscellaneous company, thrown together by chance and duty, was only too pleased to finish its evening by an unexpected hour of amusement. After which the entertainer retired to his hotel in a somewhat cheerless building tenanted only by himself and the landlord's family. As the latter invariably slept in the cellars, he had an extensive choice of bedrooms; and, having decided on his domicile for the night, he disposed himself for such rest as he might get—bearing in mind an instruction, hospitably given, to the effect that, in case of shelling, he had better remove himself hastily, as the neighbouring church was a landmark which attracted the German gunner.

Of nerve-trying experiences he had plenty during his tour; there was the night when bombardment began suddenly, and, clad chiefly in a blanket, he adjourned to a dugout, and lay there for eight lengthy hours—hours which were rendered more tolerable by the enterprise of a *padre*, who crawled out between the shell-bursts, to return not only with the entertainer's trousers but with a supply of cigarettes for the party. Nights of this kind, he confessed, made the next day's performance difficult; to keep up to the mark and hold your audience, a man needs a certain and regular amount of rest. Thus six weeks, he told me, was as long as he could continue at a stretch; at the end of that time he felt that he would soon fall below concert pitch and be unable to hold and amuse an audience as he did at the beginning of the tour.

He gave a concert in the drawing-room of a house which had been shelled three times during the day. There being only three sides to this room, as the side near the staircase had been blown away, the Tommies were able to sit on the stairs and witness the performance in comfort. There were a hundred Tommies in the room in their steel helmets, all ready to be on the move, and another fifty on the stairs, and he, the only man in "civvy" suit for miles, standing in the corner under the oil lamp.

The return journey to Y.M.C.A. headquarters was generally exciting, for the later the hour, the more activity along the line; and on one occasion the chauffeur, who was new to the road, took the wrong turning, and they found themselves going towards the line instead of going away from it.

When giving a concert to the Motor Transport of the 58th Division, the Germans were shelling with our own naval guns which they had captured in Russia. Sometimes, as the men had no opportunity of seeing the performance at night, as they were always on the move, the entertainments were given in the afternoon, and these performances were sometimes brought to an abrupt conclusion, owing to the arrival of the German aeroplanes.

Another single-handed entertainer gave 122 concerts in anti-aircraft sections, balloon sections, tank sections, aerodromes, in barns, tents, and dugouts.

Although for a time we were unable to send out parties, for there were no men to send, in January 1918 I got the good news from the adjutant-general that "the mixed parties would be allowed to perform in the line of the British Expeditionary Force as far east as the following line: St. Omer, Aire, St. Hilaire, Pernes, St. Pol, Frevent, Doullens, Beauval, Talmas, Villers Bocage, Amiens, Montdidier, Montgerain."

Shortly after receiving the letter I was in Amiens amongst other places, and found that the army was at Ham and Chaulnes, and that there were very few of our troops at Montdidier. I wrote a most earnest appeal that we might go farther east, and include Ham and Chaulnes. Before my letter reached G.H.Q., however, all our concert work in that area was hung up by the big battle in March.

The front line, of course, was the place of the greatest danger, and those who were in it ran the greatest risk; but in 1917 the air-raids all over the coast of France were a terrible experience. The touring concert parties, playing plays at Calais in 1917, must be included amongst the "firing-line" experiences.

The first performance of the plays was at a camp thirty miles from Calais and not very far from the firing line.

In golden weather we drove through charming country until we came at last to what looked like all the railway sleepers that had ever been made piled up on top of each other since the world began, backed by many ominous-looking piles of dark material, which we afterwards learnt were hundreds and thousands of shells. Climbing over these various piles there were small blue specks which, as we drew nearer, we saw were Chinese workmen, of whom there are three thousand working at this place alone. I believe there are now a hundred thousand in France altogether.

The real events of the evening did not begin till the second performance was just finished, when all lights were turned off and the warning siren sounded. Then began, and continued for four hours, such a bombing and firing as none of us had ever heard before, and the knowledge that we were entirely surrounded by ammunition dumps and poison-gas shells did not help us to enjoy the situation. We had to walk about a mile to the officers' quarters for supper, and during the walk and all through the meal, the shrapnel was falling all around us. Shells were shrieking, bombs were dropping continually with deafening explosions, and the sound of the guns at the Front was drowned by the noise of the guns around us—guns of all kinds, it seemed, including the angry 'rat-tat-tat-tat' of the Lewis guns, all doing their best to bring the Hun raider to earth.

On the way over to the mess, one of the singers took refuge with a young subaltern in some ditch during a specially violent period of the raid. She tried to carry on a light conversation of a thoroughly gay and trivial nature, but the wretched subaltern would not be amused or interested, and finally said in a despairing voice, as she chattered gaily on, 'It's all very well for you, but you don't know that this is an ammunition dump!'

The dinner itself was delightful, the room most delightfully decorated with large hollow paper fish made by the Chinese servants, who waited with silent efficiency. Many of the decorations could not be lighted, as it was necessary to have only the dimmest of dim illuminations, merely to let us find the way to our mouths. In spite of the noise outside, conversation was carried on, and the only indication that the colonel gave that things were getting more ominous was the slow clenching of his hands.

When the raid seemed to be over, we started the ride home. It was a glorious night, with moonlight as bright as anything the stage could possibly provide. The white houses with their red roofs, the distant fields gleamed with something almost like midday brightness. Ever and again we would hear ahead of us the sharp command to halt, and out of the shadows would come steel-helmeted sentries with fixed bayonets held alarmingly close to us. A dozen times on the road back to Calais we had to explain our right to be on the road at that time of night. Once suddenly we drove into a crowd of soldiers who had been turned out of their camp for greater safety, and told to wait on the road till the raiders should be gone.

In every village there was a group of frightened villagers huddled together in scared uncertainty as to what they ought to do. As we neared Calais, the crisis of our adventurous evening came. The bombs were still dropping, and the sky was full of shrapnel bursting over our heads, together with a succession of rockets or rushing lights—sent up, as I understand, to locate the enemy's aeroplanes. As we came near to the centre of the town, a crowd of men rushed at us, shouting that we could not proceed in that direction, and we saw by the light in the sky that a large fire was burning, caused by one of the bombs.

Finally we arrived by a roundabout road at the hotel, to find that it had been hit once or twice during the raid, but no very serious damage had been done. We felt that the worst of the raid must be over, and went all of us to bed, but almost immediately the bombs started again, and the babble of voices and the sound of scurrying feet indicated that some of the hotel guests were making for the basement.

It is curious that the munition dump could be bombarded from the air for four hours and no explosion occur.

Near Boulogne, on one occasion, the concert was being given in a forest. The camp was one where the poison gas was manufactured. Just as the concert was beginning the air-raid signal went, and the little party were conducted to the C.O.'s office to wait until it was over. There were seven of them in the little room, and as the bombs dropped all round, they looked at the four gas masks which were in the office, but no one liked to be selfish enough to leave three people without.

When the party went up to St. Pol, they were staying at the hotel, visiting the surrounding camps, and an officer drove some miles to persuade the party to come down to his camp, some ten miles away. They decided to go. The night they were away giving the concert the Germans got the range and wiped out the hotel; if they had not gone with the officer, they would have shared its fate. The raids on Boulogne were not to be despised. On some beautiful moonlight nights they dropped bombs very near the old Derveaux Hotel. It was a curious place which had been an arcade, which was converted into an hotel. Imagine the Burlington Arcade, with practically no alterations, opened as an hotel. The Derveaux was bigger; it was afterwards taken over by the British and cleaned up (it needed it), and was to be H.Q., but the Germans really got it then, and smashed it up.

I used to feel very lonely when the air-raid warning went, and would get up and dress, meaning to go out of my room and find out what other people were doing; and then I would decide I was too shy to face them, and so would undress and go back to bed, and then, when more bombs fell and the ambulance began to come out, I would re-dress, and try to face the unknown people who were living in the hotel, and decide that bed after all was preferable. It is strange how afraid people are of one another—it should be quite the other way, but the English seem born preferring isolation, and most of it is shyness.

CHAPTER 7

Repertory Companies

Although the first plays were played by Miss Gertrude Jennings and her party, it was Mrs. Penelope Wheeler who started the first Repertory Company in France. She had gone over in November 1916 to perform the Greek plays at the invitation of the Y.M.C.A. I did not think that the men would understand the Greek plays, and was very much astonished that she was able to interest them so successfully. On one occasion she was invited to a Sergeants' Mess. She explained that the play was a very old one and a tragedy, but the sergeant insisted that it would give great pleasure if she would recite it for them. Needless to say she went, feeling very uncertain as to the reception, but found a very interested and intelligent audience, who, after the play was over, invited her to come again, saying that if the gentleman had written any other plays they would very much like to hear them, and if not, perhaps she would be good enough to repeat the play they had Just heard. The play was *Electra of Euripides*.

It was whilst the firing-line parties were in the forward areas and the Egyptian party was visiting Moses' Well and Sinai, that Mrs. Wheeler succeeded in producing the first dramatic entertainments at Havre.

The first Christmas play was the old Coventry play of *The Three Shepherds*. It was played at the Central Y.M.C.A. with a good deal of success. There was one remark which caused a great deal of curiosity. In a discussion about the old Miracle play, one man said, "It's a wonderful play; I'm glad I've seen it, but I shouldn't like my mother to see it!" We all wondered why!

The Central was a largish building with a small stage, footlights, and proscenium, and was under the direction of Eric Patterson, Professor of Economics and Literature, an Oxford man, and a sort of

Liaison Officer between the Y.M.C.A. and the players.

Mrs. Wheeler had with her some professional actresses, but as she had only two professional actors, she relied on the talent at the Base for the representatives of the men's parts. She had always ready three different programmes, because at any moment some of the men might be called away for fatigue duty, and the officers might be wanted for orderly duty. On more than one occasion, when they were all ready to start off from the Granary to play at a camp, the telephone would ring, and the news would be given that a leading man had been caught for fatigue, so could not come. Then the car would have to be repacked with different properties, and the other men would be got hold of, and the programme altered. Everything had to be done on an emergency basis.

The first play the men played by their own choice was *A Night at an Inn*, by Lord Dunsany. This is a one-act play, in which there are three murders and four deaths. The night it was to be played at the Central, the scene was ready, and the men arrived with the news that "Albert" could not play, but they had arranged with "Richard," who had only a walk-on part, and he had been made to learn the part during his dinner-hour, and they had seen that he did it; and they explained that the performance would be quite all right if Mrs. Wheeler would show the new man whereabouts on the stage he was to die!

One curious result of military training was the complete loss of self-consciousness. There was no pretending that they could not do things. They just came along and did their best. It was also very interesting to watch the feeling for the theatre; the way they would take exactly the right amount of time over some bit of business, and the spontaneity of their emotions, made all they did most interesting to watch.

Mrs. Wheeler produced a new play every week to be played in the different camps, but every Wednesday and Friday they played at the Central, and the seats were entirely for the men; officers were only admitted if there was room. Every Wednesday and Friday the same men would be in the same seats, arriving two hours before the time so as to secure their favourite chairs. There were a great number of men to whom the theatre was an absolutely new experience; they had despised the plays and the players, never realising that there was anything of interest in a play, and having a constitutional dislike for the music halls. But once they caught the habit, they were enthusiastic and earnest playgoers.

A special *matinée* was given every Saturday for the convalescents, who were marched down from the camps with a full military band, led by a small dog of doubtful parentage. The dog, with the convalescents and the band, always attended all these performances; he was a most important person, being the mascot of the camp.

The men never let Mrs. Wheeler down. It was a point of honour amongst them to pull off the performance, however great the difficulties might be. There was no slacking, the men saw that the parts were learnt, and there was never any disrespect to the players. Once, when two men were late in arriving, they were waited for by the others and given a thorough "dressing-down" in the strongest and most lurid language, whilst the actresses retired to a discreet distance to allow them full scope for the expression of their wrath.

By October 1917 there were seven soldier companies giving performances of plays in that base, and it was a great distinction to be numbered amongst the players of the plays.

I saw a very interesting performance of *The Younger Generation*, by Stanley Houghten—a play which the men thoroughly enjoyed, as it gave them a great deal to discuss. As the work grew under Mrs. Wheeler's direction, scenery was painted and properties made by the men. Drawings had been sent by Mr. Charles Ricketts, which had been enlarged and copied for the painted back-cloths. The centre for all this work was an old granary which had been a warehouse for selling sacks, and had long been disused. It was a very old building in a side street off the main thoroughfare in the middle of the town. The warehouse itself was a large room with a concrete floor, high walls, and glass roof, which was very far from weatherproof.

When it was not too cold or too wet, the scenery was painted, properties manufactured, clothes were made, and scenes rehearsed. In the corner there was a wooden staircase, which led to three or four small rooms used for office work and the wardrobe. But these premises were not devoted only to the interests and needs of the repertory; the place was shared by the Morris dancers, under Miss Dakin. At one time there was quite a big vogue in France for the country dances, folk dances, Morris and sword dances. All this work was started by Miss Dakin, and there were a number of teachers in different bases who undertook to teach these dances to the men. Some of them were wildly enthusiastic, and thoroughly enjoyed the dances; of course, some of the men were "bored to tears."

There were weekly demonstrations in many of the huts, but the dancing was especially used in convalescent camps. In November a demonstration was given at Trouville; special permission was given for six men to have a night out from camp, and they went from Havre by boat. All the dancers were naturally a little seasick on the voyage. At the evening demonstration, in a large space cleared in the centre of the hall, sawdust was scattered, and there were five or six oil-lamps hanging from rafters just above the dancing-ground, and the rest of the hall was almost without light. There were about fifteen hundred men sitting around, the back rows perched on forms put on the dining-tables.

When the party walked out from the camp across in the dark and over the mud, the men lined themselves along the duck-boards, and handed them along, pretending that the girls were a firing party going up to the front line: "Mind the wire, Miss! Shell-hole at the next corner!" The O.C.'s at the convalescent depots were only too glad to have anything that would make the men smile when they were on parade, so gym. instructors learnt the dances, and I heard delightful stories of the band playing on the sands of Trouville, whilst the convalescents danced themselves back to health. There were in all about fifteen teachers in France.

Several performances were given at the theatre at Havre which were very successful: *Candida, You never can tell*, Galsworthy's *Joy*, *Sir Anthony*, by Haddon Chambers, *The Marriage of Kitty, General Post, The Mollusc, Cousin Kate*; but the great effort was the production of *The Merchant of Venice*.

It was a great help to our work that Mrs. Wheeler was able to enlist the interest and sympathy of Mr. Charles Ricketts, who not only designed, but himself stencilled the dresses which were made under his direction. No words can express our deep sense of gratitude to Mr. Ricketts for his generosity in this matter, for with his help we had a full wardrobe for the productions of *The Merchant of Venice* and *Twelfth Night,* which could also be made to serve for the productions of other plays, notably *Two Gentlemen of Verona*. Thus he not only made it possible for us to play Shakespearean works in France, but has made it possible for us to do a great deal of valuable work since.

After the Armistice there were serious riots in the camps in the Harfleur Valley. We heard that the trouble arose over food. Rations had been cut down, as there was no longer any fighting, and the full ration for a fighting man was not considered necessary. A great deal of irritation was caused in some places by the manner in which the new regulations were enforced. There was a great deal of trouble over the hard biscuits, which were all right for men with sound teeth, but many of the men were not able to eat them. The men complained, and were put off; complained again, and finally broke into an army canteen, where they found bread, for which they longed, and which was to be sold to them.

The outbreak was instantaneous. They burnt the canteen and other huts. The riot lasted all night, and there was some shooting. The next day the men were, to put it mildly, in a difficult mood. The Repertory Company was telephoned for. Their arrangements were already made for the evening, but it was urged that they must cancel their previous engagements. After some deliberation they decided that the triple bill was not suitable, as the change of subject prevents the concentration of interest.

The only three-act play they had ready was *Candida*, by George Bernard Shaw. They drove up from Havre to the valley, feeling very uneasy and nervous of their powers. The signs of the outbreak surrounded them, and though the hut was full, the feeling was electric. Anything might have started fresh trouble. They began the play, and for the first five minutes it seemed uncertain what might happen. Gradually the men grew interested, and the evil spell was broken. The expressions of gratitude from those in authority were very sincere; they said the play had been invaluable, for it had changed the current of the men's thoughts. There is something very delightful about using Shaw to quell a riot!

When it was proposed to produce *Fanny's First Play* there was trouble amongst the hut leaders. Some of them said that this play was the last ditch, and they were going to fight it. They spoke of the immorality and want of religion of the play, and a conference was called. On the way to the conference Mrs. Wheeler tried to secure a second copy of the play, but found everywhere that though they had had copies, they had all been bought. At the discussion it was plain that there were only two out of the twenty-five to thirty men who were really antagonistic to the play. It was pointed out that there was no attack on religion in this play, but a very big attack upon the people who put respectability in the place of religion. Mrs. Wheeler was able to point out that the artistic conscience is very often more exacting in its demand for truth at any cost, in its search for what is highest, than other sections of the community, who are somewhat afraid of truth. The conference decided in favour of the performance of the play.

Two of the leaders, who had been up the line, spoke of the help the plays had given them. There was one leader in France who was intensely bigoted on the question of the theatre. No Puritan of the time of Cromwell could have been more anxious to destroy all signs of this pernicious art. At one time he was sent down for a rest from the line, and was unable to find any. He could not sleep. He walked about by the sea and saw nothing but dead bodies in the waves; he came back to London, and went from church to church and from sermon to sermon, hoping that he might escape from his misery. One day he passed a theatre and went in. He came out cured; he is now writing plays himself.

In Havre there were a great number of mine-sweepers. They formed a little colony apart. Their drifters lay alongside their own private quay, mixing neither with the native French fishing boats nor with the miscellaneous merchantmen, not even with the British destroyer. The quay was theirs, reserved for their interest only, for their sheds and stores, for their necessary offices, for all that pertains to the business and peril of mine-sweeping. One had to pass through gates, and without a pass there was no admittance. From this quay the trawlers and drifters, and the men who once fished for herrings and mackerel, went trawling for a prey more dangerous. The men had rough lives full of peril.

The stage was eleven feet by nine. There was only one dressing-room, which was used by the women; the men, to the intense joy of the audience, dressed, made-up, and changed on the stage in full view. It was a labour of love for these men to make this tiny stage and equip it as well as possible. They also painted a back-cloth. The first performance there was a mixed entertainment—two one-act plays, *The Soup and the Savoury* and Allotments, with various musical items to fill out the programme. The evening was a thundering success, though the men were very shy at first, and stood about outside the door waiting to be invited in. At last, one more courageous than the rest asked if the party was ready for the audience, and they filed in, about 120 officers and men.

The supper afterwards was arranged on the deck of a very smart and gaily decorated drifter berthed at the quay.

The moment it was found that the plays were so helpful there was a demand for the nucleus of Repertory Companies in many other bases. The rehearsals and the interest created by them was extremely helpful to the men. Very often shell-shock cases were sent us from the hospitals; they would sit about during rehearsal, gradually becoming interested, then be invited to bring on a tray, eventually to say a few words, and finally it would be found that in their interest they had overcome their fear. In several cases this interest saved the lives of men. One man, who had been an actor, was deaf and almost unable to speak from shell-shock; his headaches were intolerable. When first admitted to a rehearsal, he sat motionless in a chair, deaf and indifferent; when the others walked over his outstretched legs, he gave no sign of life— he was, to all intents and purposes, mentally paralysed. Gradually the interest of the rehearsals got hold of him, and it was not long before he was one of the most active workers in the productions and played many parts.

Another man was reported as half-witted. His mouth was twisted on one side, and he could hardly speak. After one or two rehearsals he returned to the camp an entirely changed man. When asked what had happened, he smiled and said, "I've got a part!"

The Second Repertory Company was formed at Abbeville, under the direction of Miss Cicely Hamilton. There was the same great difficulty with regard to the men, which was met in the same way under even greater difficulties, as Abbeville was on the edge of the fighting line.

Amongst other plays they played *The School for Scandal, Quality Street, Just to get Married, His Excellency the Governor, Much Ado about Nothing, The Taming of the Shrew,* and Miss Hamilton wrote and produced there that most delightful of all modern miracle plays, *The Child in Flanders,* which was played in connection with the W.A.A.C.'s stationed at Abbeville. This Repertory Company also gave a special performance at G.H.Q.

During 1918 the air-raids on Abbeville were so frequent and so violent that no one was allowed to sleep in the town at night. The house which we had as a hostel for the artists had a small hall, a kind of miniature theatre, in which many entertainments were given and all the rehearsals took place. A bomb destroyed this, and broke all the windows in the hostel. Every night both the Repertory Company and the concert parties after their work slept in the forest of Creçy in the open, or in some hut outside the town.

It was, no doubt, through these experiences of agonising fear that Miss Hamilton found she was able to describe so wonderfully this kind of warfare in *William, an Englishman*.

Of course, there were all kinds of humorous incidents in the experiences they had, but perhaps the most amusing was when they were camped close to the search-lights outside Abbeville, and at the exact moment of the arrival of the theatre party after their evening's work, a tremendous number of enemy aeroplanes went over, dropping bombs. One actress, who was Scotch and imperturbable, kept on asking for her pink flannelette nightgown, which she declared she could not sleep without. Bombs were falling and exploding all around them, but still the plaintive cry went on, insisting that without the pink garment sleep would be impossible.

The town was fairly safe in the daytime, so that after reaching camp, say at half-past twelve or one o'clock in the morning after the performance, they would be taken in lorries back to the town to re-hearse, manufacture necessary scenery and properties, and prepare for the afternoon and evening performances; and it is their very proud boast that, with all these difficulties to contend with, they never failed to turn up or carry out their programme.

This Repertory Company afterwards went into the forward areas, and were very much appreciated there. Repertory Companies were established at Etaples, Calais, and Dieppe, and last but not least, at Rouen. I may include this letter from Etaples:

> On the eve of the departure of the Lena Ashwell Acting Party, I wish to take the opportunity of thanking you for the valuable assistance they have given me in our programme of entertain-ment in the Canadian huts. The latest play, *Cousin Kate*, made a great hit, more especially on their closing night in the new Maple Leaf Theatre, Blundellsands Hut; more than forty offic-ers were present at the performance, and all speak of it in the highest terms.
>
> I should like, if it be possible, that you convey to Miss Ashwell the thanks of the Canadian Y.M.C.A. for the entertainment given, not only by the present party, but by all those who have visited us since our establishment at the Canadian Base some months ago.

At Rouen the party was under the direction of Miss Rosemary Rees, a New Zealander, and a very clever and delightful actress. They played a number of plays, including *A Woman in the Case, Leah Kleshna, Cousin Kate,* and *The Marriage of Kitty.*

On one occasion they took these plays to an Irish regiment who had just come to France from Mesopotamia, and the excitement and joy of the regiment, who had had no entertainment for three years, almost reduced the company to tears—not the best frame of mind in which to play a comedy.

Like the other Repertory Companies, the Rouen one undertook to get the men interested and encourage them to play plays themselves. They drilled them and rehearsed them, often with the best results, and, just when things were getting fairly smooth, the wretched producers would be reduced to despair, for the military authorities transferred members of their cast to other places!

The great achievement at Rouen was the production of the *Mikado*, produced by Miss Mary Barton and Mr. Bevan. There were only three professionals in the whole of the production. The orchestra was composed from men at the Base, the chorus represented some one. from every unit in the vast camp, and representatives of the Red Cross, W.A.A.C.'s, W.R.E.N.'s, and Y.M.C.A. workers.

It was very amusing to watch the men rehearse in their khaki uniforms with their thick boots, manipulating their tiny little Japanese fans. Because of the severe drill they had been through, they were much quicker in picking up movements than the women, and much less conscious of themselves. I have sometimes wondered if women would not be the better for a little drill and quick obedience, without *discussion*, to all sorts of orders.

They had a great success with *Billeted*. Of course we all knew the men would love the play, but hardly to the extent that they did.

> Really last night at the M.B.D. they whistled and cheered as if they had never had any entertainment before. I wish you could have heard them. Officers and nurses sitting on the floor right up to the stage.

All the Repertory Companies had a great number of one-act plays, which were easier to do very often in the cramped condition of the huts. But all the work of the parties was hampered by this difficulty of obtaining actors. In nearly all plays there are more men than women, and there are very few good plays written entirely for women. We never had more than two or three professional actors in any company, and, having to rely upon the talent to be found amongst the officers and men, the amazing thing is that we were able to do as good work as we did. Amongst the one-act plays that were produced were *The Twelve Pound Look, Rosalind, The Old Lady Shows Her Medals, by Sir James Barrie, Poached Eggs and Pearls, The Bathroom Door, The Rest Cure, Five Birds in a Cage, In the Fog, The Pantomime Rehearsal, The Fourth of*

August, Box B., The Monkey's Paw, The Bishop's Candlestick.

Amongst other delightful letters I received, showing that the plays were useful, were the following:

The general officer commanding this brigade has directed me to write to you to convey the appreciation of officers, N.C.O.'s, and men from this brigade, who were present at the entertainment provided by your party which visited us today.

In a building not devoid of shell-holes, two audiences, each of 500 men fresh from the trenches, were entertained by your party, whose members would be able to tell you, perhaps better than I, the appreciation with which their performances were received. . . .

The following was received from the Headquarters of the Fourth Army:

I beg to express to you our warmest appreciation of the services of a concert party and a dramatic party that bear your name. The concert party gave us two entertainments, and the dramatic party performed to us eight times. . . . Without resorting to apparent exaggeration, it is difficult to describe what a profoundly stimulating effect the two parties had upon our spirits and enthusiasm. They brought England and home very near to us throughout several delightful hours, and the pleasure they afforded us will remain with us for many a day.

I feel that you would like to know that the men to whom the parties gave such real pleasure were really fighting troops men who were sent at Christmas time to the rest area for two months, after having taken a not inconsiderable part in the operations on the Somme in 1916, and at Arras, Vimy, Messines, and Ypres last year. The majority of those who attended the various entertainments had taken some part in most, if not indeed in all, these battles. . . .

In June 1917, when I was in Paris, the city was filled with troops on leave, and I heard many regrets that there were no places of entertainment where the troops could hear their own language, and there was no place where continuous entertainment was given, except, of course, the French theatres. General Phillips, who was in command of the Paris area, approved of the suggestion of opening a theatre to meet this need, and in a letter to me said: "It is not only Colonial troops who come to Paris. On a rough average we have three thousand a day coming and going, and a good theatre such as you suggest would be an undoubted benefit in every way."

It was not possible for the Y.M.C.A. to co-operate in taking a theatre in Paris, though they gave me every assistance in their power. The rents of the Paris theatres were very high, and it was difficult to make the decision as to whether we should take a small theatre a little out of the main thoroughfares, or undertake the risk of a large theatre such as the Bataclan. It seemed better, owing to the uncertainty of Paris leave being continued, to undertake the lesser enterprise, and so I took the theatre in the Rue du Rocher, quite close to the Gare St. Lazare, renamed the Théâtre Albert 1er. The theatre was opened by the Repertory Company on the 29th June 1918, and Lord Derby and the Corps Diplomatique were present at the opening.

All the arrangements with regard to the theatre were made by Mr. Worthington. Having been refused by the army, he had worked for some time with the Y.M.C.A., and finally the Information Bureau in Paris was under his direction. The organising of trips for the men to see Paris, the answering of endless questions all day long, the meeting of the men on leave and trying to invent amusement of some kind to keep them out of mischief, and when they had got into mischief, to use every effort to get them out of it—all these were his especial concern. Although at that time he had less than half a lung, and endured the miseries of that terrible disease, tuberculosis, he carried off all these efforts in the merriest way, and so plucky was he in concealing his ill-health that during the many times he helped me in Paris—and without his help we really could not have managed the work—I never knew that he was suffering. There are more ways than one of giving up one's life for one's friends.

But when we had finished all the arrangements, taken the theatre, rehearsed, and the company had arrived in Paris, there were very few British troops. All leave to Paris had been withdrawn, "Big Bertha" was unloading those terrific shells in the city, a church as well as an orphanage had been destroyed, the Germans were again approaching perilously near, all Paris was making every kind of excuse and explanation to try to get away, the railways were crowded with refugees, and there were long queues of people down the streets outside the railway station. There was a very delightful story told of Sacha Guitry, who, looking at this tremendous crowd, said:

155

I am not going for the same reason that all these people are: I am going because I am afraid!

At this most inauspicious moment the little party arrived in Paris, and it was a sort of joke with us that their arrival seemed to turn the tide, and the German Army retreated.

I was unable to procure passes in May 1918 through the Y.M.C.A. There were various difficulties with regard to scenery, the lease of the theatre, the billets of the company, etc., which had arisen, and my presence in Paris to arrange these matters was most urgent. I therefore applied for a pass through the Ministry of Information. Lord Beaverbrook was in charge of this ministry at the time, and was at this moment considering the advisability of using the living forces of drama and music in propaganda instead of the mass of printed matter that had been scattered over Europe to very little advantage. I had before been asked for help in propaganda, but without anything materialising. There had been urgent requests for some good representative artists to go to neutral countries, and on one occasion a special demand for a fine representative singer for a music hall; but when I made inquiries as to the exact requirements, it transpired that the singer was to be an expert in rag-time. I could not feel that rag-time was really representative of the music of England, and so gave up the job.

But Lord Beaverbrook listened most sympathetically to my account of the work we were doing with the armies, and at any rate did not *veto* some suggestions that I made. It appeared to me that if the *Comédie Française* would be generous enough to invite a British Shakespearean company to play in their historic and world-known theatre, the company could afterwards visit neutral countries with this hall-mark of artistic excellence, and also this sign of co-operation between the two great nations would be invaluable in neutral countries. A good deal of propaganda was being done by the Germans in neutral countries through music and plays, and amongst others, Reinhardt's productions of Shakespeare plays.

On arrival in Paris I adjusted the difficulties of the theatre and, armed with an introduction from Sir Henry Austin-Lee, called on the Minister of Beaux Arts, who was most gracious, and obviously interested in the suggestion. He was good enough to arrange for me to have an interview with Monsieur Fabre of the *Comédie Française*, and with a hospitality and courtesy which indicated their very real wish to co-operate, they said it would be possible for all the rehearsals to take place at the *Comédie Française*, that they would place everything possible at the disposal of the English, and invite such a company to play some *matinées* at the invitation of the *Comédie Française*, a unique honour, that such a scheme would be very welcome to the French people, and they especially recommended the playing of the Shakespearean comedies, as they had had no opportunities of seeing these works, which they knew so well by reputation.

The French people had been able to represent the tragedies of Shakespeare with considerable success, but had no knowledge whatever of the comedies. It is important for English people to remember that during all the years of war, although on more than one occasion the Germans were practically at the gates of Paris, their national theatres, the *Comédie Française* and the Odéon, were kept open, as well as Opera, and the *Opéra-Comique*; and that besides these theatres being kept open, there were four productions of the plays of William Shakespeare—a somewhat different record than that of the greatest city of the greatest Empire that the world has ever known, London.

I was so delighted at the success of my mission that I went down to the Ministry filled with excitement, to find, however, that the door was closed. During my absence the aspect of affairs had entirely changed. Lord Beaverbrook would not see me, and the ministry issued a statement that neither English music nor English drama would be used for information or propaganda. The cinema was to be used instead. There are some events in life which fill one with unspeakable rage because of their crass stupidity. The theatre in Paris carried on through the summer, producing *Smith, General Post, Mrs. Gorringe's Necklace, Billeted, Wanted—A Husband, The Mollusc, The Tyranny of Tears,* and, at the time of the Armistice, they were playing *The Man who stayed at Home*, and actively rehearsing *Twelfth Night*, which was to be the next production.

After the signing of the Armistice we disposed of the theatre to the Americans and moved the company to Lille. At Lille there is a very beautiful municipal theatre, which was on the verge of completion when the Germans entered the town in 1914, and remained in occupation until November 1918. From Lille the theatre party visited the surrounding towns, such as Tournai, Roubaix, and Tourcoing. They worked in co-operation with the military. When playing in theatres, half of the takings went to the mayor, two-thirds of what remained to us, and one-third to the army. Owing to the danger from the electric plant the authorities closed the Lille theatre in February. The evacuation was carried out with great speed. So the company returned to

England from Tournai in March 1919.

The weather in January was intensely cold, the theatres were like ice-houses, no heating, and the journeys, of course, were made in open cars, and several of the company had to go to hospital.

There was a very curious coincidence with regard to the moving of the theatre party from Paris up to Lille. Although I had applied that Paris and the forward areas should be on my pass, as it was necessary for me to see the conditions and the kind of work which would be expected of us after the Armistice, when I received my permit I was horrified to find that none of the necessary places were included on it. I went to General Danielson at the Permit Office, whose kindness and help to all the parties it is impossible adequately to acknowledge, and told him of my difficulties. He explained that it would be impossible for him to help me, but urged me on landing at Boulogne to make every effort to proceed to Montreuil G.H.Q. to see Captain Morley Reed, in whose hands the arrangements of these matters lay.

I knew it would be quite impossible for me to get from Boulogne to Montreuil. None of the Y.M.C.A. would have been likely to understand the omission from my white pass, and there was no one at the Base I knew sufficiently well to appeal to. It was therefore with a very heavy heart that I got into the train for Paris. It was the second one to go from Boulogne to Paris after the reopening of the line. I saw no solution whatever of my difficulties. Apparently the company was to be hung up indefinitely in Paris, and feeling quite hopeless I went into the dining-car.

There were two staff officers sitting in the car, and one of them came and asked me if I would not dine with them. I was only too delighted, and during the conversation he said, "You don't remember me?" to which I replied, "I remember we met at Etaples, but I don't recall your name." It really did take my breath away when he said, "My name is Morley Reed."

On the long journey to Paris I was able to explain all the difficulties we were working under, all the rearrangements we would like made, and I left the train rejoicing, with a letter to the A.P.M. in my pocket.

The idea I had hoped to be able to work out was that the different Repertory Companies producing different plays might take their repertory up to the small theatre in Paris, and a system of exchange in the different bases would have led to more satisfactory results, but we did the best we could; though not entirely satisfied, we feel that we were better than the curate's egg.

During the early part of 1918, owing to the great movement of the armies, the permits came through very erratically. Very often a whole party would be arranged for, and the permits at the last moment would be cancelled. There was one delightful well-known music-hall artist who cancelled all his engagements to go out, and at the very last moment he had to be told at the office that the permit had been cancelled. Of course we dreaded a few recriminations with regard to broken contracts, wasted time, etc., but he most delightfully said, "Well, they have all been put to a great deal more inconvenience than I have."

It was owing to this difficulty that it seemed advisable to have a small base for work in England, somewhere where the artists could be employed during the time that their permits were held up. I therefore in 1917 took the small Palace Theatre, Winchester, where we played plays and gave concerts, and from there visited the surrounding camps, such as Lark Hill, Warminster, etc. Hospital work was very necessary around Winchester, and General Slater expressed his opinion that the parties were the best form of medicine the men could have. Of course we were delighted to help in this way, but our main object was to keep the parties together, so that when the passes came through they would be ready to start off immediately for France.

We went to Portsmouth and gave entertainments to the fleet. Concerts were given on H.M.S. *Terrible*, H.M.S. *Redoubtable*, and at the Naval Hospital, and we took the theatre party several times to Harwich to give entertainments on H.M.S. *Dido*.

In February the mixed parties went up to St. Omer from Calais, and there were two parties of ladies that went up to the forward areas from Amiens, and another party that was performing at St. Omer got audiences of men down from Ypres and that neighbourhood.

We were invited to send entertainers to Switzerland, and had hoped to follow them up with dramatic companies, but permission never came through. Still, the singlehanded entertainers gave much happiness to the men who were very home-sick, at Berne, Mürren, Château d'Œx, Lesin, Saanen, Rougemont, and the detention camp at Lausanne. We were also asked for parties to go to Italy, but there again arrangements were never completed.

A certain amount of work was done for the interned and repatriated officers and men, and in September 1917 they went on board the *Carisbrooke Castle*. A little piano covered with a Union Jack had been discovered and brought out on to the upper deck in readiness. They fixed up a small table in a corner of the lower deck for the play, *Between the Soup and the Savoury.* The dresser consisted of a raft, and the back-scene was the bulwarks. A companion ladder made a suitable "exit." The audience, besides being on the deck, climbed into the booms and the tops of the deck-houses, whilst the officers occupied the upper deck.

Of course the enthusiasm was wonderful, and the men were in a great state of excitement at being again on British soil. The items were all announced from the upper deck, for the two plays were part of the programme, which included music before and after them. No points were lost of the plays. They were a continual roar of laughter from start to finish. One of the men who had offered to help in the concert played a violin solo, so our violinist contented herself with playing accompaniments. The finish of the concert was the most wonderful moment in the show. The last item was a song, "There's a Ship that's bound for Blighty." The cheers which followed its announcement were deafening and indescribable.

After the Armistice we were able, in England, at the invitation of the Prisoners of War Committee, to give several concerts and entertainments to welcome men on their arrival in England, during those two or three days of camp or barrack life which had to intervene before they could return to their homes. The artists who undertook this work will not easily forget the three rousing cheers that paid them for their evening's work. For many miserable months they had been without music, without singing, and they sat with their eyes intent upon the singers and players, a crowd intent upon its enjoyment. They applauded the announcement of each item not perfunctorily, but for the sheer pleasure of knowing there was more to come.

Nothing could divert their attention from the platform as long as the concert lasted, but when the final song had been sung, and the curtain had gone down, they were quite ready to tell their German experiences. This one had made his way through Waivre, through Valenciennes, to the Canadian lines at Mons, let loose with a loaf and a hunk of unsavoury sausage. Another had set out from Luxembourg, and struck a French regiment near Verdun. He started without rations of any kind, but had only to say he was English to be sure of help from the Belgians.

One, a slow-spoken boy, a long time captive in Germany, told grimly how Fritz used to jeer at our men when they tried to stay their hunger with turnips. That was when first he was taken. Later, Fritz had been glad enough of turnips himself. There was a man who had worked at felling trees and sawing planks in the Ardennes, and who, out of six hundred fellows, had seen sixty die in four months—die of overwork and underfeeding; and there was his neighbour, who had seen a comrade killed in mere wantonness, and the German lieutenant, when appealed to, dared not even rebuke the unauthorised crime, since the German officers had begun to fear for themselves.

On one point the narrators were all in agreement—the crumbling of the German war machine—some even regretting the granting of an armistice to enemies rotten with indiscipline and incapable of further resistance. One keen-faced lad said gleefully he had long known things were going badly with the Central Empire; being told off for work in the orderly-room, and having more than a smattering of German, he was able to satisfy his natural curiosity by a surreptitious perusal of documents not intended by their owners and authors for the use and enlightenment of prisoners. Two events, he said, were unexpected blows to his jailers—the defection of Bulgaria and the fall of Cambrai.

I suppose it was sheer happiness which had wiped away from most of their faces the signs of recent misery. You heard tales of wretchedness, of cruelty, and hunger, but the boys who told them were eager and bubbling with energy—they were home, and the Germans were beaten, and what for the moment could a reasonable man want more? Perhaps there would be no more splendid hour of their lives than the first few hours of freedom. Clean clothes and good meals were in themselves a blessing, and with a comfortable cigarette between their lips, they listened to the music that gave them a welcome home.

CHAPTER 8

The Devastated Areas

Christmas morning 1918, Mr. Pleasance of the Y.M.C.A. and I left
Paris for Lille. The train was packed to suffocation, and I had, the day
before, waited several hours in the queue at the Gare du Nord to get
the necessary *visées* and permits. There was a struggling mass of people
trying to return to their homes, or rather to the places where their
homes had been.

We arrived at Lille at about half-past three, having passed through
in the train a great deal of the devastated area. In those early days
of traffic on the damaged railway lines we travelled very slowly. The
signs of the war began just before reaching Amiens. There dug-outs,
trenches, and shelters began on both sides of the line, and the first little
white cross, right down by the side of the railway, gave me a sick feeling: it looked so piteous and so small. Sometimes there was only one
alone, sometimes a group of three or four, but in the fields there were
groups of twenty, and sometimes many more.

As we went north, the desolation and destruction increased. There
were literally miles of destroyed villages, and the country was riddled
with shell-holes that ran into and overlapped each other. Many of the
holes were filled with stagnant water.

Passing through St. Eloi, I thought of the terrible battle, and of the
men wounded and dying in the streets of Boulogne, through Albert,
the remains of which seemed to me almost more impressive than
Lens, which is so completely destroyed that it might pass for a rubbish-heap; but because in Albert one sees a little more clearly what the
town once was, its present desolation strikes home with greater force.
From Albert, through miles of destroyed villages, past Vimy Ridge and
many a wretched farmhouse, the train crawled on till we came to Lens
and Bethune—Lens, wrecked houses here and there only, although

the large buildings and machinery connected with the mines are in a hopeless condition of chaos. I heard that the French Consulting Engineers said that the mines cannot be worked for the next seven years.

As one approaches within three or four miles of Lens, the destruction gradually becomes worse. For at least three miles the houses and shops which lined the roadside were mere ghosts of their former selves, and were all in too battered a condition to allow the possibility of any one remaining in them, except where, here and there, the inhabitants were creeping back to this mixture of bricks, stones, broken wood, barbed wire, stoves, telegraph wires, kitchen utensils, and wall-paper; and over that scene of desolation lay the silence, like the stillness in the chamber of death.

As I stood on the remains of what had been a large iron building, the stillness was broken by the intermittent blows of a hammer on iron, and I started at what seemed like the sound of human effort to commence the work of reconstruction. But it was nothing more than a piece of loose iron hanging from the remains of a roof and striking as the wind swept it to and fro on a drunken-looking iron tank. There it will swing till it rusts off and falls on the rubbish-heap beneath it. To say there was no whole house left in Lens is to say nothing. There was not a whole brick, stone girder, joist, or floor board from one end of the town to the other, and it required an effort of imagination to believe that it had ever been a town with living men, women, and joyous children in its streets, its houses, and its gardens. Its soul had fled, and nothing but the mangled, unrecognisable remains were left.

The silence of the place was broken before I left by the passage of a battalion of French soldiers, with many guns and waggons, passing in a long, almost unending line through the ruins. They took the road towards the north, leaving the town once more to its terrible silence.

Through these broken shadows which were once prosperous towns we went up to Lille, and to me the most awful place of all was the little village of Guinchy. I heard afterwards that at this point the line had hardly varied during all the years of the war, which no doubt accounted for the peculiar horror of the place.

On arrival at the best hotel in Lille, which had been occupied by the German Staff, I was given a splendid suite of rooms, including a luxurious bathroom. We had to walk up the shabby staircase; the lift had been put out of order by the Germans, and on every side we saw evidence of the careless disregard of other people's property. In the bedroom the telephone did not work, the bells did not ring, and there was no water for the luxurious bath. When leaving, the Germans seemed to have done as much damage as they could, both great and small, and water could only be used in Lille during stated hours, owing to the injuries to the water-supply.

In the morning I had to search the hotel for some one to bring me breakfast. At last I found a kindly *femme à tout faire*, who brought me black bread, no butter, no salt, no sugar, no milk, and coffee which was not even a good substitute.

The manageress of the hotel had remained in the Bureau all through the German occupation. She was very neat and trim, with a splendid black wig most carefully arranged; but a few words about the miseries of these years, cut off from the rest of France and under the dominion of the Germans, and all trimness and neatness disappeared, her face became livid, the wig rose and balanced itself at a rakish angle as her white hair stood on end beneath it. Poor people of Lille; their sufferings were terrible, and the years must have seemed endless! All the people had that drawn, white look which continuous underfeeding produces.

So much has been written about the devastated areas, and so many pictures trying to represent their desolation have been painted, that it is perhaps unnecessary to dwell again upon it. But as the train passed through the blackened, tortured fields, the horrible stagnant water, the poisoned earth, the ghastly remains of distorted trees, the skeletons of houses, the disused factories, the great overlapping holes of bombarded corners haunted with black fear, one was filled with a nausea quite indescribable. Leaving our manufacturing towns so full of life and prosperity, to see the hideous destruction and feel the ghostly silence of such large towns as Lens and Bethune, made one's heart ache for the French people.

Motoring out from Lille northwards, we went through Armentières, once a great educational centre, now empty of inhabitants, all that remained a few unsafe, broken walls. Bailleul, now only a pile of bricks, almost level with the ground, an archway left of the old church, and two or three broken remnants of houses standing still amongst the ruins, and one black cat on his way to tea with the town major the only sign of life. Locre, Dickiebusch, all ruins, on to Ypres, through country so destroyed that there was not a vestige of life left. Mud, black grass, shell-holes filled with water—even Dante in his *Inferno* did not draw a picture of desolate misery to equal this.

Through Poperinghe and Bergues on to Dunkirk, which was

packed with troops, and there were no rooms to be had. At the hotel there were kind officers who offered me their bedrooms, and proposed cheerfully to sleep in the bathroom, but it was impossible to accept hospitality which meant such great inconvenience. After a desperate search outside the town, in a tiny hotel I found accommodation in the smallest and dampest of bedrooms, and my kind escorts were allowed to sleep on the floor of a sitting-room which belonged to an officer who had, mercifully, retired to rest.

The next day we passed along the canal where Rawlinson went with his army, on through Furnes and Nieuport, along shattered roads with the ragged, painted camouflage screens still fluttering in the wind, masses of concrete on the roadside—used, I believe, greatly for building the little pill-boxes so much used in later warfare; the roads marked on the motor map were cut across by trenches, and impassable. All the fields were deep under water, all the towns and villages in ruins, nothing standing anywhere except a few roadside Calvaries.

We went through desolation on broken roads and rough tracks to La Panne and Pervyse to Ostend; from Ostend to Bruges the fields were cultivated again, and there were cattle browsing, and no sign of destruction; but at Bruges, though the town appeared little damaged except near the canal, the bridge had been blown up, and we had to go a long way round to find a temporary wooden bridge, where crowds of refugees with bundles begged for a lift to take them on their way to their homes.

We took up a nurse whose home was at Ghent. She had a small bundle in which were all the possessions with which she was returning to the home she had left on the outbreak of war. The road to Ghent is straight along the water bank, and in the darkness and the rain she pointed out the way. Quite suddenly the driver stopped dead, and taking off one of his headlights, he said he did not like the look of the road, and went to investigate. A few yards ahead there was a deep chasm several yards wide where the Germans had blown up the road. We should certainly have been killed but for the uncanny instinct of the driver.

At last we arrived in Brussels, a blaze of light, the first city I had seen for years fully lighted. From Brussels we returned to Lille, passing near Waterloo, through Tourcoing and Tournai. The destruction in Belgium, with the exception of the areas round Nieuport and Pervyse, seemed very slight compared with the devastation of France. When we get annoyed with the French because they will not see eye to eye with us, I think every English-speaking person should remember that there was nothing in Europe to compare with the destruction and desolation of that great strip of France, in which millions are buried. To this one must add the wanton destruction of the coal mines, factories, houses, libraries, museums, and churches. Then there is the devastation of the land itself, and no Englishman can love his country as deeply as the Frenchman loves the earth of his own fields. The ruins may be partially covered now, for the earth soon hides her scars, but the poison and misery is still there.

During the war I have heard people say in desperation that the English could not hate. Now it would be good for Europe if it might be said that the English could sympathise and understand. We have fought for freedom side by side with a nation that has struggled and suffered for freedom, and we can love and admire them, even if we cannot see our way to agree.

In these devastated areas the Repertory Companies of players and musicians went on working till the armies were evacuated, and these desert places were left to the burial parties; and we carried on with the burial parties till they had almost completed their grim work.

I was present on Christmas night at a concert in the casino at Lille. The vast place was packed to suffocation with over two thousand men, and outside there were others battering on the doors, clamouring to be let in. It was exhilarating to be spending that especial day with the men who had set Lille free.

At Le Cateau the plays were played in the former Boche theatre, which, after he had been turned out, brother Boche thoughtfully blew most of the roof off. The rain pattered on the audience and the players, making so much noise that they were almost inaudible.

The cold all those months was intense, the platforms like ice-houses. The people giving concerts sat in blankets and coats. They were luckier than the players in the plays.

It was from Abbeville that the parties always went to St. Valerie, Candas, Doullens, etc. Fifteen hundred Byng Boys of the Third Army were at this rest camp in 1918, and presented a small statuette of Joan of Arc as a tribute of their gratitude. The little statue was presented to the dramatic company for the house at Abbeville in which all the artists lived. "Joan of Arc was once in St. Valerie; that is why we offer you this particular souvenir." The gift was accompanied by a little souvenir for each member of the party. "They relate Ypres and Poperinghe, where we have all been, and that is why we have chosen them."

The road to Cayeux, the great rest camp, goes through St.Valerie, a little village lying alongside the rapid-flowing Somme. Of course, St. Valerie used to be on the coast, but it resembles Sandwich in that the sea is now a long way from the little town, and the great rest camp in the middle of the sandy dunes; there is a convalescent hospital which holds four thousand men, and where they changed a thousand a day.

From here William the Conqueror set out with his little fleet of five hundred sailing ships to conquer England, and did it, which seems so comic now. This we know, because there is an old barn-like building with a royal inscription on the house: "The Duke William set off with five hundred sail," etc.

The road runs level with the edge of the bank and there is no side walk, and the drop into the Somme is about fifteen feet or more. It was here, in February 1918, that the only fatal accident happened, though we had all of us been many times where there was grave danger. On a winter night after a successful concert, the members of the party were packed into the cars to travel back to Abbeville. On the first car were two drivers, because the chauffeur who had driven out from Abbeville had asked the best driver of the camp to start him on his way, as the roads were so slippery, the night so dark, and the turnings of the road so sharp. Perhaps he had a premonition of what was coming.

The singers were packed into the back of the touring car; the hood was up; they were well wrapped up with heavy coats and warm rugs. The road headed straight towards the Somme, turning sharply to the right at the bottom of the street. One of the wheels went over the side of the river bank and, owing to the icy condition of the slope, failed to right itself; the car slid backwards into the Somme, and Miss Emily Pickford, Mr. Vincent Taylor, and the driver lost their lives. Their bodies were not found, and the one comfort their relatives had was that they, too, were doing their best to serve their fellowmen.

Although still, I fear, feeling somewhat rebellious at his being cut off, at the commencement of a career he was looking forward to with such pleasure, we are solaced by the knowledge that he met his death while doing something for those who have given so much for us all, just as he might have done had he been able to join them at the Front, which he was prevented from doing by constitutional weakness, and that his work was appreciated . . .

So this was the feeling of Mr. Taylor, who came to the office with his wife, when we had to break the tragic news. I went to Cardiff and saw the relations of Emily Pickford, whose husband felt so terribly his loss.

The Repertory Companies came up from Havre to the devastated areas; from Rouen they went to Douai and the surrounding districts. The old *château* at Douai, which was run by the Y.M.C.A. as an officers' club, had been a magnificent house, and the Hun officers lived there for over three years, but it had lost something of its original comfort and luxury. There was hardly any glass in the windows, and the linen and paper which had taken its place did not keep out much of the wind. There was no water except what was painfully pumped up, and no light except candles, stuck up without candlesticks on tables and windows. The garden was littered with slates from the roof, and there was a shell-hole in the wall of the passage leading to the bathroom, where there was no bath, but only small wooden wash-hand stands. There was no furniture at all in the cupboardless, shelfless, bookless bedrooms, where the walls were papered with old newspapers. They slept on camp-beds with army blankets and no sheets or pillow-cases.

From Abbeville they moved up to Valenciennes, Charleroi, Arras, Peronne, Namur, and Mons, where the retreat of our armies began in 1914, and where the Armistice was signed. The following letter was received from a chaplain at Charleroi:

> I write this quite unofficially and informally to say how in-tensely grateful we chaplains feel for the help you gave our men in this division by your splendid concerts. I never realised before the tremendous power which music has to raise and uplift character. I am certain that concerts of the kind that you gave—healthy, artistic, bright, and inspiring—are the greatest possible assistance in keeping these men true to the best and noblest ideals. And here, in a district such as this, and in a restless time of reaction such as the present, when temptations many and great surround these men, I feel confident that your efforts, tiring and wearisome though they must be to you, do untold good, and bring back thoughts of home life and true ideals to every one who hears these concerts. Thank you ever so much for what you have done, and are doing, for the men.

The base at Winchester was closed that the Repertory Company there might be transferred to Amiens.

In the snow there was something awful in the whiteness, the

dark figures of the men standing up in the endless pits in the snow.

The transport was most difficult, and the conditions of the country appalling. The Abbeville Repertory Company went up into Belgium, and in May 1919, the first concert party went up to Cologne and worked for the Army of Occupation for seven weeks.

From Charleroi onwards it was noticeable that all the coal mines were in partial working order. The first concert was to the boys of the East Lancashires, and they were boys, all about eighteen; none of them had seen active service. At the mess the concert party were entertained by a German orchestra, who had bargained for payment in food instead of money. Their need was written on their faces, and the officers of the East Lancashires, to their credit, engaged them more because they looked hungry than for their talent. The mess was in the *burgomaster's* house, which had been handed over to the English by the German Authorities as a punishment to the *burgomaster*, who had been something of a profiteer, and had ridiculed the food ticket system.

They saw Marshal Foch come down the line from Mainz, the headquarters of the French Area of Occupation, on an official visit to General Robertson at Cologne. His coming was heralded with a series of artillery salutes which crept nearer and nearer, until they saw the Rhine Flotilla of motorboats, looking rather like water gnats, and manned by extra large bluejackets. Then there swept into view a flight of aeroplanes, followed by the old Rhine pleasure steamer, by name the *Bismarck*, and on the bridge Marshal Foch, acknowledging the cheers of the hundreds of troops who lined the banks. The airmen were doing "stunts "over and under Bonn Bridge, and as the *Bismarck* disappeared from sight there was a thunder of cheering and artillery from Cologne.

There was an amusing incident when the party played to the 32nd Division, which was under the command of General Lambert. When the Peace celebrations took place in Paris, General Lambert led the English troops in the march through, and he has since been shot in Ireland. Before the concert began he made a nervous inquiry as to whether the artists would like him to make a speech before the concert. His speech was brief:

Boys, in 1917 we were going up the line, and the Lena Ash well Concert Party was announced. When the curtain went up, I regret to say there was a groan: they were all men. I can only

169

say, 'Look upon that picture, and on this.'

And he pointed to the party, who were all of them women.

Some of the concerts were given to gunners who were scattered in the little villages; the party generally gave the concert in the largest village, and the men walked, rode, or drove from all the country round. They commandeered the strangest vehicles. On one occasion there was a *mêlée* of khaki legs and arms protruding from an old-fashioned *diligence*.

In Germany there is in every village an excellent concert hall, with full lighting equipment and scenery, where it was possible to play any play or give any kind of concert.

During the week in which they played every night at the Deutsches Theatre, Cologne, there were labour troubles, and during one performance there was a call for the machine gunners. Mercifully, however, these precautions were not necessary.

They met many old friends from France, and were billeted and drew rations, and had an orderly detailed to cook their food. They were constantly challenged with fixed bayonets and surrounded by road patrols.

In June the Peace was signed, and very soon our work with the armies was over. In the Blue book issued by the Ministry of Reconstruction, on Adult Education, there are several references to the importance of our work, and one paragraph concludes with this sentence:

We believe that the work accomplished by Miss Ashwell's organisation was not only recreational but educational in a high degree, and that the remarkable results achieved in the citizen armies are practically valuable in indicating what might be done in introducing good drama and music to the home population in normal times.

The great bases of the army dwindled, and finally closed one after the other, and I cannot, I feel, wind up the story of the work better than with the letter of the end of May 1919, from the engine repair shops in Rouen:

Now that the last show has been given, I feel I should like to write and let you know on behalf of every one here, how very, very much your different parties, both dramatic and concert, have been appreciated by this unit.

On every occasion they have played to a crammed house. The dramatic party, with Miss Rees in command, are specially old and well-established favourites, and it devolved on them to ring down the curtain for the last time on many most delightful entertainments with the *Mollusc*, which went with the usual bang. I am sure it is not too much to say your parties have been a godsend to us out here, and if I may do so, I should like to congratulate you on sending us such *good* and appropriate stuff. I know that has been specially commented on, and was particularly the case with the dramatic party plays. Speaking with a good many years' experience, I can say that the men *are* keenly appreciative of high-class entertainments, and certainly in the case of my own men here, any old thing is *not* good enough for the 'hired assassins.'

I feel I also personally owe you a great debt of gratitude in that your parties have helped me so much in combating in these big works that insidious and deadly complaint, staleness and boredom, where men are called upon to work very hard as they have been here.

Again, for myself and every one, thank you very much indeed; you must have had much hard work, but it must be some compensation to know, as you must do already, how much it has been valued.

When I speak of what I have seen and experienced of the tastes of the masses of our nation, I am often contradicted by writers who have not perhaps had so much experience of the subject as has been allotted to me. So this letter may possibly shake the prejudice that exists that the poor in this world's goods are necessarily poor in spirit, that the well-to-do are naturally and inevitably the best judges of what is noble and fine in art. It is true that for a just appreciation of art, education is necessary, but for simple enjoyment of beauty, one only needs the simplicity and sincerity of children.

CHAPTER 9

Work at Home and Demobilisation

Everywhere where the foot of man could tread the Y.M.C.A. had opened huts. People now perhaps forget what these huts meant to the men. Everywhere in France, and elsewhere with the armies, there were these free clubs for the men, where at any rate they could come in out of the rain. There was a place to sit, notepaper to write on, and the nation paid for the transport of letters, which were all censored and marked "On Active Service." There were always hot tea and coffee, buns, biscuits, and cigarettes to be bought at the counter, and behind the counter there were always pleasant, friendly people to sell the goods, and help with advice if it was asked for.

The organisation spread and spread, but it had always been an institution for men, and though the women who were working for it were roughly a thousand to ten men, the Y.W.C.A. was supposed to meet the needs of the women. Both these organisations were under the spell of the early Victorian ideal of fitness of things. They were bound down with the idea of keeping the sexes gracefully apart lest in any way they should influence each other on the downward path which leads to ruin. The idea of companionship, friendship, equality of status and interests was undreamt of.

When properly educated you entered a world where a member of the other sex was not referred to except as a strange and dangerous being who apparently made rare visits from a distant planet to spread havoc and destruction. There was every effort at first to follow this strange prejudice which strove to separate the two halves of the human race. There was much talk of the fearsome fact that the men who had come from the Colonies had, no doubt, wives and sweethearts whom they had left behind, and the men must be saved from the intriguing women who waited for them here in every street, behind every lamp-post.

The Y.M.C.A. naturally resisted for a long time the organising of a club where men could naturally give their womenfolk a cup of tea, and sit down in a friendly way for a chat. It was a tremendous departure for so conservative an organisation, and there is something delightfully ludicrous in the fact that when they had to take the plunge, they had to go off the deep end, and for lack of a more suitable building, take over the supper and dancing club known as Giro's. There was a certain undercurrent of excitement attached to the venture, as the club had been raided at some time or other. I was talked to about the necessity of changing the atmosphere and the difficulties of effecting a complete transformation.

When the Y.M.C.A. leader stopped for suitable words to express his disapproval of the past history of supping and dancing, I filled in the pause by saying, "Its offence is rank and smells to heaven."

He looked at me severely, and said, "No, no. I would not go so far as that!"

So many only know the name of William Shakespeare and nothing of his works. Once in a hospital there was a weary, mournful patient, who was too full of pain even to care to be interested, and when the visitor distributed the books, he languidly consented to take the smallest, a little copy of *Twelfth Night,* issued by the Chiswick Press. His neighbour, who was not quite so wretched, encouraged him by saying, "Go on, matey; you don't 'ave to read it!" The following week the visitor was collecting the books, and the languid man said he would like another of the same. The visitor asked what book it was, and who was the author. His answer was, "The book was called *Twelfth Night,* by the Chiswick Press."

Giro's was the first Y.M.C.A. hut where the women were welcomed with the men. The not altogether unnatural fear that the innovation might be abused, and that the men might bring in a class of women that were unsuitable, proved to be without any basis. I always feel that there is a danger of underrating the good manners of men. If it is understood from the beginning that in a place of this kind good manners are expected, they are generally there; but if people are expected to behave badly, they generally do. At Giro's it was understood from the beginning that it was a place where self-respect and respect for the other fellow were expected, and there never was the slightest infringement of good taste, even though Giro's is situated in Leicester Square, the very heart of London.

Sir Arthur Yapp was good enough to suggest that I should undertake the entire management. This, however, I felt was quite beyond me, though I gladly undertook the concerts.

It was a very happy experience. The quartet was led by that most brilliant musician, Mrs. Withers, and so good was it that the place was haunted by musicians. Roger Quilter was often there, and he and Gervase Elwes gave the men a Quilter concert. Martin Shaw also gave special concerts. Opera-singers, ballad-singers, reciters, and entertainers came over and over again. The quartet played all the really classical music as well as the best of modern works, and the men listened with intense interest. "We needs must love the highest when we see it" was a platitude there. The music began in the afternoon, and continued until the closing of the hut at night. The general direction of this work was undertaken by Mr. Paget Bowman.

While an appeal to popular taste for selections from grand and light opera was made, they gradually introduced into their repertory works by British composers such as Frank Bridge, Sir Edward Elgar, Percival Fletcher, Edward German, Percy Grainger, Roger Quilter, Coleridge Taylor, as well as the works of Bizet, Delibes, Grieg, Massenet, Mozart, Rachmaninov, Saint-Saëns, Sibelius, Tschaikovsky, Wagner, and many others. The best works were quickly found to rival the others in popularity, and in 1918 the quartet began a series of Chamber Music in the small hall underneath the larger hall, at which the works of Beethoven, Brahms, Dvořák, Fauré, Schumann were given. The audience at these concerts increased to such an extent that it became necessary to give them in the large hall, and they became an outstanding feature.

Thus for a time there was established in the centre of London a concert hall in the nature of a music club for the people, where the evening could be spent in a most enjoyable and musically intellectual way. Hundreds of men testified to the influence it had on their lives and on the lives of their comrades, and expressed the opinion that such an institution is a most practical method of combating the evils of drink in our streets. The quartet and their colleagues endeared themselves and their work to thousands of people.

In 1919, as the demobilisation of the army continued, there were fewer and fewer troops passing through London, and finally Giro's, too, closed as a Y.M.C.A. hut, and was reopened as a dancing and supper club.

On the closing night of the concert work there, I was asked by the artists to come and recite and make a speech. The little hall was very crowded, the gallery packed, and a very great number of the six hundred modern troubadours were present. There were flowers and cheers, and much concealed agitation. At last Mr. Bowman and Mr. Flint drew me aside, and the latter, in an agitated undertone, said:

We are presenting you tonight with an address, and an illuminated list of the subscribers who have bought you an emerald and diamond pendant, which we are sure you will like, but it has not come, so don't show any surprise when we present you with one of your own jewel cases. We have just sent home for one. It will be empty, so for goodness' sake don't open it, or the men in the gallery will see there's nothing there!

It is indeed a very beautiful pendant of splendid workmanship and design, and I love it; but I was so thankful that this comic situation saved me from making an idiot of myself. I was so grateful to them for their love and splendid loyalty to their art all through these terrific times of hectic effort. Their persistent, continuous, and arduous work made me feel very humble and horribly emotional at being treated, if only momentarily, as a leader and head. I treasure my pendant and the illuminated address, and they have departed their several ways, carrying in their work a deeper knowledge and a certain faith in what they are able to do, and what their mission is as servants to the public.

The work with the armies slowly dwindled, and with the sending out of fewer parties it was obvious that it would be essential to have some form of demobilisation work. Many of the artists had been for four years cut off from their work, their places at home had been filled, and to enable them to live until they had an opportunity of picking up the threads of the professional work again, some form of demobilisation plan was necessary.

The Charity Commissioners allowed us to use the small sum remaining of the fund called "Concerts at the Front" for demobilisation purposes. We ran a number of concerts in hospitals, and took the Baths at Bethnal Green from Oxford House on a weekly rental.

There is no public hall in that great borough, no place of meeting for the people; in Stepney and many other boroughs of greater London there is not even a bath available in which to arrange entertainments. It was some time before we succeeded in getting an audience, though we changed the programme every week and our charges were very small; but gradually our audience increased, and we were full of hope for the following season, having done a good deal of pioneer

175

work before the Baths had to reopen as baths. In spite, however, of the good work we had accomplished, which the Oxford House authorities acknowledged, they decided to turn the Baths into a Cinema, as they felt there was more money to be made in that way.

On leaving Bethnal Green we found a small hall at Hanwell, not far from the Lunatic Asylum; the lunatics did not find their way to see our plays, but the Labour Mayors did. Major Attlee, who was the Mayor of Stepney and chairman of the Labour Mayors, came down to Hanwell and saw what we were doing. He was delighted, and arranged a meeting of the mayors, and an agreement was come to on these lines: that I should find a company of players who would play in their town hall, or, where there was no town hall, in the public baths, during the autumn and winter months; that I should be responsible for all the expense of the performances, the company, authors' fees, music, printing, transport, etc., and that the mayors and the council would let us have the hall at a nominal fee, one night in the week, for this period; that they would help us by making our effort known in the neighbourhood, and in every way give us their support; that we should show our books at the end of the season, or, in some cases, monthly, and pay a percentage upon the takings.

As we were visiting each borough every week on the same night of the week, we called ourselves the "Once-a-week Players." Financially it was only possible to make the efforts self-supporting if we played every night, with a minimum of £30 per night. Even with the help of the mayors and their councils it was difficult to secure the halls consecutively throughout the season, and we opened without the full number. Owing to the death of the Mayor of Hackney we were unable to arrange for one night in the week, and the People's Palace, which the Mayor of Stepney took and himself paid for a short time, proved very unsuitable for our work. This vast hall was built solely with the idea of concerts, and is so arranged that when playing plays the artists cannot be seen or heard, so we were very soon compelled to abandon playing there.

This first season we went every Monday night to Fulham Town Hall, Tuesday to Battersea Town Hall, Friday to Shoreditch, and Saturday to Camberwell. We struggled on with two vacant evenings up to the beginning of the New Year, when all the money was finished. At the request of a few of the artists we have struggled on since on cooperative lines. Last winter was our second season, and showed a substantial improvement, though we were not entirely self-supporting.

This second season we played every Tuesday at Battersea, Wednesday at Canning Town Town Hall, Thursday at Deptford Baths, Friday at Greenwich Town Hall, and Saturday at Camberwell Baths. It was our second year at Battersea, Greenwich, and Camberwell.

The reason we were not self-supporting this second year was due to the fact that the arrangements made for the Monday, which we had hoped would be most satisfactory, we were obliged to scrap, since, as we approached the opening date at Plaistow, the original arrangement suggested was so altered that it was impossible for us to accept.

The closing of the season this spring was remarkable for the enthusiasm and friendly appreciation of the audiences, who throughout the entire season, many of them, had been in their places every week to welcome the players. The Mayor of Greenwich, in saying goodbye to me until the autumn, said it was very remarkable that, though in Greenwich there had always been a great difficulty in getting any civic feeling and co-operation, the meeting of the people every week to see the plays was creating the civic feeling that was so much desired.

In October we are starting again in the same boroughs, but have added others to these. We shall have twelve places instead of six, and of the satisfactory growth of our effort in co-operation with the mayors and councils of the boroughs there is now no doubt.

In the report of the Departmental Committee appointed by the President of the Board of Education, published in 1921, called *The Teaching of English in England*, the work is referred to on page 325:

We note with satisfaction that Miss Lena Ashwell, who organised a most wonderful series of entertainments for the troops during the war, is continuing in peace-time her efforts to popularise good plays by arrangement with the mayors of some of the London boroughs, and a Repertory Company under her direction, the ' Once-a-week Players,' has given performances in some of the town halls. We hope to see this co-operation between the stage and the municipal authorities extended to other parts of the country.

The distinctive importance of our work is the effort to demonstrate to the boroughs that it is necessary to have a building which can never be diverted from the purpose of supplying recreation which can be considered of a standard which meets the needs of the people themselves. The work, of course, from the point of view of the actor, leaves a great deal to be desired, but the smallness of the platforms, the difficulty of proper lighting, the lack of facilities for any scenic effects are deprivations which are far outweighed by the responsiveness of the audiences in the different boroughs. Nevertheless this work could never have been initiated or carried out but for the experiences which we had in France.

It was because we were accustomed then to play anywhere, under any conditions, that we have been able to work continuously in the baths and town halls, and it is because we are haunted with the memory of those years with the armies, because we recall the great use we were in healing the sick and encouraging those who fought, because we broke the deadly monotony of life out there, that we know we can be of use to the masses of the people in this country. Our work now is done in memory of those who fought, and the great army of those who died, and of those still with us who have come back to the bitter struggle for existence.

CHAPTER 10

Recreation and the National Life

It is impossible for me to have any idea of the opinion which will be formed by the readers of this account as to the fundamental necessity of real recreation. In any case, this' effort to give an impression of the experiences of over six hundred people during four years must necessarily be entirely inadequate.

Many, I am afraid, will brush the whole matter aside as of no importance, merely a phenomena of the human spirit under the stress of war, living under extreme conditions of bodily discomfort and physical misery. They will also very likely dwell on the fact that there was little to do when not fighting or drilling except to write letters home, and play the childish gambling game called "House." They will feel that in ordinary civilised life there is nothing parallel to the needs of war. There is, of course, a great deal to be said in support of this point of view, but is not our whole civilisation at present founded on war, and is not our industrial system an open warfare? Not so obvious as air-raids, big guns, battle, murder, and sudden death, but none the less a deadly struggle for existence, which it is harder to realise since much of the struggle takes place in the intangible field of man's psychic life.

Does not civilisation need to try a different method to put into practice the new outlook which is very slowly creeping into man's idea of what is wisest and best? The practical demonstration of the scientific experience that we individually are very much a part and parcel of the whole community, and that however hard we may try to live for ourselves and our families alone, ignoring the world outside our own safe walls, we find that it cannot be done. The world outside has a very definite effect on our small world, and it is plain common sense to recognise that civilisation has come to the turning of the ways.

We have found that workers cannot strike without the nation suffering, that people who do not toil with their hands but with their heads cannot shut themselves off and live in separate compartments, that the rich have a great obligation to fulfil or perish, and that in modern civilisation isolation is impossible; that the ignorance and stupidity of the minority dominating one country may throw the whole of the balance of civilisation out of joint. But we are very slow to realise this, and our modern education so far has not helped us much. The "isolated fighting unit" idea is still prevalent in our idea of education, although human experience has passed beyond it; and we know we should be educating "citizens of the universe."

The theatre can be an invaluable power in making the audience understand the point of view and the suffering of different sections of the community, and all the difficulties and the different emotional outlook of other countries.

But there is an idea which prevails in the great daily Press of London that, as long as there are some good plays running in the theatres of the City of Westminster, there must automatically be a healthy condition of affairs in the rest of the country. This may have been so once, but it is certainly not true now.

Let me take the last point first. As many years ago as 1905 I was on tour, gaining my first experience in management. I was in Sunderland, and Sir Henry Irving was in Middlesbrough. I felt then, and have always continued to feel, the very deepest love and affection for him. He was not only a great actor and a great man, but was one of the few people who put his calling first in his measurement of values. The beauty of fine work and the dignity of the theatre were always first with him. Although the London public wearied of him, and he had to leave the Lyceum, it was considered in the theatrical profession a hall-mark of artistic work to have been engaged at that theatre. I had played with him on three occasions, and when that tragic dissolution of the great partnership between him and Ellen Terry took place, he had sent for me to take her place, and I, with a very heavy heart, had refused, because it was to my mind hopeless even to try and follow Ellen Terry in her great roles. And although when I said, "It is no use a star trying to be the sun," he said, "That's very nice, but you might learn," I stuck to my guns and only played in his new production at Drury Lane of *Dante*.

I went over from Sunderland to pay my respects to him, and sent up a note to ask if I might say good morning, hoping only for a few minutes' talk, but he kept me with him for some hours. He told me then of the gradual death of the theatre in the provinces, of the gradual extinction of players of Shakespeare, the shrinking of support and interest. He was concerned not from the personal point of view, since he was playing his farewell tour, and his great record assured his success, but he was considering the art of acting itself, and the great loss he felt the public would suffer through the withdrawal of their support of the theatre.

I have thought much of the subject since, and I have wondered if, when education became general, there did not creep in a standard which regarded learning only from the point of view of its material use. I have noticed when suggesting that discontent might be met by the study of some interesting subject, merely for the enjoyment of the increasing of one's powers, the reply is generally, "I don't think I can use it, it would be no use to me," the idea being that nothing is of any use unless there is money in it, and, of course, with that outlook one shuts the door on living. The theatre did not, I suppose, appear a useful method of learning how to be an efficient "isolated fighting unit."

Another factor in the decline of the theatre was the lack of continuity. Few people who are actors have any continuity of work. They drift here and there from one management to the other, and are very much in the same position as the casual labourer. The managers, the employers of labour, generally lack any objective except commercial success. Therefore, there is a constant wobbling in policy. Theatres in the City of Westminster constantly change their entire policy from season to season in the search of what the public wants. The City of Westminster feeds the provincial theatres.

These theatres are under different controls in small groups: thus one man will have under his control three or four theatres in different counties, and the booking of the companies is on a percentage basis. The sitting manager naturally wants to get as big a return for his money as possible, and as big a percentage as can be dragged out of the manager of the touring company. His object is to book as many as possible of the London successes, or he gives that up and turns his theatre into a cinema or dancing hall, according to the vagaries of the partially educated youth of the country.

The interest of the public is focused as much as possible on the advertising of the spectacle, the expense of the show, the grandeur of the production, and the phenomenal drawing capacity of the play. The actor has almost entirely disappeared and, with a very few exceptions, is unknown in the provinces. People go to see a replica of the London

181

productions. The public, therefore, have little opportunity of seeing actors in different parts, and therefore can have little idea of what acting really is. The travelling player, not belonging to any place, is cut off from his fellow-men.

It seems to me that the old Stock Companies, where the actors were part of the life of the town, known by the people, liked by them, when it was possible to see the same actor play many different parts, that there was more human interest; and those Stock Companies are not so very distant from us, since both Ellen Terry and Mrs. Kendal began their professional careers in stock.

I wonder if the nation has any idea how much it is indebted to the Repertory Companies, which have replaced in some towns the Stock Companies, indifferent as they often are, lacking in spontaneity and finish from overwork? These efforts of the actors themselves, such as the Repertory Theatre, Glasgow, which gave us, I believe, the first of Arnold Bennett's plays; Miss Horniman's splendid enterprise in Manchester, which gave us Stanley Houghton and the Manchester school of playwrights; the Birmingham Repertory, from which *Abraham Lincoln* came to spend a short holiday at the Lyric Theatre, Hammersmith, and stayed for over a year—these and many other enterprises of the same kind, however, are as water on the sand, for when they pass, the community, having done nothing to co-operate, having made no effort of its own, takes no interest whatever in the continuance of the work.

Thus the Gaiety, Manchester, is now a cinema; the Glasgow Repertory, broken up by the war, has no theatre in which to play. When the desire came to reconstruct it, the theatre had gone and there was no building in which they could work. There can be nothing which will ensure the natural and healthy growth of the theatre amongst the people except the co-operation of the people themselves.

There is something to be said for having a continuous effort with an object in view. It gives the actor a chance of becoming acquainted with those "two boards and a passion" which have been spoken of so much lately. The trouble is that those isolated efforts make little impression. The public accepts no liability, does nothing to co-operate, goes to the theatre if it is the fashion of the moment, or stays away with equal unconcern and indifference. So long as the public cannot see any real use or value in the theatre, there will never be any real basis on which to work.

In those good old days of "Merrie England," which led up to the great Elizabethan literature and its climax in the work of William Shakespeare, the Court, the Nobles, the men of Science, the men of Letters, the men of the Church realised the importance of great literature in the theatre, acknowledged it and made use of it. There could never be a controversy as to the authorship of Shakespeare Plays if Francis Bacon had not been at any rate in touch with the life of the theatre. In these present days the Court, the Nobles, the Church, give their support to games. There never was a time when racing, football, boxing, tennis, dancing, and all forms of games had so much influence behind them.

But the greatest powers in the evolution of the races have not been always those distinguished for the greatest physical prowess. The greatest literature does not concern itself much with these things, but with the education of the greater powers of man. We might realise that our emotions are a finer part of us. The soul of each one of us is what we have felt. But it is this great power in every human being, the power of feeling emotion, which has been regarded with so much fear and suspicion by the community.

We have just passed through a long period influenced by the Puritans, when a definite effort was made to stamp out this inconvenient force, and the result has been that it has not been stamped out, but there has been a partial atrophy. Evil emotions can never be wholly conquered, except by education. We understand each other so little because we are living from different emotions, and when we can understand the emotion of the other fellow we begin to pity or admire him, as the case may be. *Tout comprendre, c'est tout pardonner,* may be said of nearly every occasion when time is wasted on criticism and anger. Increased understanding is the law of evolution of the soul, and exists from the lowest to the highest that we can know, for are we not forgiven by the Crucified because we know not what we do?

Feeling is not just for the sake of feeling, it is an organ of knowledge, and is good because it is useful. We grow with our capacity for feeling; we increase our powers by enlarging our understanding of the feelings which lead to actions, and the theatre is for the purpose of representing emotion in action. We can see in the theatre that what we feel becomes our limitation, and we are stimulated to try to feel constructively instead of destructively.

We acquire knowledge of a very definite kind when we feel moved by fearlessness, compassion, friendship, love, and we can see how tiresome the cross, worried, fearful people can be.

Let us have every kind of play—those that appeal to the intellect, those that appeal to the soul—but let us know when the play is one which appeals to the animal sensuous nature, and let us have the common sense to face the position fearlessly. Let us know what emotions are being stimulated, in the same way that when we are studying, when learning languages for instance, we do not pretend to ourselves that we are studying typewriting. If we want to have our intellect put aside and the greater powers of the soul deadened by an exhibition of sensuous animalism, let us just say, "We are so weak and dull that we are running on the lowest gear, and afraid, or too lazy, to run on top, using the full powers of our organism."

In the calling together of all the arts, the art of the theatre should, in the end, be the completest form of art, and take the leading place in the evolution of the masses in the future.

Quoting the lovely words of Bacon in *The Advancement of Learning*:

For although in modern commonwealths stage plays be but esteemed as sport or pastime, unless it draw from the satire or be mordant; yet the care of the Ancients was that it should instruct the minds of men unto virtue. Nay, wise men and great philosophers have accounted it as the archet or musical bow of the mind, and certainly it is most true, and as it were a secret of nature that the minds of men are more potent to affections and impressions congregate than solitary.

Poesy cheereth and refresheth the soul, chanting things rare and various and full of vicissitudes. . . . So, as poesy serveth and conferreth to magnanimity and morality, therefore it may seem deservedly to have some participation of divineness, because it doth raise the mind and exalt the spirit with high raptures, by proportioning the show of things to the desires of the mind, and not submitting the mind to things, as reason and history do. And by these allurements and congruities whereby cherisheth the soul of man, joined also with consort of music whereby it may more sweetly insinuate itself, it hath won such access that it hath been in estimation even in rude times and in barbarous nations when other learning stood excluded.

Dramatical or representative poesy, which brings the world upon the stage, is of excellent use, if it were not abused. For the instructions and corruptions of the stage may be great, but corruption in this kind abound. The discipline is altogether neglected in our times.

For the education of the soul, the taming of the passions, the awakening of interest in other people living under other conditions, in other nations, for the understanding of other people's difficulties, and for the stimulating of all that is highest and most adventurous in the desires of the human spirit, there is no more powerful agent then the theatre. The continuous representation of the finest dramas, including not only the great masterpieces of William Shakespeare, but the finest modern work, should be continuous, easily accessible to all the people, and public opinion should feel that in the growth of the organism and the development of the mind, there is something splendid.

Then the archet or musical bow of the mind would be used for the creation of loveliness in the minds of the people, and life would be a freedom of growth instead of a suppression and negation.

In recent years a number of eminent people have tried to awaken interest in the establishing of a national theatre, the founding of a dignified building where the finest expression of all the complicated modern machinery of the drama might have a fitting shrine, and where a noble company, representing art and literature, painting and the fine arts and crafts, music and acting, working together, would demonstrate the power and beauty of dramatic work, the synthesis of all the arts, devoted to the expression of the complicated emotions of the human race.

A most worthy cause. It must surely be regretted by every member of the English race that we alone in Europe are without any national building for this purpose. We have our museums, our art galleries, not only in London, but in our great provincial cities. The other nations of Europe have these as well, but to them is added, not only in every capital, but in every great provincial town, a building dedicated to the use of drama and music; and it is curious that the nation supreme in dramatic literature should be without any national building in which it can be represented.

But when we have—if we ever do—achieved one national theatre as a memorial to the greatest poet of the world, William Shakespeare, we shall still be far from achieving the real object of the drama; that will still remain unexpressed. It is not only the few who live in the capital who need the theatre. Many of them are jaded, and their critical faculty is far greater than their power of response. Perhaps the respectable, comfortable class have no need of a physician; they do not know how sick they are.

There are forty odd millions of people in this Island, most of them workers, many of them manual workers. They have a desperate hunger and thirst for some healthy, emotional stimulus. They are restless and miserable, for their education, which has only just begun, has entirely ignored the awakening power of their emotional life. They are bound down by our industrial system to maimed and blunted lives, with little to lift the cloud that surrounds them, the dreary greyness of the conditions of their work. After a few months, when learning the mechanism, they have, most of their day, to make no mental effort, the work being purely mechanical. Man cannot live a healthy life of industrial toil unless his mind is interested. For happiness he must climb the Jacob's Ladder of unfolding awareness of beauty, wisdom, and strength. If he can see something beautiful to admire, he grows more and more in tune with what attracts him.

In the modern drama there is much that can widen his sympathy and interest in other people's lives, and occasionally there are glimpses of something larger and greater than himself. He can, through the medium of the theatre, not only understand the conditions of his own country, but become interested in, and aware of, the difficulties of other nations.

The remarks of a schoolmaster of great distinction after seeing last year *The Government Inspector*, by Gogol, were very striking. He said that he had read every bit of literature he could get hold of with regard to Russia—the novels of Tolstoy, Dostoieffsky, Tourguénieff, Gorky, etc.—but it was only when witnessing the play as played in the theatre that he began to understand the reasons which underlay the Russian Revolution.

No one would say that the modern theatre is ideal, not even those critics who desire to bolster up the present system, which is entirely governed by the commercial standard.

The education of the power of the soul should not be left entirely to the standard of financial success. If our national education had been left to the people who were able to attract the greatest number of students and make the greatest amount of money by looking at education as a financial enterprise, where would the nation stand? It is because Parliament was made to see that however many schools existed, run upon the principle of being self-supporting, it was necessary for the life and development of the nation at large that education should be taken out of the hands of commerce and undertaken nationally.

To make the representation continuous and accessible to the mass of the people, it is necessary to have many places of recreation. There should be civic or municipal theatres in every dignified town, and there should be theatres feeding groups of villages. These civic or municipal theatres would not at first be absolutely perfect or fulfil all the opportunities which dramatic expression can represent. But at least the people of the town would be able to protect themselves, and achieve a standard of what they considered wholesome food for the imagination, and it would not be left, as at the present time, to extreme sensationalism and the flogging of atrophied emotion, which so much of the present cinema represents.

The success of thieves and murderers, the tortures, the shooting and killing, without any sign of consequences or the horror of suffering, and the shedding of blood, cannot be good for any nation, and it is significant that lately, when criminals have been arrested, and they have said, "I had no idea it was done so easily" (in the case of a murderer), or have shown a pride in inventions for robbery and other offences against the community.

A little while ago some one told me that Bernard Shaw upheld the cinema at a meeting of the Fabian Society, saying that, at any rate, "*it showed the poor people how nicely the rich people eat.*" The other day he asked me if I had been in Wales, and expressed himself as horrified at the films he saw. There is no doubt in this country there are towns that now no longer have any other form of recreation for the people than the cinema, and it is not satisfactory that there should be only one form, even if it were entirely and completely a satisfactory one.

For the artist self-expression implies, for its full realisation, somebody on whom the impression, sooner or later, is to be measured, for the purpose of achieving a better understanding of the emotion itself, and gradually the expression takes a more or less complete form. All art, since it is art, must take place within a form of some kind, and the form is only a danger to growth when the desire for perfection of form takes the place of the desire for the expression of emotion.

If Plato concluded that the four cardinal virtues which comprised the All Virtue were Wisdom, Fortitude, Temperance, and Justice, it was left to Benedetto Croce to discover that the four primary concepts in the ideal are Beauty, Truth, Usefulness, and Goodness, and these taken together supply the complete basis of the All in terms of Qualities. It therefore appears that a complete work of art should contain these four concepts, and that the artist who is indifferent to goodness and usefulness is limiting his powers for the expression of beauty and truth.

As before in the history of England, the great movement of the revival of the theatre is beginning amongst the people themselves. It is not amongst the well-to-do so much, though there are signs of it there, but in the masses of the people who are bestirring themselves and trying to find some outlet for the consuming desire for beauty which is deeply rooted in the people. Responding to this there is a very real movement amongst the educationists to include in the teaching in the schools some knowledge of plays as a method of expression and as a means of using the imitative power.

When one recognises that Marlowe was the son of a shoemaker, Ben Jonson of a mason, and Shakespeare the son of a butcher, dealer in skins, or farmer—the children of the workers—it is with hope that one thinks of the workers in Sheffield and other great towns, the many efforts through the Women's Institutes for the playing of plays. The community is essential to any work of art, and it is this movement in the community itself which should be the hope of the modern artist, to be on the look-out for this stirring of the people, and try to help and co-operate with it.

There is not only for an artist the immense interest and joy of self-expression, and the pursuit of perfection in the art that he has chosen, but the recognition that he is there to help and lead by his knowledge. He may be willing to sacrifice himself and his family to achieve success in his art, but it will bring him no happiness, and be but a three-legged affair unless it is of use to the community. The greater the artistic value, the greater the use, not in terms of commerce but in terms of quality. Surely no business man, no soldier, no writer, no financier, has ever been to the world of greater use than William Shakespeare? His plays have not only given to the British Empire some understanding of the love of country, splendour of friendship and love of one's fellow-men, but are now of untold value to other nations in Europe where his plays are played, understood, and appreciated.

It is very noticeable that it was in Vienna that *Troilus* and *Cressida* was produced, also *Richard II.*—both plays very little seen in this country. There are many productions of *Hamlet* and the other tragedies in almost every country in Europe. In Serbia, before the war, they found room for continuous playing in the State Theatre of his great works. In Paris, throughout France, Germany, Switzerland, one can see the plays of Shakespeare.

In England I do not believe it would be necessary to subsidise the

188

company, but it is necessary and will always be of vital importance that there should be a building belonging to the community in every town and large borough. If the public bodies had no control over our museums and picture galleries, all the treasures of the National Gallery might be hurled out to make room for new impressionism or photographic wonders of the people who wish to be famous. There should be buildings for the performance of music and drama which the nation feels are representative. Civic theatres would not interfere with private enterprise. Public education has not interfered with colleges and universities, but has added to their power and importance.

Modern works should be acquired by the nation and accessible to all the community, for the use of all companies working with the authorities. The workers in science and medicine do not hold up their discoveries for private gain; their tradition is otherwise. Plays such as *Abraham Lincoln*, by John Drinkwater, John Masefield's *Nan*, Bernard Shaw's *Candida*, and *Back to Methuselah*, to mention only a few, are as water to the thirsty soul of man. The inhabitants of every town should be able to see Shakespeare and modern plays continuously. The drama season should be followed by seasons of music and opera. There are always hungry people needing mental food, and there is such a thing as mental food, however much there may be attempts to kill the fact by ridicule.

The trivial Press tries to deaden the hunger of people with the transatlantic word "highbrow," but words don't alter facts. With our physical food we are careful. We have laws to prevent adulteration and the mixing of poisonous elements into our daily diet. Bad food is thrown away and burnt when it becomes infested with the lower form of life. If people try to sell it, they are put in prison or heavily fined. But with the minds of men, in our insistence on freedom of ignorance, for money, men may sell the foulest most poisonous food for the mind, and no one ever mentions that such is tainted. No effort is made to ensure the distribution of good food for the hearts and minds. Everything is left to the freedom to be poisoned by the person who thinks money is the only good to be found in life.

As there is no pure bread distributed, people acquire the habit of preferring the strong taste of what is at best a dope to deaden the soul.

Whilst other countries in Europe make haste to protect small children from the evil things in the cinema by laws which prevent admittance unless grown-up people take the responsibility of taking them there—the age of youth being as high as eighteen in some countries—we, with our shrieks for liberty, leave all the children to be fed on the poison of sensational murders, robberies, tortures, animals tearing human beings to bits. The foolish *cliché*, "*the camera cannot lie*," goes on being repeated, but is a cover to the stupidest of lies; nothing lies like the camera, for the impression is given without results. People are torn and there is no blood; people are tortured—no sound conveys the agony; people are killed, and it is not death—it is only a picture.

And all that is needed is a standard. We have a standard in education.

The importance of the theatre for children is exceptionally well put in the life of Mark Twain in his amazingly interesting letter on the Children's Theatre, in which he says:

> A children's theatre is easily the most valuable adjunct that any educational institution for the young can have, and that no otherwise good school is complete without it. It is much the most effective teacher of morals and promoter of good conduct that the ingenuity of man has yet devised, for the reason that its lessons are not taught wearily by book and dreary homily, but by visible and enthusing action, and they go straight to the heart, which is the lightest of right places for them.

Also in Frank Crane's book, called *Just Human*:

> One of the most vital discoveries of this age is that in well-ordered amusement there is more power to change the character and affect the morals than in any other thing. . . . We see the awakening of the immense moral dynamic force of the theatre. The most important moral element of a nation is its amusement.

And there is a most remarkable tribute to the power of entertainment of even the most primitive kind in *Red Dusk*, the book on modern Russia, just published, by Sir Paul Dukes:

> The '*Internationale*' was not sung when he concluded. There was too much sincerity in his speech, and the bombastic strains of that tune would have been sadly out of place. The rest of the programme consisted of two stage performances, enacted by amateurs, the first one a light comedy, the second a series of propagandist tableaux depicting the sudden emancipation of the worker by the Soviet Power, heralded by an angel dressed all in red. In one of these Comrade Rykov proudly participated.

In the concluding tableau the Red Angel was seen guarding a smiling workman and his family on one side, and a smiling peasant and family on the other, while the audience was invited to rise and sing the '*Internationale.*'

Of conscious political intelligence in the cultural-enlightenment committees there is none, nor under 'iron party discipline' can there possibly be any. All Communist agitators repeat, parrot-like, the epithets and catch phrases dictated from above. None the less, despite their crudity and one-sidedness, these committees serve a positive purpose in the Red Army. By the provision of entertainment the savagery of the soldiery has been curbed and literacy promoted. If they were non-political and run by intelligent people with the sole object of improving the minds of the masses they might be made a real instrument for the furtherance of education and culture. At present they are often grotesque. But representing an 'upward' trend, the cultural-enlightenment committees form a welcome contrast to the majority of Bolshevist institutions.

It should be remembered by the community that by the provision of entertainment, the savagery of the soldier has been curbed, which shows that the emotional life is capable of being used on the primitive animal plane. But surely it is clear that there are other sides to the human soul, and there is a great joy in the quickening and growth of the higher powers in the emotional life.

As we become accustomed to enjoying the feeling of expansion and the growth of power which free us from the littleness of ourselves, we can gradually be led back to an understanding of the great mainspring of life itself, and we shall look for a pouring out of the knowledge of the Invisible, which will then become real to us.

We need so desperately to take all our art back to the heart of things, to bind ourselves on to the tree of life instead of always eating of the knowledge of good and evil. Some day dramatists will write and poets will sing of the cosmos as part of our little lives, and we as a part of the cosmos, and the audience will see and understand. We shall be big enough and simple enough to sing and play as part of the great company passing on the moving staircase of evolving life with the angels and archangels and all the company of the Invisible.

We have lost our way in civilisation. The Churches would not use the artist or help him or support him. The State will not acknowledge anything of importance except the business man, the efficient worker in supplying industry. Intellect is the god of man, and it was a significant truth that the writer of Proverbs insisted on, when he pointed out that the demand of the Creator was for the heart of man. The heart is the place of life, emotion, feeling; the intellect is to control and guide this living force. Without vision the people perish, and Art is the beginning of vision, the early steps, the little light appearing like the will-o'-the-wisp in the surrounding darkness.

Let us use the gifts we have been given, and together with the importance of the intellect show an equal encouragement for the expressions of the heart. For those whose religious limitations make them turn from the theatre, let them consider the words of the great mystic, Jacob Behmen:

> Art is really the tool and instrument of God, wherewith the Divine wisdom worketh and laboureth. Why should I despise it?

List of Artists

A

Zoe Addy. Edwin Adeler. Julian d'Albie. Harry Alexander. F. J. Allen. Claude Allister. R. Andean. Elsie April. Dora Arnell. Florence Arnott. Dorothy Atkinson. Lilly Augustus. Marie Ault. Una Austin. Marjorie Ayling.

B

Alfred Barber. Frances Barnard. Harry Barratt. Annie Bartle. Edith Bartlett. Mary Barton. Olive Bastow. Doris Bateman. Doris Bates. Barbara Battishill. Elsie Beanland. Margaret E. Beanland. Harold Beaumont. Lottie Beaumont. Maud Bell. Stanley Bell. Lela Bellaudire. Nannie Bennett. Sternedale Bennett. George Benson. Will Bentley. Margery Bentwich. Thelma Bentwich. Arthur Besoni. Cyril Best. Grace Best. Beatrice Betts. F. J. Blackford. Phyllis Elaine. Norah Blaney. Ivy Blew. Dorothy Bond. Ina Bosworth. Phyllis Boulton. Basil Bowen. Paget Bowman. Orton Bradley. David Brazell. Henry Brearley. W. H. Brereton. Elsie M. Bridgeman. Phosbe Bridgeman. Betty Broadfoot. M. A. Broadfoot. Winifred Broadfoot. Sydney Brooks. Eva Hunsdon Brown. Winifred Browne. Jean Buchanan. Maud Buchanan. A. O. Buck. Rawson Buckley. Madge Burbidge. Bennett Burleigh. George Burrows. Thomas Burrows. Miss Butler.

C

E. M. Calladine. Meda Callander. Mercia Cameron. C. Cannock. Alfred Capper. Henry Carlisle. Bernard Carodus. Julia Caroli. Christine Carrol. J. C. B. Carter. Nell Carter. J. Rice Cassidy. F. W. Cavanagh. Mrs. Cavanagh. Helen Cavell. Yourke Challoner. Elsie W. Chambers. Florence Chambers. Kate Chaplin. M. Chaplin. Nellie Chaplin. Frederick Chester. Gladys Chester. Tom Child. Lillie Chipp. Nellie Chisholm. Goldney Chitty. Valerie Christopher. Alick Chumley. Esmé Church. Florence Clare. Gladys Clark. Winifred Clark. Elizabeth Clarke. Su-

193

san Claughton. Kate Coates. Gladys Cockeroft. L. Coles. Dr. Houston Collisson. Charles Compton. May Congdon. Evelyn Cooke. Phoebe Cooke. Ida Cooper. Alice Coppin. Zoe Corner. Charles Cory. Mabel Crichton. A. Cromartie. Sybil Cropper. Jean Cross. Lilian Crow. Muriel Crowdy.

D

D. C. Daking. Ralph Darlington. Charles Davenport. M. Ffrangcon-Davies. Hilda Davies. Madoc Davies. Muriel Davies. Olive Davies. Dorothy Davis. Dr. H. Walford Davis. Dorothy Day. Marjorie Deacon. Gene Dell. Nora Delmarr. Paula Desborough. Roma Detmold. Adah Dick. Eve Dickeson. Lillian Dillingham. Maud Dixon. Biddy Doyle. N. Drake. John Drinkwater. M. Drury. Elspeth Dudgeon. Albert Dudley. Margaret Dudley. Lola Duncan. Winifred Dunning. —— Durie.

E

Molly Eadie. Charlotte Eastgate. M. Echevarri. Melisane d'Egville. Sybil Elliott. David Ellis. Kenneth Ellis. Gervase Elwes. Eva Embury. David Evans. Edith Evans. Beatrice Eveline.

F

Arthur Fagge. Winifred Fairlie. Lilley Fairney. Charles Fancourt. Nancy Farmer. Phyllis Farmer. Gwen Farrar. Joseph Farrington. W. D. Fazan. Ettie Ferguson. Alexander Field. Ben Field. Miss Fleming. Noel Fleming. Theodore Flint. Vera Florence. Theresa Foote. Beryl Forbes. Wilfred Forster. Megan Foster. Joan Fowler. Kennedy Fraser. Beryl Freeman. Percy French. E. Fry. Herbert Fryer. Gertrude Furness. Jean Fyans.

G

Nellie Ganthony. Gale Gardner. Dorice Gay. Sylvia de Gay. William Gellatley. A. Gentry. Harry Gilmour. Miss Girdlestone. Frank Gleeson. Alma Goatley. Elma Godfrey. Marguerite Godfrey. Olive Goodwin. Elsie Gough. Daisy Grace. Greta Graham. Kathleen Grahame. E. A. Graves. Erica Green. Janet Grieg. Elsie Griffin. Dorothy Griffiths. Jessie Grimson. Ernest Groome. Fred Grove. Betty Grundy. Edith Gunter.

H

Joan Hailey. Edith Bingham Hall. Elsie Hall. George Hall. Jessie Hall. Cicely Hamilton. Douglas Hamilton. N. Hammond. Paul Hansell. Edith Hanson. R. C. Harcourt. Cyril Hardingham. Rex Harold. Charles Harris. Francis Harris. Frank Harris. John Harrison. Julius Harrison. Olga Hartley. Brenda Harvey. Sir John Martin Harvey. Phyllis Hasluck. Edith Hately. Christine Hawkes. Moreland Hay. Bret

Hayden. Alfred Heather. Kate Hellewell. Janet Hemsley. Miss Hepburn. F. Herries. George Hewson. Gertrude Higgs. Archer Hill. Harrison Hill. Miss Hilliard. Clytie Hine. Amy Kitchen. Percival Hodgson. Gwen Hodsoll. C. Holbrow. Florence Hood. Arthur Hopper. Alderson Home. Dorothy Home. Elsie Home. Clara Hubbard. Frederick Hudson. Henry Hull. Elsie Hulme. E. Leigh Hunt. Rachel Hunt. H. Hurry. May Huxley. Reginald Hyde. Walter Hyde. Audrey Hylton.

I

Elsie Illingworth. Ernest Ingram. Beryl Ireland. E. Ireland: Grace Ivell. Harry Ivimey. Constance Izard.

J

Gladys Jackson. Nelson Jackson. C. W. James. Dorothy James. Winifred James. Marion Jay. Ruby Jenkins. Gertrude Jennings. Mary Jerrold. Reginald Johnston. William Johnston. Auriol Jones. B. Griffith-Jones. Dilys Jones. Ernest Thomas Jones. E. Wynne Jones. G. Joslin. A. F. Jowers. Amy Joyner.

K

Norah Kaye. Wilfred Kearton. Christian Keay. Hilda Keen. Harry Kemp. Ward Kemp. Katherine Kendall. Niel Kenyon. F. Kiddle. Dennis King. Herbert Kinze. Olive Kinze. C. Kirton. Ethel Kitchen. Bernard Knowles. Amy Knyvett. Miss Kyle. M. Kyle.

L

Dorothy de Lacey. Frederick Lake. A. J. Lancashire. Vivian Langrish. Miss Latta. Jessie Leete. Frederick Lennard. Adelina Leon. Lawrence Leonard. Hubert Leslie. Hilda Lett. Olive Lett. Phyllis Lett. Philip Levine. Alice Lilley. Mary Lincoln. Barry Lindon. James Little. Fewlass Llewllyn. Charles Lloyd. Rosina A. Loader. Basil Lofting. Mr. and Mrs. Lomas. M. Lomax. Elsie Loubert. John Luxton. Benita Lydal. Joseph Lynn.

M

Lilian M'Carthy. M. M'Carthy. Isa M'Chlery. Annabel Macdonald. Enid Macdonald. Frank Macey. Miss Parker Machon. Mary Mackie. Mrs. May Mackintosh. R. MacLennan. Alice Mandeville. Effie Mann. Gladys Mansfield. Kathleen Markwell. M. Marriott. Mr. and Mrs. Oswald Marshall. Margaret Martin. Olga Martin. Samuel Masters. Joan Maude. Elsie Mavis. George May. Margaret Mayne. Florence Mellors. Arthur Melrose. W. A. Merrells. L. Miles. Bertram Mills. Fred Milner. Irene Milton. Lily Mines. Robert Minster. Muriel Mitchell. Doris Montrave. Carey Morgan. Nesta Morgan. Fanny Morris. Herbert Morris. Harry Morton. Helen Mott. C. Murphy. Jerome Murphy.

Margaret Murray. Maud Murray. Robert Murray. E. W. Musgrave.

N

Blanche Napier. Dorothy Nash. Phyllis Nash. John Needham. Lettice Newman. Marjorie Nield. Mary Nilsson. E. Ninimo. Robert Noble. Jean Nolan. F. Norris. Nellie Norway. Ivor Novello. R. Nugent.

O

Margaret Oakden. Olly Oakley. Sylvia Oakley. Winifred Oakley. Barry O'Brien. Madeline O'Connor. Una O'Connor. Kathleen O'Dea. F. O'Farrell. Jessie O'Grady. Margaret Omar. J. O'Neill. Valentine Orde. Evelyn Osborne. Henry Oscar. Evelyn O'Shan. Tudor Owen.

P

Blanche Padden. Cusha Parker. George Parker. Patterson Parker. Peggy Parker. Phyllis Norman Parker. Gladys Peck. John Perry. Hilda Perry. W. A. Peterkin. May Peters. Thelma Peterson. Dorothy Phillips. Emily Pickford. Muriel Pickupp. Yvette Pienne. Robins Piercy. Bantock Pierpoint. C. Piers. A. Pilkington. Robert Pitt. Ernest Platts. Patric Playfair. Monigue Poole. Muriel Pope. Archibald Potter. Anita Powell. E. Powell. Lloyd Powell. Dorothy Pratton. Moira Prendergast. Winifred Primrose. Vincent Print. Margaret Prior. Mary Purcell. Isabel Purdon.

R

Marjorie Raine. Frederick Ranalow. Una Rashleigh. Joseph Reed. Annie Rees. Rosemary Rees. Louis Rhill. Adelaide Rhind. Amy Richards. Dan Richards. David Richards. Dorothy Richmond. Susan Richmond. Pett Ridge. George Riley. M. Riseley. Paola Rivers. Ena Roberts. Evelyn Roberts. Turner Robertson. Alice Robinson. W. V. Robinson. Muriel Rogers. Rose Smith Rose. Estelle Ross. Irene Ross. Sophie Rowlands. Arthur Royd. Rosa Rubery. E. Ruegge. Dorothy Rundell. Claude Russell. Edith Ryland.

S

H. A. Saintsbury. Mr. James Saker. Mrs. Saker. Mrs. Foster Salmond. Marjorie Samuels. Eveline Sanders. Hadyn Sandwell. William Scott. Percy Sharman. Coutance Shearer. Buchanan Sheill. Tom Sherborne. Craighall Sherry. Ida Shirley. Violet Shirley. Sara Silvers. Alexander Sim. Hebe Simpson. Hilda Sims. Joan Simson. Phyllis Sinclair. Peggy Skelton. A. Skidmore. A. J. Slocombe. Enid Smith. Ulph Smith. Muriel Snow. Miss Keighley Snowden. Eva Sparkes. Sybil Sparkes. Sylvia Sparrow. Sybil Speed. Bessie Spence. Earl Spicer. Elsa Stamford. Frank Stanley. Mr. and Mrs. Stayton. Miss Steadham. William Storry. Eleanor

Street. Vera Struggles. Phyllis Stuckey. Dorothy Sturdy. Olive Sturgess. Mary Sumner. Dora Sutton.

T

Vincent Taylor. Gwendoline Teagle. Corrie Telford. Olive Temple. Arthur Thomas. Charles Thomas. Kathleen Thomas. Marie Thomson. Edina Thraves. Grace Thynne. Ernest Tomlinson. Charles Tree. Enid Trevor. Edgar Tripp. Carrie Tubb. Beta Tudor. Bernard J. Turner. Norah Turner. Henry Turnpenny.

U

Bessie Unwin.

V

Fred Vallance. Doris Vane. Marjorie Vane. Marjorie Verel. Katherine Vincent. Gladys Voile.

W

Allan Wade. Gerald Walenn. J. Dundas Walker. Jock Walker. Marion Walker. Mildred Walker. Ada Ward. W. M. Ward. Elsie Warner. Madeline J. Warner. Dorothy Warren. Dorothy Hayward Webb. Dorothy Webster. Frank Webster. Mackay Webster. Mrs. Weekham. Constance Wentworth. Elsa West. Doris Westall. Ethel Weston. Penelope Wheeler. A. P. Whitehead. Marguerite Wickham. Harold Wilde. Ulrika Wiley. Maud C. Wilkinson. D. J. Williams. Eric Williams. Foden Williams. Frederick Williams. Furness Williams. Hilda Williams. Gordon Williams. Grace Williamson. May Windsor. Herbert Withers. Minna Woodhead. Randall Woodhouse. Emily Woodward. Stanley Worrall. Mrs. Stanley Worrall. Charles Wreford. Lindon Wyatt. Wish Wynne.

Y

Margaret Yarde. Clifton Yates. Alfred Young. Helen Young.

Z

Deric Zoya.

My Greatest Adventure

Ada L. Ward

Contents

The Call to Action   203

"Crowded Hours of Glorious Life"   206

Sunshine and Shadow   211

Au Revoir   217

CHAPTER 1

The Call to Action

It came in a very ordinary way, just as a telephone call. I was sitting in my office one Monday afternoon, when my telephone bell rang, and a voice said:

"Can you be ready to go to France on Saturday? We are sending out a concert party to entertain the soldiers. We have already a quartette of two ladies and two gentlemen singers, a violinist and a pianist, and we are just short of—a well—*a comic turn!!* We have already had a conjurer, a ventriloquist, and an elocutionist, and now the boys are wanting a change. One of them has written from France to say: 'Try and get hold of Ada Ward and her blackboard and send her along.'"

Within half an hour of receiving that telephone message, I was being interviewed by Miss Lena Ashwell, a brilliant English actress, who is the very soul of this great work of entertaining our troops on active service. My only previous acquaintance with her had been as a distant admirer on this side the footlights. It was good to meet her face to face and to find her a gracious, charming and loving woman, as well as a clever actress.

I think I must have given a certain amount of preliminary satisfaction for she told me to go to the Foreign Office next day and put in an application for my passport. I did so and was told it would be ready for me in forty-eight hours. In the meantime, I had to be interviewed by another lady, Princess Helena Victoria, President of the Society of "Concerts at the Front," who takes a keen and active interest in the work, and sees and hears each artist who goes out there.

I cannot say I looked forward to that interview. I am not nervous, but I think I approached nervousness as nearly as ever I shall that Wednesday afternoon, when I drove up to that West-end mansion in a taxicab, with my blackboard, easel, pegs, chalk and duster.

Miss Ward and Her Blackboard

When I was shown into the drawing room, there was an audience of two, both women, the princess and Miss Ashwell. That surely was an ordeal. I am happiest in large rooms with crowded audiences. I like a platform, and an easy exit. Yet here I was in an ordinary drawing room, no platform, no eager, crowded audience, no comfortable exit. I was on a level with my hearers, just two individuals of my own sex, always the most ruthlessly critical, one a royal princess, the other a brilliant actress. I felt stupid, awkward, artificial. I felt as if I were wearing cotton gloves, with a hole in every finger, and elastic side shoes with flat heels, square toes, and the elastic all worn out!

I need have had no apprehensions. The princess was just a lovely, womanly woman, keenly interested in my blackboard pictures and stories. Miss Ashwell was merry and bright, my little entertainment "passed" these two critical censors, and I was told to be ready for France on the Saturday. Before leaving England, my passport had to be vised by both British and French military authorities, who granted me permission to enter the war zone of the combatant armies.

I met the rest of the *artistes* at Waterloo Station on the Saturday evening. We were soon *en route*, soon across the dreaded Channel, soon landed in fair, sunny, war-worn, shell-shattered, weary France, and our work began at once. No slackers there!!

CHAPTER 2

"Crowded Hours of Glorious Life"

Our first concert was given to an audience of wounded soldiers in a large hospital tent. When we arrived they were already assembling. Some were being brought in on beds and stretchers, some were being wheeled in, in bath chairs, some were limping in on crutches, some, alas, groping in. All were battered, shattered, broken and bandaged. When I saw them, those dear boys, who had left us so well, so strong, so physically fit, saw them there so helpless, I wondered how I was going to be a "comic stunt," with a lump in my throat and tears in my eyes. It was my first experience among the wounded, and I shall never forget it. Since then, I have entertained hundreds, nay thousands, of them, but that first audience stands out in my mind clear as a "movie" film.

There was one poor boy close to the platform. They brought him as near to us as they could. All we could see of him was just one eye! The rest of him was bandages. Really, he looked more like a mummy than a living human being. Yet bandaged and shattered though he was, he managed to give me a wink with his one eye!! Two other boys were sitting near. One had lost his right arm, the other his left. They arranged to sit together, so they *might clap each other's remaining hand*. Another boy came to me with his thumb and two fingers gone from his right hand. With a twinkle in his eye, and a chuckle in his throat, he said: "It doesn't matter, 'cause I'm *left-handed!*"

Such is their spirit. Never was there a brighter, cheerier audience. Every boy had done his duty, his bit. He had faced Hell in those awful trenches. Surely the hospital is Heaven. It was indeed a privilege, a joy to do anything to make them forget their sufferings, even for one brief hour.

After the concert, we had afternoon tea with the matron and sis-

AN AUDIENCE OF CONVALESCENTS BEHIND THE LINES

ters of the hospital, those charming women in that pretty uniform we love so well. Truly if the hospital is Heaven, these are the ministering angels. Doctors and surgeons were present too, keen and clever, devoting their knowledge of medicine and surgery to the service of the wounded, full of enthusiasm for their work, never weary of telling of the marvellous cures being wrought, of the patience and courage of the men under their care. To meet these wonderful medical officers, to talk to them was a delight and an inspiration. I could have spent the rest of my tour at that one hospital centre.

But there was much work waiting for us to do. As soon as tea was over, automobiles were waiting to take us miles away to a military camp where our evening concerts were to be given. When we arrived at the hut or tent, we found it packed, crammed to the very doors, with eager, excited, perspiring, suffocating Tommies, *all smoking*, every single one of 'em! Think of the atmosphere. It became thicker and thicker, and bluer and bluer until by the end of the evening, we couldn't see across the room. It was like pea soup! What an audience that was, and what a concert.

Our artistes were on their mettle. The magnetic attention of those soldier boys brought out the very best in us. We gave them the lovely quartettes from Gilbert and Sullivan's operas, the best songs in our language and beautiful instrumental pieces. For the time being war and its sufferings, its horrors and discomforts were completely forgotten. The appreciation was intense, the demand for encores insistent and tremendous, not one or two, but three, four, five and even six. Often and often our artistes have sung as many as fifteen songs a day each. And if you are going to France, you must have a pretty extensive repertoire. For Tommy chooses his own encores, and woe betide the artiste who cannot comply. From every part of the room come requests:

"Give us 'Annie Laurie' please miss." "No, don't. Give us 'A Little Bit o' Heaven.' We've had so much of the other place." "Sing us 'The Rosary.'" "'Perfect day,' please miss." "No, sing us 'Ipswich' miss, then we'll all join in the chorus." "Yes, 'Ipswich,' 'Ipswich'"!! This was a great favourite on our tour. It was an experience to hear those big men roaring out the chorus:

Which switch is the switch, Miss, for Ipswich?
It's the Ipswich switch which I require.
Which switch switches Ipswich with this switch!
You've switched my switch on the wrong wire.

You've switched me on Northwich, not Ipswich,
So now to prevent further hitch
If you'll tell me which switch is Northwich
And which switch is Ipswich
I'll know which switch is which.

Of course, by the end of the song, they had lost all count of the "switches," and it was just a series of "Switch, switch, switch." Never mind. Tommy had his own way, and that's everything to a soldier.

But when they saw my blackboard coming on to the platform, they didn't like it. They had had blackboards before, and they didn't associate them with a comic stunt. In fact, I believe they thought they were going to *learn* something, and that *would* have been a tragedy! I believe they expected a map, or some arithmetic, or a plan of the trenches. A storm of schoolboy protest invariably greeted the little "school marm" and her blackboard. So, in order to win their confidence, and to assure them I was not there for their *good*, I always used to begin my little turn with some funny little stories and some quaint little pictures, such as they themselves used to draw on the dear dirty old slates of long ago. Thus:

These quickly allayed their apprehensions, won their hearts, just turning them into big laughing, rollicking schoolboys, ready to enjoy any further sketches I could give them.

Then came our National Anthem, sung as only an army of soldiers can sing their country's great hymns. That closed our entertainment.

209

The room was cleared and ventilated for a few minutes. Then another crowd of eager, excited, perspiring boys poured in, all smoking, every one of them. Those at the first concert had had pink tickets, these at the second house had yellow ones, so that no boy should see the show twice. *But many did!!* So, we went on with our concert again, right from the quartette down to the National Anthem. That was our work every day, three times a day, hospital and convalescent camp in the afternoon; at nights huts, tents, hotels, wharves, docks, casinos, theatres, schools, convents, monasteries, deserted factories, laundries, railway trucks, under the ground, in the open air, wherever there were soldiers we took our music and our fun. It wasn't easy.

It was difficult. It was trying. By the end of the tour, we were tired out. Our voices were almost gone, and we were absolutely smoke-cured, kippered!! Our hair, clothing, handkerchiefs, everything smelt of tobacco smoke. But we loved our work, every minute of it, and I think the joy of my life came next year when the "boys" wrote for Ada Ward to go again, not as a ten minutes' item on a concert programme, but as a *one-man show.* So, I went out again with my precious blackboard, and month after month I gave my illustrated entertainments, week in, week out, Sundays and week days alike—week days my funny pictures and merry stories, Sundays my Bible pictures and stories. Never have I thanked God so much for my gifts of humour, of caricature and for my splendid health as in those amazing days when I was privileged to minister to the finest audience in the whole wide world.

Truly it was the greatest adventure of an exciting and adventurous life, stirring the blood, quickening the pulse, making one feel that after all life had been well worthwhile.

CHAPTER 3

Sunshine and Shadow

Such then was our work, but of course it was varied by many wonderful experiences, some intensely pathetic, some thrilling, some comical, some heart breaking, all fascinating, all interesting.

I shall never forget one very dramatic incident. It happened in the very midst of one concert. The boys were in a most uproarious mood that night, singing "Ipswich" at the very top of their voices, when suddenly I saw a big, fine, handsome sergeant pushing his way right up the middle of the room. Now the boys are so keen on these concerts, so anxious not to miss a single word, that the slightest unnecessary interruption is vehemently resented. So, when I saw this big fellow elbowing his way through the crowd *unchallenged*, I realised there was something serious, though what it was I could not tell.

But as soon as the men caught sight of him, the silence that fell over that merry throng was terrible. The music died away into a deadly stillness, and I could almost hear my own heart beat as the dread messenger approached the platform. As he drew nearer, I could see every member of that khaki-clad audience bend forward to catch the words that were to fall from that big sergeant's lips. It was like the wind blowing across a field of grain. We who were sitting on the platform were the first to hear his message. Saluting the colonel, who was taking the chair for us, he just said: "Coldstream Guards, Sir."

The colonel stood up and said: "Any men of the Coldstreams present? FALL IN." Without a moment's hesitation, big, grand, splendid fellows stood up, and went out. *They were wanted immediately in the trenches.* Think of the contrast: Indoors, music, merriment, comradeship, light; out there darkness, death in a hundred terrible forms. How could we go on with our concert, how pick up the threads of our merriment? I said to the pianist: "Play the National Anthem, let's finish." Some of the men caught my words. "Did she say 'National Anthem. Finish?' halfway through a concert, because a few chaps were called away on duty? No fear. Go on, Miss, it's all right, Go on. Carry on!"

They gave a clap and a cheer for the lads who were leaving. There was a little more room for those who were standing. Such is the world's way. We cannot stop because a few slip out into the dark. Carry on! Go on! God grant when the last great call comes to each of us to "Fall in" we may be as ready, as willing and as prepared as those splendid boys who that night left our music to face that other deadlier music.

An amusing incident occurred on another evening. I was giving my illustrated lecture: "Faces in the Crowd." The rush was terrific. The men surged into the hut and filled every available space. They crowded into the window seats, swarmed on to the platform till there was barely a square yard of space left for me and my blackboard. Some of them even climbed on to a rafter supporting the roof. Others followed their example. They clung to one another's legs, they squeezed and crowded till at last the rafter could stand it no longer. Down it came with its cargo of wriggling humans. Part of the roof came with it. I surely brought the house down for once in my life! I surveyed the dusty mass of squirming Tommies struggling in a heap on the floor. I feared some of them were hurt. But the others called out eagerly: "It's all right, Miss. Carry on. Go on. No casualties! Go on!!" Again, that cry: "Go on, go on."

Our longest day, our hardest day and I think our happiest, was the day when the automobiles came for us just after breakfast, and took us away from the camps, the bases, the towns, away from civilization altogether, up, up towards the firing line. Here we entertained the men who are working at a horse's hospital behind the trenches. Every week there is an average of five hundred wounded horses sent to this hospital, suffering from bullet and shrapnel wounds, broken limbs, shell shock, and here they are tenderly nursed back to health. When I say *nursed*, don't conjure up a vision of sweet-faced women in white caps and pretty uniforms. They are very rough men. In many cases, the only reason they are there at all, is that they love and understand a horse, or they can manage a mule and if you can manage an army mule, *you can manage anything on the face of the earth!*

Their appreciation of our visit was tremendous. Very rarely do they come in touch with the outside world. Our concert was an event, a red-letter day. The crowd was so great, that neither hut nor tent would

A TYPICAL CONCERT PARTY AT THE FRONT

hold them. We could not disappoint them, so solved the problem by giving the concert in the open air. The men sat down on the grass, and we artistes entertained from a little hillock. I shall never forget that sea of upturned, eager faces. They loved every minute of the entertainment. When it came to my turn it began to rain! Now talking and chalking in the open air in a rainstorm is not at all an easy matter, and my pictures began to weep in chalky streams. I hesitated for a moment, not knowing what to do, and the men thought I was afraid of the weather.

"Go on, Miss, carry on. It's only rain. 'Taint bullets. 'Taint shrapnel. We don't stop for rain in war time. Go on!"

Then one of them suddenly realised my dilemma. He picked up a big horse blanket, held it over the blackboard, a pal held the other end, and so I went on under this little improvised tent. And it was just then that a tiresome, ubiquitous Press photographer took a snapshot, and I never knew until I returned to England and saw my picture in the newspaper! Never mind, Tommy had *his* picture and nothing else mattered. At the close of the concert a special treat was offered to us. We were invited to witness an operation on a horse!!

After tea, we motored another twenty-five miles nearer to the firing line, where we entertained another section of the same army corps. These men were engaged in even more monotonous work than the ones we had just left. All day long from morning to night they are just dealing with fodder, loading and unloading, chopping up hay and oats for the horses. Just hay and oats, oats and hay! It gets on one's brain like a delirium. Think what our concert meant to these men, many of them taken straight from the docks of England and put into khaki. Many a rough face softened, many a furtive tear was dashed away with toil-worn hand as the tender strains of the home music swept from our hearts into theirs.

Yes, they may be rough, but they are lovable as children, gentle as women. I remember one big fellow tenderly nursing the dirtiest, stickiest, tiniest, wretchedest, blackest and smelliest kitten I had even seen in my life. The poor little thing had lost its mother and wandered in among the soldiers. It could not have chosen a better sanctuary. I said to him: "What on earth are you doing with that awful kitten?"

"Why Miss," he said, "A bloke must have summat ter love. The wives ain't here, the kids ain't here, and yer carn't love one another, can yer? Who could love that silly blighter?" affectionately indicating a pal close by."

Their gratitude for our work was pathetic. At the close of the concert one dear, big, shy boy came up to me in a very mysterious, embarrassed manner, and said: "Can I speak to yer for a minute, Miss?"

"Certainly," I replied. Often and often the boys had made me the *confidante* of some little love affair, and I thought it was going to happen again. But no. This one was different—so anxious to get me away from his comrades, from my fellow artistes, and at length successfully manoeuvred me into a quiet little corner behind the tent. Here he stood first on one foot, then on the other, while I waited ill at ease. Really, I don't know which of the two of us looked the sillier! Finally, he blurted out: "Well, are yer keepin' company with anybody?"

There's gratitude! So keenly had he enjoyed my work that he was willing to bestow his hand, his heart and his name on a poor, unworthy travelling concert artiste! It was beautiful!!

We had our supper in a little dark tent, just illumined by stable lanterns. No tablecloth adorned our repast, but our kindly hosts had made the table as attractive as they could. They had gathered sweet peas, just nipped the heads off, and arranged them in pretty patterns all over the table. It was charming.

They had an idea, too, at the back of their dear, rough heads that artistes, lady artistes, should have bouquets. So, they presented me with a wonderful bouquet, which they had made themselves—and their idea of a bouquet was how many flowers they could get into it. So, they had gathered thousands and thousands of sweet peas, crammed them, jammed them, squashed them, put a mighty holly-hock in the centre, and tied the lot together with an enormous piece of white ribbon. Tears and smiles struggled for the mastery as I saw their offering of love approaching. The flowers have died long ago, but the memory of that kindly action will never die, and among my most treasured possessions is that famous bow of white satin ribbon which brings back so gracious a recollection.

When supper was over, we found the men lined up in a double guard of honour, from the door of the tent, to the door of our car, singing their regimental song: "Here we come gathering oats and hay, oats and hay, oats and hay!"

Just as we were going to step into the car, one of them said: "I say, mates, let's take the 'orses out, and shove." Well, there are no "'orses" in an auto, so they persuaded our driver not to start the engine, and *they pushed us for a quarter of a mile!* Such is their gratitude. Such was our experience all along the line, sunshine and shadow, tears and smiles, joy and sorrow, life and death all strangely blended into that great adventure.

CHAPTER 4

Au Revoir

A very memorable day was the 4th of August, 1916, the second anniversary of the declaration of war. To commemorate the occasion, we arranged to decorate the crosses on the graves in the little cemetery where our fallen heroes were laid to rest. A fresh wreath of flowers was made for each cross. Never shall I forget the sight as the afternoon sunshine flashed a golden glory over those cross-crowned, flower-laden graves. When the beautiful ceremony was over, I walked round and read the names on those crosses, the regiments, the dates of death, and most pathetic of all, the ages—boys of eighteen, twenty, twenty-two, twenty-five, all laid here silent and still, their work over, just at life's beginning, dear, young lads who would have made such good fathers, such splendid citizens.

Yet here was no sense of death, but rather a consciousness of vigorous life, a glorious triumphant abounding vitality. The very air seemed vibrant with their pulsating electric influence. They are not dead; they are alive, working, watching, waiting, hoping. And I had rather be with them, rather my body were laid with theirs in the fields of France, Flanders and Gallipoli, and have my SOUL FREE, than have my body well, and my soul crushed under the heels of Prussian militarism. Honour and liberty are grander than life, greater than death.

Our last night in France was memorable. We gave our concert in a big French theatre. This was the only concert in our whole tour where a small charge was made to help our funds. The place was packed from floor to ceiling. To me that night was the realisation of a childish dream. As a tiny girl in a northern moorland village of England I had mused on this. I meant to be an actress—a great actress—not merely in England, but in France. My dream was to act in a French theatre, to see it packed with admiring crowds, all listening to *me*, and above all I must be wearing a pretty dress! And here it was realised! Little did I think under what conditions it would be consummated, and that the steady boom of the thundering guns would be its dread accompaniment. Here I was in a French theatre—crowded—everybody listening. I had a pretty dress on, yes, and the dream went on, for I saw a movement in the wings, I saw a lovely bouquet of crimson roses coming to me, brought by a boy in khaki, such a charming boy, and as he presented the bouquet to me with such a gallant salute, I nearly said to him: "Are yer keepin' company with anybody?"

At the close of the concert the brigadier-general of the whole district stood up and said: "We want to thank you for the splendid work you have done. It has been a tonic for the sick, a stimulant for the well. We wish to say 'Thank you' in a special way. So, we have had a little collection among the officers. We haven't given much, but we have succeeded in raising two hundred pounds (one thousand dollars). Here it is—a cheque—only *a scrap of paper*, but IT WILL BE HONOURED. Take it back to England with you, give it to Miss Ashwell, and tell her to use it for her splendid work, to go on sending out more of these concert parties."

So ended my tour on that note: "Go on," the slogan, the watchword of our boys over yonder, the message they gave me to all you over here. GO ON! Anyone can go on for a month, anyone can keep the steam up for six weeks. It takes big men, big women to go on through the weary months and years, to go on when the first enthusiasm has died away when the first thrill, the first glamour of patriotic ardour have passed away. The testing time comes when the heart is stricken and bleeding, when sacrifice and suffering have taken their toll.

Go on! I charge you by the sacred memories of the dead boys out yonder, by the mute appeals of the maimed and suffering, by the splendid courage and patience of the living and the strong, go on!

Go on till oppression and injustice shall be crushed under the feet of a righteous and victorious peace, till a noble democracy shall rise triumphant, "till the day dawn and the shadows flee away." GO ON!